Advance Praise for

The Social Organism

"*The Social Organism* is a remarkable hybrid: a riveting history of mass media, a convincing guide to the landscape of digital platforms, and an indispensable window into our future world. It's a must-read for business leaders and anyone who wants to understand all the implications of a social world."

—Bob Iger, Chairman and Chief Executive Officer, The Walt Disney Company

"In less than a decade, social media has gone from fringe to mainstream. In the next decade, it will reorder the ways people communicate, work together, trade, and pursue ideas. Luckett and Casey have written the quintessential guide to understanding our social future."

—Marc Andreessen, Co-founder, Netscape and Andreessen Horowitz

"Social media is the most obvious recent way that human life is being forever changed by technology. This book's brilliant unifying metaphor, the Social Organism (which is the converse of my mentor Marvin Minsky's book *Society of Mind*) illuminates how the ground is shifting beneath our feet. As Luckett and Casey conclude, social media will begin to act more and more like a global brain. The implications for our way of life, our governments, and our businesses are immense. I cannot recommend this book enough."

—Ray Kurzweil, inventor and futurist; Director of Engineering at Google; *New York Times* bestselling author of *How to Create a Mind*

"*The Social Organism*'s exploration of social media goes far beyond a recipe for clicks and 'likes' and presents a deeply convincing theory of how life is changing in the digital age, and how you can use social media not only to transform your business but to help change the world."

—Arianna Huffington, Co-founder and Editor-in-Chief, *Huffington Post*, and #1 *New York Times* bestselling author of *The Sleep Revolution*

"Social media and its complexity may appear to be disordered chaos, but, using a natural and biological lens, *The Social Organism* helps us make sense of this powerful new system. Important reading for anyone trying to understand the world."

—Joi Ito, Director, MIT Media Lab, and co-author of *Whiplash: How to Survive Our Faster Future*

"As individuals, we are the authors of our own thoughts. But social media has triggered emergence. The sum of our public thoughts has become greater than the whole—a new life has manifested. *The Social Organism* brings context and perspective to this, our hyper-connected ecosystem."

—Biz Stone, co-founder of Twitter, Medium, and Jelly; author of *Things a Little Bird Told Me*

"When I started my first business in 1992, there was no social media. Today, no successful business is launched without a social strategy. This book is the best guide out there. Want to build a brand or a cause? Start by reading this."

—Daymond John, CEO of FUBU; CEO of Shark Branding; co-star on ABC's *Shark Tank*; bestselling author of *The Power of Broke*

"I saw how humankind can use the Internet to bring about positive change when Oliver Luckett helped register 2 million new voters for the Declare Yourself campaign we initiated in 2004. Since then, social media seems to have delivered such transformative change again and again. In their deeply insightful new book, *The Social Organism*, Oliver and Michael Casey make sense of it all. Finally, even this ancient clunk of an Internet user has some sense of what it's all about and where we're heading."

—Norman Lear

THE SOCIAL ORGANISM

A RADICAL UNDERSTANDING OF SOCIAL MEDIA TO TRANSFORM YOUR BUSINESS AND LIFE

OLIVER LUCKETT
and MICHAEL J. CASEY

NEW YORK BOSTON

Hachette Books
Hachette Book Group
1290 Avenue of the Americas
New York, NY 10104
hachettebooks.com
twitter.com/hachettebooks

First edition: November 2016

Illustration credits: (page xxix) Birgir Breiðfjörð; (page 7) Birgir Breiðfjörð; (page 21) Paul Baran and Birgir Breiðfjörð; (page 50, top) Birgir Breiðfjörð; (page 50, bottom) Barrett Lyon/The Opte Project and Birgir Breiðfjörð; (page 67) Flemming Funch and Birgir Breiðfjörð; (page 88) Birgir Breiðfjörð; (page 103) Jonah Berger, Katherine L. Milkman, and Birgir Breiðfjörð; (page 106) World Health Organization, Centers for Disease Control & Prevention, Wikipedia (Chris55), and Birgir Breiðfjörð; (page 107) Birgir Breiðfjörð; (page 108) Birgir Breiðfjörð; (page 110) Deen Freelon, Soroush Vosoughi, Deb Roy (MIT's Laboratory for Social Machines), Twitter, and Birgir Breiðfjörð; (page 165) Birgir Breiðfjörð; (page 169) U.S. Department of Justice Statistics, Forbes, and Birgir Breiðfjörð; (page 170) Bloomberg.com and Birgir Breiðfjörð; (page 243) Birgir Breiðfjörð; (page 244, top) Birgir Breiðfjörð; (page 244, bottom) Birgir Breiðfjörð.

Library of Congress Cataloging-in-Publication Data has been applied for.

ISBNs: 978-0-316-35952-8 (hardcover), 978-0-316-35954-2 (ebook), 978-0-316-43121-7 (int'l trade pbk.)

Printed in the United States of America

LSC-C

10 9 8 7 6 5 4 3 2 1

For Scott

—OL

For Pete

—MC

There is only one corner of the universe you can be certain of improving, and that's your own self.

—Aldous Huxley

CONTENTS

Preface: Purging Hate *xv*

Introduction: Epiphany in the Desert: The Seven Rules of Life in Social Media *xxiii*

Chapter 1 THE ALGORITHM OF LIFE: HOW WE PROCESS INFORMATION AND EVOLVE AS A SOCIETY *1*

Chapter 2 FROM STEEPLES TO SNAPCHAT: THE DARWINIAN MARCH OF MEDIA *14*

Chapter 3 THE AGE OF HOLARCHY: THE INTERCONNECTED, DECENTRALIZED CELL STRUCTURE OF SOCIAL MEDIA *48*

Chapter 4 CRACKING THE MEMETIC CODE: HOW IDEAS SPREAD LIKE VIRUSES *75*

Chapter 5 BALANCED DIET: THE ORGANISM MUST BE FED HEALTHY CONTENT *114*

Chapter 6 THE IMMUNE SYSTEM: HOW SOCIAL MEDIA RESPONDS TO UNWELCOME THREATS 142

Chapter 7 CONFRONTING OUR PATHOGENS: BOLSTERING THE CULTURAL IMMUNE SYSTEM 164

Chapter 8 THOMAS AND TEDDY: THE OPEN CONSTITUTION OF THE SOCIAL ORGANISM 187

Chapter 9 DIGITAL CULTURE: TOWARD A GLOBAL BRAIN 225

Acknowledgments 257

Notes 261

Index 281

THE SOCIAL ORGANISM

PREFACE

Purging Hate

On June 17, 2015, a white, twenty-one-year-old redneck took a Glock handgun to a Bible study at a historic black church in Charleston, South Carolina, and opened fire, massacring nine people. As is customary in the public spectacle that follows these all-too-frequent moments of bloodletting in American life, creepy photos of the gunman were dug up and quickly disseminated over social media. In some of Dylann Roof's selfies, he was flanked by the Confederate flag. Having grown up in the Mississippi Delta, I found these images especially disgusting. I thought, *It's fucking 2015... why in the hell is this allowed or tolerated?* After a centuries-long struggle for social justice, that flag's continued presence in the cultural regalia of the South represented an untenable sanctioning of racism, civil war, human rights abuses, and violence. Now, in the wake of a mass shooting by a killer who later explained that he was trying to ignite a race war, here was a vile reminder of why that flag had no place in modern America.

Then, something remarkable happened. People's outrage found a clear and concise expression. It took the form of a three-word imperative prefixed with a hashtag that was widely shared across Twitter,

Instagram, and Facebook: #TakeItDown. Within days, Walmart, Amazon, Sears, and eBay had announced they'd stop selling Confederate paraphernalia; the governors of Alabama and South Carolina had called for the removal of the flag from their statehouses; and those of Virginia and North Carolina had stopped issuing license plates bearing the symbol. The cable network TV Land even halted reruns of *The Dukes of Hazzard*, the early-eighties sitcom whose lead characters' signature asset was the "General Lee," a 1969 Dodge Charger with the Confederate flag painted on its roof.

Why suddenly had the zeitgeist changed? For decades I'd watched my father, Bill Luckett, a Mississippi lawyer and politician, along with his friend and business partner, the actor Morgan Freeman, publicly battle the "stars and bars." He'd been able to remove it from our local town house, only after he became the mayor of Clarksdale, Mississippi, the mostly black town in which he lives, but the rest of the state—and much of the old South—just dug in and resisted. Now, 150 years after the Civil War, it was coming down everywhere—almost overnight.

What drove this about-face reaction? Why suddenly did we collectively start equating this symbol with hate and stop supporting it? Two words: social media. After little more than a decade in existence, this dynamic new mass communication system holds a commanding grip on twenty-first-century society. It has forever changed how we share and use information, organize communities and businesses, make political decisions, forge bonds, and maintain relationships with each other. Social media has sent into overdrive the random, evolutionary algorithm that dictates how ideas are generated, iterated, and reconceived, and how our culture takes shape. It is completely reshaping the essence of what it means to be human.

The social media developments around the Charleston massacre offer a snapshot of how this evolutionary process plays out within the new communications architecture that social media has forged. #TakeItDown was born of a mutation of #BlackLivesMatter, the hashtag of the movement spawned by incidents of police brutality against black citizens and the street protests that followed. When, amid the outrage that followed the Charleston shooting, #Black-LivesMatter activist Bree Newsome climbed the South Carolina statehouse's flagpole to take down the Confederate flag, tweets that shared one of many smartphone-shot videos of her act soon carried a new hashtag: #JeSuisBree, a variation on #JeSuisCharlie, the statement of solidarity that was adopted en masse after twelve journalists were murdered by Islamic extremists in Paris months earlier—a meme that later simply became #JeSuisParis following the still deadlier terrorist attacks of November 13, 2015.

Other meme cross-pollinations followed: As Newsome became a social media hero, she was depicted in artworks as Wonder Woman. When the Supreme Court struck down laws barring gay marriage a few days later—itself a response to social media–driven legal activism—artists leaped at the chance to mesh two highly recognized symbols into a single compelling idea. Cartoons depicted the gay rights rainbow flag being raised while the Confederate flag was lowered, and a modified *Dukes of Hazzard* poster showed the General Lee sporting a rainbow roof.

This is how ideas spread and value systems evolve in the age of social media. They morph through hashtags, photos, and shared cartoons and videos. They rely on emotional triggers to open up lines of communication. What seem like nuggets of information can amass immense power. The ones that stick arouse emotions—joy, sadness, anger—and spur people into a reaction. In this new information architecture, the most compelling and emotive ideas can transform public opinion in mere days and weeks, generating abrupt changes in attitudes and priorities that had previously lasted for decades. For better or worse, social media is making human culture less rigid, more dynamic and unpredictable, and subject to much faster evolution.

People's opinions about social media are often strong and widely divergent. To many, these networks are empowering tools of liberation. In his memoir, Twitter cofounder Biz Stone reflected on the service's usefulness for organizers of the Arab Spring uprisings, writing, "We hadn't changed the world, but we'd done something even more profound and had learned a deeply inspiring lesson: When you hand good people possibility, they do great things." In those heady days, this positive view of Twitter was widely shared. But, as I write this today, a news story about social media is just as likely to invoke fears about cyberbullying, time wasted on celebrity gossip, and how these platforms have become a tool for ISIS and other hate-mongers. No matter which of these perspectives dominates your view, you cannot deny the profound impact that social media has had on society. This undulating and amorphous new communication architecture has become the digital economy's central mechanism for how policies, organizations, and innovations are created and shaped.

And yet, as ubiquitous as social media has become, most of us have little notion how it works. It seems utterly bewildering. We simply do not comprehend its form, function, and possibilities. How is that one witty Facebook post can rapidly attract a million views while another that seems just as funny goes nowhere? Why do some political polemics manage to generate an overwhelming wave of mass hysteria literally overnight and then disappear off people's radar a few days later? Social media can feel like a giant ocean of unpredictable swells, tidal shifts, and hurricanes that surge out of nowhere. It is time we figure out how this mass complexity actually functions. That's my goal in writing this book.

Nearly all of us now have a digital persona, not just celebrities and influencers but marketing managers, politicians, business leaders, writers, athletes, and high school students. That makes us integral elements of this unique human network. We must come to terms with and figure out what we want from it. If we are to learn how to democratize it, how to deliver constructive communications that build a better world, and how to live at peace with the relentless barrage of information, we must understand what makes this system tick.

Our choices in what we do, who we have sex with, and what we buy are made through these peer-to-peer systems. In the new economic contexts of our age—the so-called sharing economy, for example, or the "gig economy"—where not only established businessmen but also ordinary people are constantly "selling" themselves, those who don't adjust to this new communications architecture will be left behind. At the corporate level, too, marketing managers will waste oodles of money if they continue to rely on systems and consultants who fail to recognize the fundamentally different social dynamics of this new system and simply recast old media tactics as if they are new social media strategies. These self-described social media "gurus," with their litany of buzzword-laden nonsense, are condemning once powerful, trusted brands to a future of relentlessly declining relevance and revenues. And finally, society as a whole will suffer if we can't collectively figure out how to harness this new model of communications for good. We can't simply leave it to the loudest, most non-inclusive bullies. (One word: Trump.) We must start by acknowledging that this sprawling, powerful new system for spreading ideas is now *the* system for everything and that it is categorically different from the previous one. Once we establish that, we can start to take a closer look at how it actually works. Only then can we design strategies that turn social media into a constructive, democratic forum for proposing, debating, and delivering new policy ideas.

We desperately need a guide, an overarching theory of social media. Coming up with such a theory is a tall ask; after all, we're talking about the functioning of something as complex as our global society. But, being the kind of audacious zealot that I am, I believe I've come up with one. And as my Aussie co-author might say, "It's a ripper."

My hero and mentor Norman Lear, the great TV producer and social activist, always told me to follow the serendipity of life. He meant that I should appreciate and learn from every twist and turn of experience that comes my way. He also liked to say that the fastest route between two people or places was the direct one. Armed with that message, I've had the confidence to network from field to field and to engage in opportunities that connected and presented themselves. As such, my career has been shaped by a mélange of microbiology research, systems engineering, art collection, talent management, music and film production, and, most recently, as an innovator at the largest media company in the world and a pioneer of social media publishing. The *Los Angeles Times* once wrote that I had "mastered the art of excess." Whether it's what the writer meant or not, I like to think it referred to my genuine curiosity about the world, how it works, and how everything is interconnected. I want to know as much about the nuclei of tiny cells as about the behavior of human communicators and the vast social and economic networks that arise from their connections with each other. In pursuing those eclectic interests, I've somewhat serendipitously stumbled upon my own "theory of everything," an explanation for how the universe's infinitely diverse components combine to forge order and meaning out of chaos, defining this wondrous experience we call life.

My theory provides a chart of existence showing how biology, technology, and culture are, quite literally, evolving together. That process has now reached a convergence point, and social media—a technological platform that facilitates organic connections through which human beings share art, words, and ideas—is its manifest expression. With this biology-framed perspective, we can also recognize that the structure and internal workings of this new system are defined by the laws of the natural world, by the biological and ecological roots from which we all come. Stated more simply, social media functions on every level like a living organism.

You want to understand social media? Or, more precisely, how human society functions in the digital age?

You need to review the essence of life itself.

It took an epiphany in the desert for me to discover that.

INTRODUCTION

Epiphany in the Desert

The Seven Rules of Life in Social Media

In March 2013, my boyfriend Scott and I traveled from our Los Angeles home to Joshua Tree National Park for our yearly digital detox and fasting retreat at a quirky spa called WeCare, a sanctuary we lovingly call Colon Camp. As in times past, we needed a break desperately. *Details* had recently bestowed a few entrepreneurs, including me, with the cringe-worthy title of "Digital Maverick," tasking us with drawing a graphic representation of the "future of social media." I wanted to provide the magazine with a thought-provoking image, and, as we began our retreat, I felt bothered that I hadn't yet conceived of an illustration that would adequately capture the immense if amorphous technological sea change happening before our eyes. What were the analogies? How could I map the interconnectedness of social media users?

I've always been a visual person with a deep love of patterns and art. But as I walked out into the desert each morning and thought of all the flow charts I'd drafted since my first digital world job at Qwest Communications two decades ago, I remained stumped. None of those stacked-up, tree-like diagrams of the first IP-telephone systems captured the nuances of the human beings connected to each other, nor did they explain the complexities of the like, the share, the retweet. My mind drifted further back into the past—to drawings from the hematology lab in which I'd worked during high school. I'd been obsessed with microbiology and had memorized the colorful images of the cascading metabolic actions that described the pathway from "cut to closure" during coagulation. The evolved system of thrombocyte factors, platelets, the shape-shifting non-nucleated megakaryocytes, and the incredible spider-like glue of fibrin had captured my imagination. As a sixteen-year-old at the International Science and Engineering Fair at Disney's Epcot Center, I won second place in the world for my work on "Further Characterization of Glycoprotein IIb-IIIA, the major Fibrinogen Receptor on the Human Platelet." Yup, I was that nerdy kid.

Since high school I'd let my knowledge of biological phenomena wane. After enrolling in summer courses in human physiology, marine biology, and molecular biology at Harvard, I'd discovered my love of weed, which helped ease my mind and synthesize my racing and rampant ADHD. At Vanderbilt, a university known for its rich cultural heritage and literature programs, I took another detour from the study of biology. I finished my major in French Renaissance literature, and became obsessed with how the Catholic Church had built and then lost its hold on information, how the Gutenberg printing press and the introduction of kindergarten forged a literate middle class, and how this all led to the twentieth-century notion of mass media into which I was born. Inspired by the music of the Talking Heads and the subversive ideas of Neil Postman, Theodore Roszak, James Twitchell, and the Berkeley counterculture movement of the sixties, I also developed a disdain for the new breed of corporate controllers.

Surveying the desert, I felt the disconnect between my life then and now was as vast as the landscape before me. I'd gone from being a closeted, Mississippi-born, nature-loving geek to sitting at the helm of a glitzy media company that I had cofounded with two of Hollywood's most colorful characters, a service that links hundreds of top-name celebrities with hundreds of millions of interconnected souls. But suddenly, in my food-deprived state, the bridge between them became clear in one of those all-too-rare bolts of insight. The knowledge I'd stored from the biology lab and my study of communication history suddenly coalesced, and, *whoosh,* a colorful image of the microscopic environments of cells and viruses that I'd seen in petri dishes rushed into my head. *That was it!* Social media was mimicking an organism. Our communication network had evolved into a living, "breathing" creature, one from which I was now deriving a livelihood. If it was a living organism, I reasoned, the rules of life should apply. I, a lab-rat-turned-"Digital Maverick," was just one of billions of differentiated cells inside this same organism. We are its cells and our interconnected, timeless, and ubiquitous Internet networks are the substrate for this new life form.*

Was this just a trippy, reductionist metaphor conceived under the

---

* I've since pondered whether the best metaphor is that of a single organism, a group of interconnected organisms within a wider ecosystem, or some kind of super-organism. We've taken to calling it the singular "Social Organism" for consistency, but all those ideas fit within it. If that sounds like the definitions are a little fuzzy, it's worth remembering that the natural world itself doesn't always conform to the rules we draw for it. Viruses, for example, are especially difficult to pigeonhole. Scientists generally don't consider viruses a life form as they have no cell structure, but they do have their own genetic information with instructions to change the host and then replicate. The intricacies of life itself are complex and not always easily classified; so too are those of the Social Organism.

duress of too much heat and not enough food? For the weeks and months that followed, I kicked the tires on the comparison between social media and biology, running it through all sorts of scenarios. And when I applied it to the work I'd been doing at theAudience—the company I'd founded three years earlier with Hollywood talent mogul Ari Emanuel and Napster founder Sean Parker—the metaphor seemed ever more apt. Our publishing outfit at theAudience was tapping into an ecosystem in which artists, brands, events, and fans all thrived because of the organic connections they enjoyed through a network of influencers that reaches more than a billion customers a month. The content we were pushing out was specifically designed to find the patterns and latch on to the human "cells" that make up those networks. These would then replicate it in a manner akin to how a biological virus will exploit a biological human cell's internal machinery to spread itself through a process of auto-replication. It was not for nothing that we boasted of having found the formula for making content and ideas *go viral.*

As I explored the metaphor further, I began to think of the world's social media users as 1.5 billion autonomous organisms, attached through the emotion-sharing machines in our hands, forging a connection that transcends time and distance. The sum of these parts, all of us fluidly interacting together, was the singular Social Organism, a ubiquitous life form that was constantly nourishing itself, growing, and evolving. In sharing and replicating packets of information as memes (e.g., sharing a video on Facebook), we—the cells of the organism—are facilitating an evolutionary process much like the transfer of genetic information in and among living things.

Soon, I was seeing the entire social media environment through this new lens. The most effective social media communication, including the #BlackLivesMatter and #TakeItDown hashtags, were transformative memes, building blocks of our evolving cultural DNA. (This connection between memes and genes is drawn from the ideas of Richard Dawkins, who first introduced the word "meme" to the lexicon in 1976.)

For several years now, the biological word "viral" has come to denote a phenomenon where online content is widely shared or viewed. In the Social Organism concept, I discovered new dimensions to this parallel concept. A biological virus will seek out receptors on the outer membrane of cells so that one might let it enter its cytoplasm. Once inside, the virus adds information to start altering the cell's DNA. That process provokes genetic mutation, a phenomenon that for the most part goes unnoticed inside our bodies. The result can sometimes be disease, but in time a viral attack can also create new resiliencies and contribute to biological evolution. Similarly, I realized, viral media content attaches itself to what I now call our personal *affinity receptors*. Once inside the human "cell" on the network, this appealing content slowly starts to alter the *memetic* code that shapes our thinking. Often the effects are inconsequential (the sharing of a silly cat video engenders a laugh and perhaps a desire to see more cat videos) or positive; sometimes they are grave, disease-like, and even a threat to the wider Social Organism (e.g., ISIS's use of social media to call others to violent acts).

As social media has grown, it has evolved into a profoundly complex organism, as if going from a simple life form such as an amoeba to the complexity of a multi-cell organism like the human body. The activity of this increasingly expanding network of interacting human beings began with a mostly static set of actions—sending an email, for example. It later incorporated more interactive engagements such as blog posts, which could be read by a much wider array of readers. Now, social media activity encapsulates a mind-boggling array of inter-relationships. In this new, more highly evolved organism, a single YouTube video can be shared a million times and, in turn, inspire countless derivative knock-offs, parodies, homage videos, memes, hashtags, and conversations, all collectively pushing the original work's cultural influence ever further and wider. This flow of auto-subdividing information can simultaneously flow outward to reach a wider audience but also behave recursively, turning back on its origins in a self-adjusting, self-corrective inflow of new ideas. It's impossible for us to map these innumerable interactions, reactions, and counter-reactions in our heads; they defy the linear, causal explanations that our brains feel inclined to seek, leaving us overwhelmed with information. But just as powerful computers now let scientists study the once impenetrably complex features of the human body, so, too, are tools emerging, mostly in the field of Big Data analytics, to investigate the workings of the Social Organism.

That work, especially the graphical illustrations that data analytics have generated around social media, helped reinforce the parallels with microbiology that I'd recognized in that revelatory moment at the Joshua Tree National Park. As such, I came to see that if we follow how biological pathways work, we could learn how to manage this unruly new organic media architecture. There was by now no doubt in my mind about the picture I would submit to *Details*:

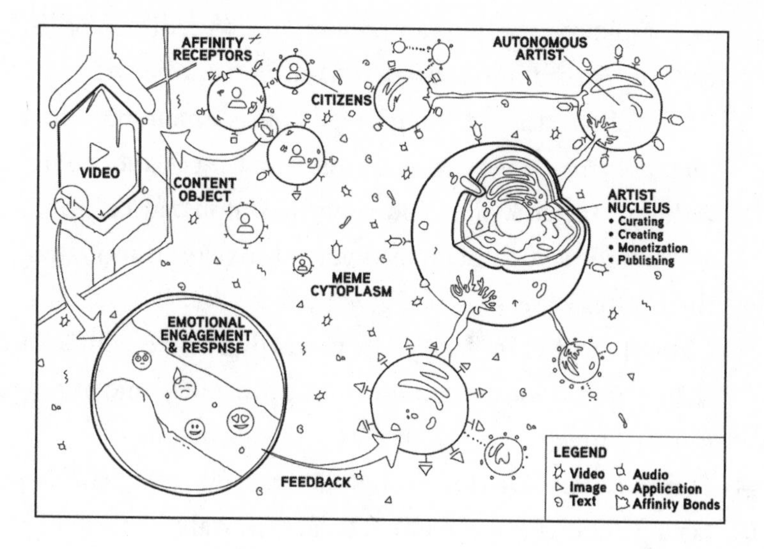

Remember high school biology? For me that was where my journey began. I was a rambunctious kid, but, thankfully, my AP biology teacher, Mrs. Franceschetti, saw something in me. (In a Facebook exchange, she recently described me as "the wildest but most intelligent student I ever had.") Mrs. Franceschetti arranged for me to work several half-days each school week at the Lisa K. Jennings Hematology lab at the University of Tennessee Hospital. It was awesome.

One of the first things anyone learns in biology class is that life has seven essential characteristics, a set of clear, essential rules that distinguish living things from their inanimate counterparts in the material world.

Here's a refresher:

1. **Cellular structure.** Living things are organized around cells. They can be simple, single-cell amoebas or occupy something

as complex as the human body, home to trillions of different cells organized into specialized roles.

2. **Metabolism.** Living things need nourishment, for which their metabolism converts chemicals (nutrients) and energy into cellular matter while producing decomposing organic matter as a byproduct. Put simply, living things need food and purge themselves of waste.
3. **Growth and complexity:** In producing more cellular matter than organic waste, living things grow over time and become more complex.
4. **Homeostasis:** Organisms regulate their internal environment, taking actions to keep it in a balanced, stable state.
5. **Responses to stimuli:** Living things respond to changes in their external environment, instituting alterations to their makeup or behavior to protect themselves.
6. **Reproduction:** Living things produce offspring.
7. **Adaption/Evolution:** Living organisms adapt to lasting changes in their environment. And over the long term, by transferring survivor genes to their offspring, they evolve.

Since that trip to the desert in 2013, I've tested these seven rules and how they relate to what we see going on in our culture and in social media and retroactively applied them to what I saw in my past work, from Disney Co. to theAudience. I sometimes describe my career as a climb up the so-called OSI network stack, from fiber and wavelengths to data systems to applications to social networks, and from there to the content that lives on top of those networks and, ultimately, to the people behind the creative output. Having seen what types of marketing, viral sensations, and publicity efforts succeeded and failed in those settings, I was convinced the seven rules apply almost as readily to social media as to biology.

Consider rule number one: a cell structure. Billions of emotion-driven human actors comprise the cells of our Social Organism. Just like the organizational structure of other complex cellular organisms, mostly notably the human body, as well as that of other community-like natural phenomena such as hives of bees or ants, the cells of the Social Organism form a *holarchy*. Each human unit on the network constitutes what Austrian intellectual Arthur Koestler described as a *holon*, meaning that it is both independent and part of a wider whole; its activity is autonomous but at the same time simultaneously limited by and dictating the rules and activity of the greater group.

This community of cells devours a constant feed of quips, comments, selfies, articles, and new ideas, all digitally conveyed in text, images, and video. Thus we can view content uploaded into these systems as its nourishment. As it feeds the Social Organism becomes larger and more complex in its intercellular connections and network reach. Here we come to rules two and three. The organism's metabolism of human emotional response processes the content, absorbing, sharing, and reshaping it to allow growth. Meanwhile, it purges itself of waste—all the unloved content that fails to achieve mass reach, the billions of tweets that get lost in the ether, the YouTube posts that wither with a view count in the double digits, and the rule-breaking social media users who are expunged from the system by pitchforked vigilantes. What fate befalls a particular piece of content or cellular node depends on whether the Social Organism regards it as healthy nourishment. Having observed the mistakes and successes of content creators from within and outside the media establishment, I've learned what types of content nourish a social media network—getting absorbed and replicated—and which do not. We'll explore these ideas in the pages ahead.

The fourth rule on homeostasis—that living things regulate their internal environments to maintain balance—brings us to the concept of metabolic pathways. In a biological organism, this refers to the chemical reaction chains along which molecular components coordinate actions within and across cells. They are the communication lines of cells and, if broken, different parts of the system won't know what the others are doing; homeostasis will fail—the organism's internal temperature will rise too fast on a hot day, or its acidity levels will blow out when a certain food is eaten. Think of what happens when the limb of a tree is damaged: Branches and leaves beyond that point can't receive the water and nutrients needed to regulate photosynthesis, so they wither and die. So, too, in social media, the lines of communication for emotional exchange must stay open. Otherwise there is no capacity for equilibrium. The system can't tolerate that.

This is not a position that today's online message managers always feel comfortable with. The first instinct of brand builders for public figures, top companies, and artists is often to cut off information flow to maintain proprietorial control and "exclusivity" of the information. It's the wrong choice. I've seen successful, profitable content suddenly lose momentum when the lines are shut, or when, God forbid, you publish it exclusively to Jay-Z's TIDAL service. Biology's rules tell us that managers of information (and copyright)—be they artists, journalists, advertisers, marketing managers, corporate publishers, or governments—need to be far more laissez-faire in their approach if they want to reach and connect with people.

To illustrate rule number five, the organism's response to outside stimuli, let us return to the Charleston massacre. To many, especially black Americans, the killings and Dylann Roof's photos were untenable. As such the overall community of social media, which at its widest encapsulates the full array of America's diverse, multiracial society, could no longer abide such a symbol of intolerance and division as the Confederate flag. I see Charleston as an example of how periodic hashtag "movements" serve as a kind of immune system response. They are the irritants, the antigens that elicit an emotional and functional response to fight against attacks from perceived pathogens.

With the sixth and seventh rules—reproduction and adaption/evolution—we witness the Social Organism's lasting impact in our culture. Memes—those vessels of culture-shaping information that comprise our social DNA—give rise to other memes and ideas through a process of reproduction. Meanwhile, the organism faces constant conflict, as the ideas propagated by new memes often prompt a backlash from people who hold countering views. But just as our bodies are made stronger by exposure to bacteria, conflict is necessary for the organism to adapt and evolve. The open petri dish of our noisy, uncensored world of social media—as jarring and alarming as it can be—is now the main driver of cultural evolution.

Evolution is not perfect. This process doesn't always result in "progress"—at least not as that word would be defined by liberals. Even as humans can communicate across vast geographic gaps like never before, differing values persist across the human spectrum and a consensus will often seem hard to find. With social media, both extreme progressives and extreme conservatives now have a megaphone previously denied them by centrally controlled media. Either side can emerge triumphant in a given conflict, depending on the message and context. This constant clash is consistent with the complexity of biological life, where conflict between and within organisms is a feature of existence. The cell structures of living things are just as capable of playing host to forces of sickness and death as they are of facilitating growth and life. Cancers thrive within the human body, sometimes overwhelming the immune system, other times not. Viruses are constantly penetrating cells and tricking their genetic DNA into allowing them to replicate themselves. But here's the good news: The daily battles in which our immune systems engage will over time give rise to important changes. In the genetic mutations provoked by viruses and disease, lasting strength is derived. These challenges are how species adapt and evolve. The same goes for the Social Organism and the human culture that emerges from it.

With my metaphor and seven rules in hand, I had the courage to begin speaking publicly about this thesis. I had always been on the business speaker circuit but had grown tired of talking about celebrities or my business, so I started throwing these ideas around. I was shocked by the overwhelmingly positive response I was getting. I realized it was time to bring the broad implications of these sweeping changes to a wide audience. I needed a collaborator with a strong grasp of how ideas spread and how network technologies and global connections can disrupt old hierarchies of power. So, I was incredibly lucky to stumble across Michael Casey at an entrepreneurs' summit to discuss bitcoin at Richard Branson's Necker Island. Here was a unique case: a recognized, serious business journalist who had also written a seminal work about the iconic image of Che Guevara, perhaps one of our most pervasive modern cultural memes, in addition to books about global economics and the blockchain—the revolutionary peer-to-peer technology behind bitcoin. Michael and I had a true meeting of minds over my concept of the Social Organism and we shared a healthy sarcasm and humor. In that Caribbean paradise, a partnership was formed.

Together, in this book Michael and I will seek not only to illuminate the organic nature of a rapidly changing media environment but also provide tools for succeeding within it. Everyone, from CEOs to military leaders to kindergarten teachers, needs to understand how the Social Organism functions. If we fail to do so, the risks are great. The lessons we'll draw from the behavior of molecules, metabolic pathways, enzymes, biochemical reactions, and genes are vital for politicians, activists, businesses, and any other individual or organization seeking to develop a corporate or personal digital persona or brand. Successful marketing strategies over this new communication architecture require us to determine how to connect emotionally with the people who function as its messengers—the artists and influencers around whom the network organically forms. There are lessons for educators, who will find that social media is becoming an increasingly important mechanism for knowledge transfer and that our top-down education system is fundamentally unsuitable to prepare children for this new world. There are also important takeaways for business managers, since the diffuse relationships of social media have rendered obsolete the hierarchical command lines of twentieth-century organizational theory. Most important, with this book I want to encourage the world's future artists, leaders, and communicators to present their "memetic differences" and have confidence in social media platforms so that they can build lasting direct-to-consumer relationships and shut out the gatekeepers who still wield too much control over our lives.

This change in mind-set is necessary because this particular evolutionary step, the one that brought us to this new, biological communications model, is the societal equivalent of those dramatic shifts in the evolution of the living world. It calls for metaphors such as those moments when living organisms first crawled out of the Cambrian swamps or when our hominid ancestors first came down from the trees.

For thousands of years before this change, information was delivered via a top-down model. Those who controlled it were powerful, centralized organizations, whether it was the church, a broadcaster, or a newspaper. Each was beholden to an editorial hierarchy that determined what messages were distributed by physical equipment that included printing presses and communications towers. Under that model, a chain of command initiated by a person of authority such as the CEO would convey standing instructions for teams of employees and their equipment to follow a preordained plan for distributing the material—be it a newspaper or a broadcast news report. In contrast, today's mass media infrastructure is defined by untethered devices connected via a decentralized, less predictable, and far more organic structure. Its distribution network is not comprised of hardware or workers beholden to their bosses' orders but of more than a billion autonomous brains. These brains are linked through personal digital connections that defy both time and distance and which in turn form cognitive and emotional pathways. Each brain functions as a kind of biological switching technology. Collectively, it is these autonomous units—not the CEO or editor-in-chief—that determine which messages the crowd gets to hear and which get buried.

Within this network of neurons and synapses, ideas such as those encapsulated in catchy hashtags or poignant GIFs can be very rapidly disseminated across wide distances. These neatly distilled vessels of thought resonate emotionally with others, who in turn share, re-share, alter, and replicate them across ever-wider circles of influence. The ideas that stick become instrumental *memes* that form what I regard as our social DNA, the coded building blocks upon which our culture evolves. The most powerful of them are calls to action that tap into events unfolding in real time, creating a sense of urgency. But they also build on top of prior ideas, our social stored memory of the past. Meme by meme, we are building a cultural framework of meaning, one that is constantly iterated, reformed, and recorded in a digital trail of social interaction. Human society has not seen anything like this before.

Michael and I will make the case that social media represents the most advanced state yet in the evolution of human communication—and in the next two chapters we'll chart how we arrived at this pivotal moment. One thing I will not do in this book is argue that social media is perfect. There is no guarantee that it will continue to develop in a way that benefits society. Already, the new players who dominate the network platforms are taking steps to control and censor information—moves detrimental to the Social Organism's development and to the objective of an open, vibrant society. In doing this, these new gatekeepers harm their own market, of course—evident in the fact that Millennials are abandoning Facebook while Generation Z is gravitating toward Snapchat and other platforms that give them more freedom and control. That self-correcting, homeostatic mechanism could be the means through which social media moves to a more decentralized structure. Other decentralizing technologies could accelerate that process. Even so, companies like Facebook, Twitter, and Google have amassed enormous control over our lives—so much so that they now rank alongside the governments of China and India as the biggest managers of people's identities in the world. If they are to have such power, it is critical that their platforms be opened up to a freer flow of information and that their infrastructure and algorithms be transparent. It's also incumbent upon us to be aware and vote with our feet to ensure that happens.

The ground has shifted beneath us. The future of social media should be one of humanity's dominant concerns. In barely a decade, the form has positioned itself at the center of twenty-first-century society. In this new world, everything from interpersonal relationships to marketing to corporate and political structures is being upended. How do we exist within this new reality? We struggle to keep up, at best. We're at once obsessed and horrified by this new phenomenon. We try to describe it in reductionist ways, but end up with a host of competing metaphors: social media as a marketing tool, as a forum for jokester Millennials to pit their wit against each other, as a way to maintain human bonds with distant friends and family, or as a giant, noisy town square full of half-crazed people yelling libelous abuse at each other. But none of them come close to capturing it in its complex entirety. So we just stay confused.

We need to operate confidently within social media, not simply hang on to the edges while it hurtles forward. But to do that, we must first understand it. We need a guide, one with a frame of reference that ties this seemingly unfamiliar, uncharted new concept to a field of inquiry that's far more deeply established and recognized. Biology, the study of life itself, is that reference.

CHAPTER ONE

THE ALGORITHM OF LIFE

How We Process Information and Evolve as a Society

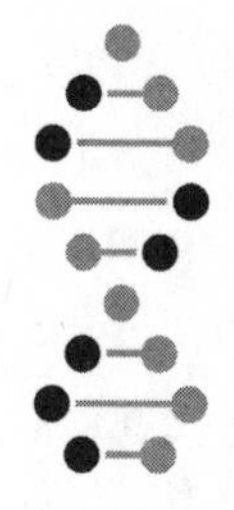

EVERY SPRING in North Mississippi and East Tennessee—the region in which I grew up—rich folks prepare their young men and women for presentation at a series of debutante parties that mark the annual Cotton Carnival. Each is organized by a grand krewe bearing an Egyptian name and an appointed king and queen. I've always seen these events as a deliberate throwback to a bygone era, its lineage drawn from a time when cotton was king, when white was white and black was black: ladies in their finest presented to the gentry of the High South in their High Cotton attire.

One feature of the Cotton Carnival always strikes me as a wild departure from the contrived order and privilege, however: Bringing up the rear in the weeklong parades that accompany the parties is the dreaded Boll Weevil Brigade. This howling group of drunken stag men turns up every year in crazy green buses and costumes to crash the parties. The Secret Order of the Boll Weevils also does charitable works, handing out toys to kids. But it is best known for the disorder it brings to the otherwise tightly choreographed krewe parties. This not-so-secret order might not be afforded official status as a grand krewe, but its symbolic challenge to the authority of Southern patriarchy and the legendary stories of debauched shenanigans associated with it are as much a Cotton Carnival tradition as anything.

Anthropologists have long noted similar, chaos-inducing elements in Latin American Carnival and Mardi Gras processions, events in which communities ritualistically perform an overturning of the established social order before submitting to the chastity of the Lenten period. To me, however, as a tech entrepreneur schooled in the dynamism of Silicon Valley and in the evolutionary development of social networks, the Boll Weevils are symbolic of the more lasting disruption that unanticipated change will bring to a society.

"Boll Weevil" is a not a lightweight label for a group of Southern men to adopt. The beetle of the same name, which feeds on cotton bolls, has been the bane of cotton farmers ever since it first migrated across the Rio Grande from Mexico in the late nineteenth century. Almost as much as the Civil War, the boll weevil is responsible for sweeping changes in the economics and the demographics of not only the American South but of the North as well. The damage it inflicted weakened the giant Southern estates that were built on the back of slavery and that once held great sway over the entire U.S. economy. The tiny beetle made a mockery of the "King Cotton" slogan, which anti-Yankee southerners relied on to explain how the cotton economy would sustain the South's inevitable secession from the Union. My home county, Coahoma, was one of the wealthiest counties in America at the height of cotton's power; today it is one of the poorest. The bug also decimated the livelihoods of the black tenant farmers and sharecroppers who'd emerged after emancipation to farm their own small cotton plots. It spurred the creation of a great diaspora, a migration northward of newly impoverished African Americans to the industrialized cities of New York, Chicago, Baltimore, and St. Louis. There, these transplants forged the communities that, now, a century later are defining a new phase in America's civil rights evolution with the #BlackLivesMatter movement, a powerful social media phenomenon that we'll return to on various occasions throughout this book.

The boll weevil's ability to outsmart the century-long eradication efforts of farmers, chemists, entomologists, and USDA bureaucrats is a fabulous example of evolution, mutation, and natural selection at work. In the 1920s, with boll weevils rife across all cotton-growing areas, farmers tried to wipe them out with powdered calcium arsenate, which proved only partially successful with the weevils but alarmingly lethal for many other living things. Then, in the 1950s, farmers tried using new synthetic pesticides such as DDT that targeted the molecular makeup of the insects themselves. After some initial success, entomologists discovered within a few years that some boll weevils were unaffected by the pesticide. And not long thereafter, entire populations proved resistant to DDT. The same pattern was repeated over and over again throughout the twentieth century as new insecticides were introduced only to find that resistant strains of boll weevil would later emerge, making the product redundant. The latest hope for farmers comes from a genetically rewritten and modified cotton developed by Monsanto that secretes a naturally occurring insect toxin called *Bacillus thuringiensis*, or Bt. Yet still, many expect it is only a matter of time before Bt-resistant weevils emerge.

The same force is at work here that occurs when drugs become ineffective against a disease they were engineered to fight. This process is no mystery to anyone with a modest knowledge of biology: Although each new version of the insecticide is deadly to most individuals within a population of targeted pests, a small number will carry a trait dictated by a mutated gene not possessed by the bulk of the species. That gene allows those lucky few to defy the insecticide. They pass on this gene to their offspring, and the survivability trait that goes with it, and soon enough an entirely new population of insecticide-resistant insects is buzzing around.

The boll weevil's ongoing battle with the USDA's entomologists is thus a classic "survival of the fittest" tale. Like so many such cases, it confirms the hypothesis at the heart of Charles Darwin's theory of evolution. (Ironically, Texan cotton farmers' future battles with boll weevils could be undermined by the fact that their state's schools are emphasizing Intelligent Design–friendly textbooks and curriculum.) Darwin's "dangerous idea" constitutes a "basic algorithm," as the philosopher Daniel Dennett put it. (I know your eyes might roll back at the use of "algorithm," but it's important to set this core computing concept as a basis of logic here.) Although Darwin had never encountered a computer, the nineteenth-century naturalist's theory can be expressed in the kind of equation structure that runs our math-driven digital world: "*if* X and *if* Y, *then* Z." More precisely, the algorithm boils down to this: *If* there is variation across species and *if* the distribution of finite resources requires a process of selection among competing living organisms, *then* those individual beings with variations best suited to obtaining those resources will survive and pass on their traits to their offspring.

The equation might seem simple but it sets in motion an unfathomably complex web of causal relationships, unleashing a never-ending series of unpredictable consequences in different directions. Have you ever heard of the "butterfly effect" theory of chaos? It used the metaphor of a butterfly flapping its wings in the Amazon, thus setting off a chain of events leading to a hurricane off the coast of Florida. You need to understand evolution in terms of such interconnected complexity. Our brains tend to avoid complexity and instead go with linear explanations that miss all the many second-, third-, and fourth-order effects that ultimately shape outcomes. To fully understand evolution—both as a biological and a social concept—we need to break free of that limited thought process.

If you get nothing else from this book, embrace the notion that the world—including its human-built social networks—is an incredibly complex system. Evolution, with its unpredictable outcomes forged out of an otherwise simple algorithm, is the ultimate result of all of that. And human society is just as, if not more, susceptible to its dynamism as simpler forms of life.

When adaption and change occurs in one species, it affects the survivability of *other* species, whether predators, prey, or competitors for food, and so subjects those beings to the same algorithmic process of adaption and change. Then, this will in turn affect *other* species with which those species compete. As cotton plantations expanded across the South, boll weevils that were competing for scarce resources in their native Mexico were drawn north. Later, the ebb and flow of the weevil population as it evolved to resist each new insecticide changed the survival outlook for Argentine fire ants, another import from the South and a predator of the weevils; in response, they, too, went through mutation-led changes. As food became scarce, a stronger strain of ant emerged; they went from forming mono-queen colonies to multi-queen colonies, which strengthened the group's ability to survive and procreate in settings of scarcity. At some point these kinds of breakaway strains become entirely new species.

Extrapolated to its ultimate end, the process offers an explanation for everything, including the organization and culture of human civilization. Across billions and trillions and quadrillions of emotionally driven interactions between randomly varied molecular structures, Darwin's relentless algorithm constantly fosters changes to the status quo, creating the wonderful diversity of the world we occupy. It is, as Dennett says, "a scheme for creating Design out of Chaos without the aid of Mind."

Growing up in Mississippi, I would hear people declare, "I ain't evolved from no ape." To fathom that we had "progressed" from primates was to embrace some notion of inferiority of origin and to deny the Bible. But perhaps one of the reasons the theory of evolution has not been comprehensively accepted, despite overwhelming evidence in its favor, is that it is erroneously described in "progressive" terms. We must distance ourselves from the simplistic idea that evolution stands for the development of things that are superior to their predecessors. It's a misunderstanding that's been around almost as long as Darwin's theory itself. In our lifetimes it has been fed by representations such as the iconic "March of Progress" illustration of human evolution, which was first published in 1965 and has been reproduced in many forms. Our version is below:

The truth is that the random interactions that trigger the evolutionary algorithm's output are not preconfigured to drive things in any particular direction. As Stephen Jay Gould has said, "life is a copiously branching bush, continually pruned by the grim reaper of extinction, not a ladder of predictable progress." Keep this lesson in mind when we discuss the evolution of the Social Organism. Social media has undoubtedly brought improvements to our world, but it has also created and exposed many problems. The greater point is that new forms arise from evolution, whether biological or social, and take shape without any purpose behind them. They just come into existence. Yet we should also recognize that humans can influence evolutionary forces—after all, it was humans who introduced cotton in the South. We need not feel entirely disempowered. Once we better understand how both biological and social phenomena evolve we can encourage their development in ways that *do* make for a better world. In effect, how do we *grow* a better world?

Many scientists have long been uncomfortable applying Darwin's powerful theory to anything outside of biology. There was a natural aversion to the "Social Darwinism" philosophies behind Nazism, Arian eugenics, and other white supremacist ideologies, for example. And other than most hardline libertarian economists, the idea that economies should be designed around a ruthless survival-of-the-fittest version of laissez-faire principles was unfathomable for the suffering it would impose on the poor. (Many still justifiably complain, albeit with inaccurate metaphors, about "Darwinian" economics forging America's extreme income inequality.) But just because the laws of evolution are a deeply flawed template for social policies doesn't mean that the evolutionary algorithm doesn't shape society. After all, the same variables—variety and the competition for scarce resources—exist in human relationships.

In recent years, as we've become more aware of the toll human activities have taken on nature and concerns grow about the sustainability of life on earth, new fields such as biomimicry—which seeks lessons from the systems that have evolved in nature to design more resource-efficient economic and organizational models for society—are giving evolution theory a renaissance in the social sciences. Evolution has become particularly prominent in computer science and network theory, but also in the embrace of "cultural evolution" concepts by the likes of British intellectual Matt Ridley. These ideas help frame many of the concepts in this book.

One compelling application of the natural laws and evolution in a social science context comes from César Hidalgo, a colleague of Michael's at MIT Media Lab. His theory on how economies evolve hinges on the idea that information is constantly "growing," bringing order and organization to matter within a universe whose natural state otherwise tends toward entropy and disorder. Everything is composed of information, ourselves included.* As the futurist

---

* Information here is defined more broadly than its colloquial usage around the idea of message content and communication. It can be thought of as a force defining the physical arrangement of matter, the embodiment of things. Information stands in opposition to the second law of thermodynamics, which tells us that the universe tends toward entropy. That means that information is the key anti-entropic element of existence. While molecules are driven toward diffuse, varied, and disconnected states from each other, information is doing the opposite: It is creating relationships that are structured, consistent and connected. Thermodynamic forces want to make matter a gas; information makes it a solid.

Andrew Hessel says, our genetic code represents both the hardware instructions and the software that runs our bodies, eventually abstracted all the way out into genetic memories and consciousness.

The point is that all matter has a computational capacity to process information and thus to produce it. Hidalgo describes a tree as a "computer powered by sunlight," which, aided by proteins organized into signaling pathways, figures out how to grow its roots toward water, detect pathogens and initiate an immune response to them, and push its leaves toward its energy source, the sun. In so doing, the tree itself becomes an embodiment of information—an organization of molecules that we classify as a "tree." Nonliving chemical reactions can be thought of as computers, too: They give order to inputs and forge more complex molecular compounds out that process. But it is human beings—and, just as importantly, human societies—that have developed the most profound computational capacity of all matter in the known universe, producing information in the form of what Hidalgo calls "crystals of imagination." These crystals take physical shape in all the triumphs over entropy that our species has achieved: in the houses, the furniture, the motorcars, the computers, the mechanics' tools, in everything that's ever been manufactured. What's driven humans to organize information in these ever newly inventive ways? The unstoppable algorithm of evolution.

Within human societies, arranged as economies, this tendency manifests in a perpetual competition to attain higher degrees of computational capacity. Individuals, companies, and economies evolve toward ever-more complex computing and networking systems to process information and create more valuable products. The greater the number of nodes and complexity in a network, the greater the total pool of computational power. It isn't a new phenomenon.

You can extend the idea all the way back to the first small tribes and early nomadic communities and through to the immense globally integrated computer-linked networks of today. More narrowly, the concept that social change is driven by demands for greater information-processing efficiency also explains the ongoing evolution of computing systems toward decentralized network structures. In the history of information technology, each new phase harnesses greater computing power than its predecessor: Mainframe computing was trumped by networked desktops, only to be outstripped by the Internet and cloud computing, with the next frontier being the distributed, decentralized systems envisaged by Tor, bitcoin, and other ownerless, open-source, and peer-to-peer systems.

We can apply similar thinking to the architecture of mass media. There, an evolutionary algorithm has brought us to a moment in which social media is surpassing all earlier iterations of mass communication systems in terms of its power to share, produce, and process information. To view social media as an evolutionary advance might seem like a leap if we focus on its most superficial attention-grabbing output: the banal pet videos, the destructive actions of warring trolls, and, of course, Kim Kardashian's "Internet-breaking" backside. Remember, not all evolution is progress. Still, any debate over the benefits of social media can't diminish the fact that its hyper-networked structure makes for a powerful information-processing system for society. Ideas and calls to action take hold far more efficiently than was ever possible with the old model of centralized media, and it's transparency and openness can hopefully identify the cancerous ideologies that pervade our culture.

Think of how quickly political movements are organized now. I witnessed this personally when theAudience worked on the social media strategy behind President Obama's 2012 re-election campaign. We quickly found we could coalesce supporters around distinct communities of personal identity: Pet Lovers for Obama, Veterans for Obama, supporter organizations in the LGBT community, regional groups such as Obamaha and Coloradans for Obama. This decentralized approach allowed the team to efficiently reach the right people with the right messages, and, in turn, these communities acted like connected nodes, amplifying the campaign's message by communicating online with their friends. We were able to reach over 220 million unique people the last week of the election by making the content that mattered and putting it in front of the people for whom it mattered most.

In his 2016 presidential campaign, Bernie Sanders experienced something similar—initially, without even planning for it. In 2013, Aidan King, a twenty-three-year-old grape picker from Vermont, launched a "Sanders for President" subreddit on the social media platform Reddit simply because he admired Senator Bernie Sanders. Sixteen months later, Sanders's staffers decided to use King's hobby site to formally announce his bid for office. Membership of the subreddit soared, forging a wave of enthusiasm that saw Sanders smash all fund-raising records to raise $26 million from 1.3 million donations in the third quarter of 2015. The "Feel the Bern" slogan that became a rallying cry for the campaign emerged out of this giant supporter group, not from the mind of some high-paid marketing professional. Throughout the primary campaign, it was clear that the hashtag #FeelTheBern resonated far more strongly than #Hillary2016. In fact, the online community that galvanized around it became so powerful that it was thought to have influenced Sanders's reluctance to concede the Democratic nomination to Clinton, even after she'd clearly sewn up the requisite number of delegates.

In this flat, horizontally structured network, where anyone with access to a smartphone or computer can easily and cheaply become a node for distributing and consuming information, we can crowd-source knowledge. Such shared capabilities didn't exist when mass information was steered through the gated channels of news organizations whose expensive, capital-intensive distribution systems created a natural barrier to entry that protected them from smaller, underfunded competitors. Now that billions of people are connected to a networked system that very cheaply allows them to become self-publishers, information can be exploited in more powerful ways.

Social media puts a much wider array of ideas in front of us, shows us solutions to problems that we didn't have access to before. In this world, serendipity, a phenomenon of random discovery that's vital to the conceptualization and crystallization of new ideas, is a bigger element in the information-gathering process.

What do I mean by that? Imagine you see a disturbing article that a Facebook friend posts about a Pacific Island community that's struggling with a lack of potable water. It gets you thinking because you'd just seen a tweet about a brand-new technology that can desalinate water for a hundredth of the cost of existing methods. So, you join a LinkedIn discussion group that's focused on some of these new ideas. That leads you to a back-and-forth private chat with someone from that group who shares your passions and has skills that complement yours. Shortly thereafter, a start-up is born. You're off to save the world.

By turning into a network of interlinked organisms, we've pushed human society's computational capacity into new unchartered territory, creating an externalized collective consciousness. And in the classic evolutionary feedback loop that we observed in the relationship between cotton plantations, boll weevils, insecticides, and fire ants, these changes are in turn unleashing their own powerful evolutionary force. They are accelerating the evolution of our economy, our society, and—as we'll discuss more deeply later—our culture.

As you progress through this book you'll learn how to harness this powerful force for your own economic and personal benefits, as well as how society at large must deal with it. But in the spirit of the past being the best teacher for the future, we must first review the millennia-long development of the underlying communications infrastructure that brought us to this point. The evolution of the Social Organism has been a long time coming. The long arc of history is profoundly present in its DNA.

CHAPTER TWO

FROM STEEPLES TO SNAPCHAT

The Darwinian March of Media

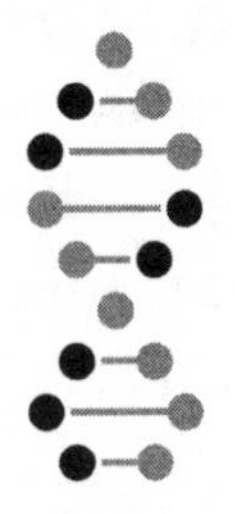

THE TERM "social organism" was coined by the nineteenth-century French sociologist Émile Durkheim, who viewed society as a living being whose health was determined by how well the core realms of economics, politics, and culture interacted with each other. Much more recently, the concept was taken on by the biologist/anthropologist David Sloan Wilson in *Darwin's Cathedral*, a groundbreaking book on religion's role in the evolution of societies and civilizations. If we conceive of societies as organisms, Wilson argues, religion can be viewed as a vital agent of prosocial behaviors that put common interests ahead of those of the individual. In this way, religion—which he describes as one kind of "adaptive belief system"—has been key to the survival, growth, and prosperity of communities. From stories of capricious gods that discouraged people in ancient civilizations from breaking their societies' defined order, or the Hindu water temple rituals that simultaneously helped Balinese society coordinate an orderly irrigation system for its rice paddies, religious practices had a unifying effect on communities. They helped societies evolve into bonded, networked communities and thus advance their computational capacity.

Until the Renaissance spurred a surge of scientific inquiry that ultimately led to the Enlightenment and the modern world, dogmatic religious ideas were the main glue bonding people together. These ideas were delivered in the form of myths and memes, stories packaged into a familiar narrative structure. The consistency of the stories' patterns and tropes—evident in how mainstream religions share strikingly similar genesis myths—ensured people could absorb them and, ultimately, act upon them.

This reflects a key point in the formation of knowledge: that cognitive skill depends on a capacity to recognize patterns. An idea simply can't take hold if there is no preceding, related idea for it to latch on to, if it is utterly unfamiliar. Until the theories of Copernicus, Galileo, Darwin, and others were burnished with the weight of scholarly curiosity and empiricism and became more widely accepted, people's pattern recognition capacity was constrained. Their in-built "computers" simply hadn't evolved to where they could comprehend and absorb the patterns in the data they were receiving. Gravity, the laws of physics, meteorology, immunology—none of these ideas existed, which meant people didn't have the foundations with which to understand the most simple of wonders.

In this environment, religious myths flourished; they were the means through which to influence the public mind. The stories told by priests represented idealized packets of conceptualization—they were memes, those basic building blocks through which ideas are passed on and which we'll explore in greater depth in chapter 4. And for their purpose, they were highly effective: Notwithstanding history's many episodes of internecine bloodletting, they mostly kept societies bonded. And yet this seemingly robust system's days were limited. Eventually, with the aid of new communication technologies such as the printing press, as well as the literacy ushered in by middle-class education, societies' capacity for sharing and processing information expanded. This meant that more scientifically founded ideas could be absorbed. Human culture evolved.

Before we delve into how the Social Organism broke free of religion's domination in the realm of ideas, I think it's useful to take a walk down history lane and look back at the early Catholic Church through the lens of mass communication. As a kid I mostly associated the Catholic Church with the domineering presence of the largest building in my hometown of Clarksdale, Mississippi. But in one of the many a-ha moments after my revelation at Joshua Tree, I came to view the Church as one of the world's earliest and most successful broadcast networks. Its bell-ringing steeples were like television towers, calling the masses to tune into the Word of God. The bell would ring at eight a.m. The congregants would gather to hear the incontrovertible truths and dogma in the building filled with religious, *memetic* iconography. Its priests were like TV anchors, the only individuals in touch with God and thus empowered to disseminate the Word. In the pre-Enlightenment Church, that was because parish priests were typically the only literate person in a village and because there was only ever a limited supply of handwritten Bibles to go around. Priests delivered a single Rome-sanctioned message, just as big news organizations hew to common rules on language style, news values, branding, and, to varying degrees, the media company's editorial line.

As a conveyer of ideas, the Church was genius. It truly grasped the power of imagery. Everything from the priest's gold-laced vestments to his elevated position in the pulpit reinforced papal power, while the iconography of Christianity gave us our most lasting memes. "Grumpy Cat" photos, the Obama "Hope" poster, and the Guy Fawkes masks of Anonymous have nothing on the crucifix, the Christian fish, or the Virgin. These images were replicated and repeated through the centuries, artists tweaking and reinterpreting the meme but staying true to a core message. Although sanctioned artists participated in this vast process of message management, most of the Church's lay community had little capacity to contribute their own content. And for centuries they had no way to safely challenge the dogma. All of this formed part of a mass communication architecture that was, for centuries, all but impossible to surpass.

Then along came Johannes Gutenberg. The first book he published with his new invention was the Bible—a wise choice, given that its themes were utterly consistent with the pattern recognition capabilities of the widest audience. But the printing press unleashed something that would ultimately expand people's access to powerful ideas very different from those laid down by Rome. It created the possibility of more widespread and rapid dissemination of information, chipping away at the timing and distance limitations of conversational communication, which demanded immediacy and proximity. Along with other sweeping societal developments—including advances in literacy from the introduction of private and, eventually, public education—the printing press broke the class structure that the Church had forged. It laid the path to a middle class, a new educated group open to alternative ideas about how to organize society and comprehend the world. And to service their need for such ideas, another powerful idea sprung forth, one that harnessed the vast new publishing power unleashed by Gutenberg: mass media. Ironically, the early literature that emerged at this time was based on the secular delights of consumption, sex, and comedy—a pattern to be repeated with the early Internet.

This new phase in the evolutionary march of society's communication architecture helped to craft a secular model for sharing information, one freed from the singular dogma of the Church. As a growing literate population demanded information that was independently delivered, a new breed of writers and editors arose: journalists. Inspired by the liberal philosophies of Voltaire, Montesquieu, Locke, and John Stuart Mill, they offered fresh descriptions and explanations of politics and culture without care for whether they complied with the worldview of authorities. And after the mid-nineteenth century, when media organizations figured out they could fund their operations by selling advertising slots to producers that were trying to reach a growing market of middle-class consumers, news organizations grew in size and influence, with on-staff writers covering an ever-wider array of topics or "beats." These publications grew in great number in Britain as the industrial revolution took hold. In the United States, newspapers sprung up everywhere in the nineteenth century. While their approaches encompassed a wide range of political philosophies and ethics, in general the industry embodied the Jeffersonian principles of free men, free property, and free ideas.

In the twentieth century, new systems for capturing and distributing information brought the media industry into another evolutionary phase. Photography, wireless, moving pictures, broadcast television, and later cable TV all offered new tools to deliver messages and spread ideas to the public more efficiently and widely. These technologies—the newspaper, the magazine, the book, and radio and television—shaped Western culture through the twentieth century; they sat at the centers of people's lives. When Americans listened to their president on the radio or watched Walter Cronkite on CBS tell them "the way it is," bonds were forged across an imagined, coast-to-coast community of co-participating citizens. Broadcast media was as much of a nation-building force as any technology before it. With no Church and no government dictating the terms, media businesses became powerful shapers of public thought. This could happen in blatant but also subtle ways, such as when TV voice modulation led the Mid-Atlantic accent to earn unofficial authority status—by default, diminishing the authority of, say, a Mississippi drawl like mine.

Yet, despite its universal reach, mass media was still very much a club. While many media business owners avoided interfering with the work of their journalists or at least paid lip service to the principles of balanced reporting, there was no getting away from the centralized power that these institutions wielded. Editorial boards and broadcast producers were gatekeepers of news. They got to decide what the public learned about and what it didn't. They defined the so-called "Overton window," a term based on Joseph P. Overton's idea that there is only a narrow range of ideas that politicians considered politically acceptable for them to embrace. These institutions' centralized control over "messaging" meant that close relationships were forged between those who made news and those who wrote it. Imagine now, in this more open era of social media, White House journalists agreeing to keep Franklin D. Roosevelt's disability out of their reporting or ignoring John F. Kennedy's sexual adventures because it wasn't in the "public interest." Whether we were better off because of those decisions, competition would make it impossible to uphold them now.

With social media, this industry has made a giant new evolutionary leap, one that I think will have as profound an impact on society as Gutenberg's printing press. Again, we are not arguing that the evolution of social media must create indisputably positive benefits. I'll say it again: Evolution is not the same as progress. What we *are* saying is that social media represents a more evolved state for society's mass communication architecture. And there is no turning back. The evolutionary algorithm has brought us to the Social Organism, within which we are now linked in a giant, horizontally distributed network. It has armed us with a far higher level of computational capacity than ever before, capable of generating, replicating, and interpreting ideas more rapidly and of spreading them more widely.

Donald Davies, Vint Cerf, and Bob Kahn are frequently referred to as the "fathers of the Internet." But it's fair to say that the Internet's grandfather is a guy called Paul Baran, who in the late 1950s came up with something he called "distributed adaptive message block switching." You might not have heard of Baran, but perhaps you've seen his oft-cited drawings of different network structures:

Network Structures

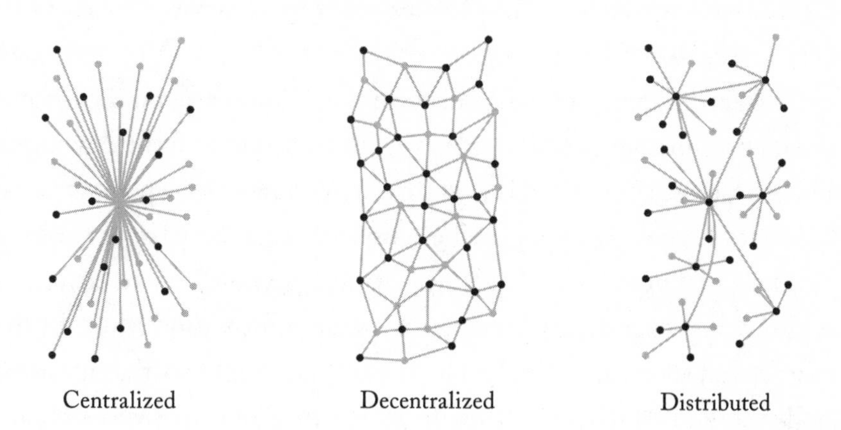

The first model represents the kind of communications relationships that has underpinned many forms of human organizations throughout history. In particular, centralization describes the telecommunications systems that persisted in most countries before the Internet era, where all traffic had to pass through a national telephone company's central hub. The second shows a system of interlinked hubs-and-spokes relationships in which various centers of coordination function as nodes within a wider, ad hoc system. It, too, is pervasive: The hardware and commercial structure of the Internet, formed around an array of different ISPs servicing multiple customers, could be described in this way. But Baran was more concerned with how information flowed, not so much how users physically connected their computers to the network or paid for access. And for that he conceived of the third model, a distributed system.

Distributed networks now pervade our communication architecture. In fact, this flat, center-less, distributed structure is the framework from which social media derives its remarkable power. Baran, who worked on U.S. Department of Defense–funded projects at the RAND Corporation during the Cold War, proposed this structure not to enhance information flow per se but because it would be more secure. The idea was that if a node went down due to attack or malfunction, it wouldn't bring down the whole network as would happen in models where everything flows through a central hub or hubs. Baran knew the structure could not be achieved without a reimagining of how we package information itself. In the distributed structure, data had to be broken into blocks that multiple nodes could simultaneously read. As it turned out, this was a bigger breakthrough than the security improvement it promised; this new system overcame the two ever-present constraints on human communications: time and distance. It would lead to the Big Bang of the Internet age, a massive breakup in the pre-existing order of the communications universe. From it we got an explosion in innovation and in new online life forms that were previously unimaginable.

Baran's idea, which he called "hot-potato routing," was at that time too unconventional for the U.S. telecommunications network, at whose center sat the all-powerful AT&T Corp.'s Bell System. That system comprised a series of hubs connecting local and long-distance telephone lines. Coordinated by switchboards, the hubs would enable point-to-point communication between two telephones, based on the codes in each phone's number. The model's legacy persists today in the NPA-NXX telephone number format of +1 (xxx) xxx-xxxx, which contains the country number, the three-digit area code, the three-digit prefix for the local region, and finally the four digits of the line owner. The model assumed a dependence on geography that Baran's idea made redundant.

A decade later in the late 1960s, the Welsh computer scientist Davies recognized that Baran's model could dramatically boost the amount of information passing over a network. "Packet switching"—the term Davies chose, somewhat less colorful than Baran's—meant that information no longer traveled point-to-point, where it would get trapped in bottlenecks. Data could now be delivered, regardless of whether there was a "busy signal" on the relevant line. Davies incorporated a version of Baran's technology into an internal communications network run by the United Kingdom's National Physical Laboratory, and, in meetings with Americans working on a Defense Department contract to build something called the Advanced Research Projects Agency Network, he convinced them to employ the same approach. In 1969 the ARPANET was launched on a packet-switching model. Four years later, Cerf and Kahn perfected two instructional protocols for managing those packet flows: the Transmission Control Protocol and the Internet Protocol, typically lumped together as TCP/IP. This system would allow virtually any other network to link to the ARPANET. The concept of the Internet was born at this moment.

With the Internet infrastructure in place, the evolution of social media could begin. While they didn't carry the label "social media," the phenomenon really began with email and instant messaging, which made sending a letter redundant and drastically cut the time for text-based communication. Then, with online mailing lists and Usenet groups organized around "threads" of conversation, a social dimension was added: Rather than one-to-one communication, these innovations allowed for one-to-many message dumps. Volunteer-run bulletin board systems, or BBS, emerged in which people with an interest in certain topics could not only share ideas but also download communal, independently created software code. These forums were popular but they required commitments from tech-savvy coordinators to stay running.

The biggest breakthrough was arguably that of British engineer Tim Berners-Lee, who in 1989 invented the World Wide Web. Building on the idea of hypertext, a term coined in 1963 by information technology philosopher Ted Nelson, Berners-Lee devised the hyperText markup language (HTML), a computing language for creating online documents that formed links over a network via special pieces of embedded code. By clicking on those code pieces, readers could jump from one document to another, "surfing" over a web of interlinked "web sites" of potentially unlimited size. It then took the 1993 release of Marc Andreessen's Mosaic browser, the precursor to the mass-marketed version known as Netscape, to bring Berners-Lee's brilliant idea to life. The Netscape browser introduced hundreds of millions to the World Wide Web with its colorful, easily navigable websites. This in turn unleashed a desire for many of them to publish their own sites, for which they now simply needed basic HTML programming skills or to acquire the services of someone who did. In time, these sites would provide the primary means of human online interaction and the foundation for the twenty-first-century version of social media.

Another formative milestone in the development of distributed communications architecture came with the Telecom Act of 1996. By mandating that Internet access would be open and economically unregulated, it unleashed rapid evolution in the digital ecosystem. Packet-switching communication over the Internet protocol now existed in a government-enforced environment of open innovation, which meant that geography and time were fully rendered irrelevant for all American participants in communications. That spurred the invention of all manner of applications to drive down the cost of publishing and consuming information.

Because they democratized access to modes of communication, these reforms encouraged the users of them to seek out ever-wider networks of engagement; the idea of "network effects" became the defining economic model for the industry. Now, you can't just order up a network; success depended on *organic* growth. By extension, that meant that the organizational structure and development of the systems and platforms that underpinned this expansive industry began to follow patterns seen in the natural, biological world. Whether or not it was part of a deliberate strategy, biomimicry found its way into Silicon Valley's organizational DNA.

Unlike the command-and-control structure of vertically organized human corporations, no single authority orders a colony of termites to work together, dictates how proteins and other molecules should interact within your cells, or orders a mushroom to grow. The constituent parts in an organic organization are autonomous. It's an apt descriptor of how individuals within a distributed communications network function together. This horizontal, autonomous, and organic system would become even more relevant once the invention of blogs gave rise to a new form of citizen journalism and even more so once social media messaging platforms gave the idea of the "public voice" a new, organic distribution system. From that emerged the Social Organism as we now know it.

Before we go there, we must reflect on the economics of the IT industry, which were driven throughout this period by the laws of physics and mathematics. In particular, a powerful combination of what became known as Moore's and Metcalfe's laws was unleashed.

Former Intel CEO Gordon Moore's idea—by now an article of faith in Silicon Valley—states that computational capacity, measured by the number of transistors that can fit on a microchip, doubles every two years. Ethernet co-inventor Robert Metcalfe's law states that the value of a network is equal to the square of the number of nodes. Because of the perpetual pressure from these mathematical growth functions, the cost of publishing and accessing information on the Internet kept falling as computer storage, Web hosting, online bandwidth, and access speeds became ever-more efficient. And as the infrastructure improved from painfully slow dial-up modems to the near-instantaneous broadband connections of today, so, too, did the ability to search the Net. Search engines went from the early cataloging and query functions of AltaVista and Yahoo! to Google's all-powerful algorithm.

The audience grew exponentially along with the technology, which greatly enhanced the potential economic impact from publishing information online. A powerful feedback loop of technological improvement and network effects took hold as more and more people logged on to access ever richer content and then in turn fed more content back to the emerging Social Organism. Soon websites became interactive, allowing readers to engage with them via comments or by posting in specially designed public chat rooms and forums. It was a new paradigm: People were sharing their thoughts with the world at large without requiring the authorization of a publishing gatekeeper.

The defining content vehicle of this new age was, initially at least, that of the weblog—or blog, as we now call it. Using dynamic websites, writers would provide anyone who'd listen with a chronological stream of updates on their lives and thoughts. The concept soon morphed into a kind of would-be journalism—although most bloggers were more like op-ed columnists. With the release of the Rich Site Summary, or RSS, feed format, an entire industry of citizen journalism was spawned around low-cost, user-friendly publishing services such as Wordpress and Google's Blogger. With more lured by Google Ads' promise to micro-monetize their content, swarms of bloggers descended onto the Internet.

To this day, the vast bulk of blog posts are just floating in the ether, crying out for someone—anyone!—to read them. And yet a big enough cadre of super-bloggers amassed such followings that they singlehandedly shook up the traditional media model—trailblazers like video game expert Justin Hall, political blog pioneer Andrew Sullivan, and gossip mavens like Mario Armando Lavandeira Jr., aka Perez Hilton. They were unhinged from the traditional journalism rules of style and ethics, employing a free form of expression to which readers gravitated. All of this posed a major challenge for established news organizations, which now faced stiffer competition for the limited resource of reader attention span and the corresponding advertising dollars. With these declining revenues they struggled to afford the high cost of gathering the news that, somewhat unfairly, the bloggers got to read, recycle, and comment on for free.

Many decided to fight fire with fire, carving out space on their websites for in-house blogs staffed by writers who opined in a more colorful style. But as independent blog empires such as the Huffington Post and Gawker emerged, the labor and distribution costs on traditional newspapers became almost too much to bear. Newspaper journalists were forced to do more with less: writing for both print and online, providing accompanying blog posts, and doing online

TV spots. The time for deep, quality journalism shrank. Layoffs grew, bureaus were shut down, print editions were canceled, and many newspapers simply perished. Despite the online advertising industry's promise of a revolution in smarter, more targeted ads, the overwhelming competition for "eyeballs" dramatically drove down "cost per impression" (CPM), the metric used to price ads. The same effect came from the measurement of click-through rates, which strengthened advertisers' bargaining power by demonstrating how effective or otherwise each media outlet's reach was. More competition and more transparency—newspapers were hit with the two most powerful deflationary forces in a market economy.

All of this plays out in some striking numbers: From Ian Ring's first online e-journal in 1997, the number of blogs soared to 182.5 million by 2011, according to NM Incite. Now, with Tumblr alone claiming 277.9 million blogs, the true total is far greater. Meanwhile, newspaper revenues are less than half what they were ten years ago and the number of newsroom employees in the United States has dropped to below 36,700 from 56,400 in 2000. This is what extinction looks like when our communication architecture undergoes rapid evolution.

It was the bloggers' content that disrupted the old media order, but it was the new Internet-based technologies that gave them the *means* to do so—much as Gutenberg's printing press gave Renaissance thinkers the tool they needed to challenge the old feudal order. And at the turn of the millennium, another new innovation in the distribution of content would arguably make an even bigger impact on our mass communication system, giving even greater opportunity to those outside the establishment to make their voice heard. With the arrival of social media platforms, the Social Organism finally had the distribution system it needed to start defining the shape of our increasingly digital society.

The rise of social media platforms created a vibrant market that locked publishers into an even more aggressive competition for audience attention. In permitting people to share any piece of communication in a collective, communal way, this new architecture took us from the twentieth century's centrally managed *mass* media system to a *social* system founded on virtual communities. It meant that the machinery that carried the message was no longer defined by printing presses and television towers but by the neurons and synapses fired by emotional triggers in billions of digitally interconnected brains. Information distribution was now about biochemistry, psychology, and sociology.

The new model depended on the organic growth of online networks, which leveraged people's personal connections to build ever-wider circles of connectivity. These interlinking human bonds became the metabolic pathways along which the Social Organism's evolving communications channels would form. It meant that the most lucrative business in publishing shifted from producing content—since everyone could now do that at much less cost—to facilitating publication, primarily by expanding social networks via dedicated platforms. In a sense, these platforms—with which entrepreneurs like Facebook's Mark Zuckerberg and Twitter's Jack Dorsey would eventually build highly successful business models—were like cable TV services, although their "equipment" was composed of human relationships rather than coaxial cables.

Encouraging ever-wider webs of human interconnection became the MO of any social media platform company. As per Metcalfe's law, the bigger the network, the more information would travel over the platform, from which revenues could be extracted in fees for advertising and data analytics. This spawned an intense burst of innovation and competition among wannabe platforms. All breakthrough innovations that lead to paradigm shifts tend to create a fluid marketplace of start-ups and flameouts, but in this case the cycle of creation and extinction was very short indeed. For our purposes, that's useful, because we can learn a lot about what makes the Social Organism grow by looking at the rise and fall of early models.

One of the earliest social media sites was SixDegrees.com, founded in 1997. It was named for the notion—popularized through the parlor game "Six Degrees of Kevin Bacon"—that all human beings are connected to each other by no more than six degrees of connection. (Incidentally, a recent Facebook study has found that everyone on that platform is now an average of only 3.5 degrees separated from each other; social media truly has made the world smaller.) Six Degrees users would list their acquaintances and, as it grew, could post messages and bulletin board items to people in their first, second, and third degrees of connection. The company swelled to one hundred employees servicing around 3 million users and was sold to college campus media and advertising company YouthStream Networks for $120 million in 1999. But in 2001, Six Degrees fell victim to the bursting of the dot-com bubble, as the gold rush–like mania that had unquestionably poured money into Internet companies with the flimsiest of business models turned into the exact opposite: a rush for the exits. Whether Six Degrees was worthy of the same newfound cynicism, the end of the gravy train of money meant the end of its business. YouthStream itself was forced to sell the following year for a measly $7 million.

It wasn't just the dot-com bubble that doomed Six Degrees. It was also confined by the limits of the dial-up modem and by a BBS structure. As discussed above, these bulletin-board systems required the time-consuming involvement of tech-savvy moderators. All of this meant that the entire premise appealed mostly to geeks. It took Friendster, which launched in 2002, to take social media mainstream. Much as Facebook would do later, Friendster allowed users to invite their contacts to join a network on which to share online content and media. In just three months, the site had amassed 3 million users, many using it for online dating and for discussing hobbies. Within a year, Google had offered Friendster's founder, Jonathan Abrams, $30 million for the site. He rejected it, partly because various Silicon Valley advisers told him he had an opportunity to turn Friendster into another Yahoo! worth billions. It was a fateful decision. Shortly afterward, Friendster also lost momentum, surpassed by another newcomer, Myspace.

There's been much business school ink spilled on Friendster's failure, and it tends to focus on the deal-making obsessions of Silicon Valley. But in essence it comes down to how well it competed for user participation, and some of its policies were antithetical to the Social Organism's growth demands. I remember visiting Friendster's offices to find staff members deleting all the Jesus avatars. Why? I asked. "Because they are not real; they can't fuck," came the colorful explanation from Abrams. He wanted to limit Friendster to identifiable people, which meant excluding anonymous avatars. This dogma opened up an opportunity for a more laissez-faire competitor. Myspace, which allowed thousands of artists and other users to create inanimate profiles, helped to build an important new model for sharing music, including direct-to-consumer music releases, social fan clubs, and efficient ticket sales. By curbing the creativity and self-expression of its many users, Friendster had hindered its own distribution network.

The Friendster-versus-Myspace story confirms an amalgam of at least three rules in our playbook from the seven characteristics of life that we introduced in the Introduction and which we will discuss in other parts of the book.* In order to grow, maintain homeostasis, and adapt to survive in the event of a change in the environment (in this case, the arrival of a competitor, Myspace), content delivery systems need to keep the Social Organism's metabolism nourished and its pathways of communication open. Curtailing creativity works against that goal.

So what about Myspace? It was also launched in 2002, but really took off in 2003 and 2004, soon attracting, and accepting, a whopping $580 million offer from News Corp. By 2008, the service peaked at 75.9 million monthly unique visitors, pulling in as much as $800 million a year in classified ad revenues. But shortly after that, the site began to decline. The reason? It comes down to the incompatibility of a giant corporation's proprietary instincts with a free-content system that requires organic network expansion.

Here, too, I have personal experience. In 2006, News Corp. began to shut off non-proprietary applications from the Myspace platform: which meant, for example, that the revenue-sharing video content site that I'd created, Revver, could no longer distribute videos over the Myspace network. I took the view—and of course continue to—that the addition of any new exciting content would have

---

* In case you're wondering, we're not going sequentially through the seven characteristics. As normally stated, the order of those rules doesn't cooperate with our narrative structure. But over the course of the book, we'll hit all of them.

widened Myspace's user base, to the firm's advantage. But News Corp., like so many old-economy companies, takes a very proprietorial view of content, subjecting decisions about it to lawyers and committees that worry about the projection of the corporate brand. Back then, such companies' instincts were to reject arrangements that didn't give them ownership of the content (even if that material was not produced by anyone on payroll, as was the case with the bulk of Myspace's content-providing users). The upshot was that when a Myspace user typed in "revver.com," they would just see an ellipsis: "..." More important, this act of curtailing content expansion went against the interests of the Social Organism's organic growth.

When News Corp. imposed its draconian rules, Myspace was left with all the gaudy mishmash of personal ads hailing from its laissez-faire roots but none of the innovative verve that should have cemented its status as a vibrant forum for artistic creation—the worst of both worlds, in other words. This failure opened the door for Mark Zuckerberg and Facebook to claim the crown as king of social media. In 2011, News Corp. sold Myspace to a group of investors that included singer/actor Justin Timberlake (who, ironically, played the part of my former business partner Sean Parker in a film about Facebook, *The Social Network*). The deal came in at $35 million, more or less the same puny sum that Google had offered to Abrams for Friendster.

Once broadband connections took hold—and later, streaming technology—video became the next big social media battleground. In that one, I played a direct part via Revver. We realized—as did the three former PayPal employees who founded YouTube—that you needed a separate site to host people's videos, since private websites usually couldn't handle the bandwidth. But what I'm most proud of is that we pioneered the idea of revenue-sharing, setting a standard for paying providers a portion of the advertising revenue that their work generated. We saw it as a way to encourage good content. The idea won us some innovation awards early on. Still, in the end it was YouTube, which Google acquired in 2006, that became the dominant platform for video. YouTube soon started rewarding people for revenue-generating content, too, and its model has since become a critical source of revenue for filmmakers and musicians. Google has done a good job developing tools that allow artists to register their works under YouTube's Content ID system, which seeks to ensure that all copies of their work are covered. However, a lot of stuff slips through, meaning that rightful owners aren't properly compensated and the calculation of revenues and how they are distributed is less than transparent. Start-ups such as Los Angeles–based Stem are working on bringing transparency to this space. The next step, I believe—not only for music and videos, but for all art—is a truly decentralized system in which artists, and only artists, have a say over who sees their work and how they get paid. Blockchain technology, which we'll discuss in chapter 8, could help to bring us there.

This brings us to Facebook, which since its launch in 2004 has swelled its user base to a mind-numbing 1.5 billion. *The Social Network* did a number on CEO Mark Zuckerberg, painting him as an uber-ambitious control freak who will stop at nothing to get what he wants. I don't know Zuckerberg well personally, but the movie's portrayal of him fits my impression of how he has allowed the platform itself to develop. I'm not at all a fan of Facebook. As I'll explain later in the book, I regard the way it manipulates and controls our access to information as dangerous to the health of the Social Organism.

Still, in terms of the evolutionary process, Facebook has adapted brilliantly to the needs of the Social Organism—to a point. Within the evolutionary confines of the marketplace in which it has operated until now, Facebook has so far been the fittest survivor.

What did it get right? For one, since those early days in a Harvard dorm, Zuckerberg has opened his network up to the widest possible community. It has been designed to be deliberately mainstream. There's a feel-good impression people get from using Facebook and an ease of use that makes it accessible to people far outside the tech-geek world. Everyone's mom is now on Facebook. It's a place where former high school classmates catch up, where families separated by oceans keep in touch, and where neighborhood communities share tips on lawn-mowing services and babysitters. It's also where companies targeting that very same giant middle-class market of users can set up shop with a friendly page engaging in a "dialogue." Facebook's rosy veneer allows people to tell the story they want to tell. They construct an idealized version of themselves. *Here's me, with my face-tuned smooth skin and my perfectly beautiful family, living our happy and safe but also sufficiently exciting and varied life.*

The platform is geared for this rose-colored form of expression, which for some time will create a comfortable arena for a mainstream market. Facebook's subtle restriction of supposedly offensive content—a draconian posture that I personally experienced when they shut down my account after I'd cracked a joke in a private message—is also focused on the same goal: a sanitized, comfortable community. But my experience tells me that over time, they can't have one with the other, that censorship ultimately constrains the Social Organism's growth and leaves those providers that practice it vulnerable to conquer by more open platforms. It's one reason I'm concerned about Twitter, Facebook, Microsoft, and YouTube's agreement with the European Union that they censor hate speech. It's hard to argue with the goal—I'm certainly no member of the #ISTAND-WITHHATESPEECH movement—but executing on it becomes extremely complicated and can breed authoritarian instincts. As we'll explore in chapter 6, trying to censor any speech is not only likely to fail but is harmful to our cultural development. It's like spraying boll weevils with DDT. To eradicate hate we need to constructively boost empathy and inclusion, not censor it. As we'll discuss later in the book, this approach matches that of contemporary cancer research, which is to train our immune system to recognize the disease and eliminate it with its own resources. By the same token, if we don't expose ourselves to the sadness and pain of hate, we can't recognize it and reject it.

This challenge to Facebook's crown is already playing out. A host of new platforms has recently arisen, many of which deliberately flout the kinds of controls Facebook imposes. They reflect the next phase in the evolution of this life form. Right now, Zuckerberg's empire is well entrenched and very unlikely to topple any time soon. But as the diversity of social media platforms expands, leading to greater competition for audience attention—much like the arrival of new, fitter species that compete with the old ones for resources—Facebook will eventually have to adapt or go the way of the dinosaurs.

Facebook's biggest competitor, Twitter, might not end up the winner, but the difference in its approach is telling. It's not well documented that Twitter—that quirky publishing system for messages of 140 characters that encompasses 320 million users and a staggering 500 million tweets per day—draws its ancestry from a community activism idea hatched down the road from Zuckerberg's Harvard dorm. According to early Twitter engineer Evan Henshaw-Plath, one of Twitter's stem technologies was the "TxtMob" SMS messaging solution for protesters that MIT Media Lab student Tad Hirsch first launched for anti–Iraq War activists who crashed the 2004 Republican National Convention. That edgy past is still in Twitter's DNA, even though multiple pivots since have bent it to the commercialization demands of its investors. Arguably, Twitter came of age during the Arab Spring of 2009, when it was a vital tool during the street protests that led to the ouster of Egyptian strongman Hosni Mubarak. Those events forged a positive impression of Twitter—and social media generally—as a democratizing force that could foment political change. It's uncertain whether that label still fits for a service that launched a $14 billion IPO in 2013 and is constantly trying to keep advertisers happy. But it does seem that Twitter's more hands-off stance on censorship and privacy gives it a better chance of engaging with the fringe-dwellers—whether in Silicon Valley or Tahrir Square—who disrupt the establishment.

Then there's the far more button-down LinkedIn, now owned by the white-washed Microsoft, which has focused on building business relationships. Yet in its own way, LinkedIn has had a decidedly disruptive and democratizing effect on how individuals form professional networks. In widening the market of searchable job candidates it has brought more meritocracy to recruitment, giving the Old Boys' Clubs less clout. LinkedIn's profitability stems from a business model that escapes the dependence on advertising by charging premium fees for special features. Depending on what happens with a bunch of new financial innovations, this subscriber-based model may become the template for other iterations of social media. (Not that it does a better job of encouraging people to show their "real" selves, warts and all. I chuckle every time I read the parade of inflated, grandiose résumés, each replete with the awe-inspiring buzzwords of "innovation," "transformation," and "disruption.")

The other big names of social media show that there is much innovation under way outside of the heavy footprints of Facebook, Twitter, and LinkedIn. A form of digital biodiversity is forming in the sector. Whether each newcomer survives will depend on how well it adheres to the seven rules of the Social Organism.

Photo-sharing network Instagram, now a part of Facebook, might struggle in the long run. It instinctively censors content, which, we will repeatedly argue, denies nourishment to the Social Organism. Instagram's policy of barring all forms of nudity has drawn derision for its heavy-handedness and, in particular, for its sexist double standards in differentiating between men's and women's nipples. Despite the company's insistence that breastfeeding images are permitted, advocates for public breastfeeding say such photos continue to get blocked. The company claims its policy stems from rules set by the Apple Store for apps available to people under seventeen years of age, but those restrictions don't seem to apply to the Twitter app and others that permit nudity. The bigger problem is that enforcing arbitrary rules depends on the discretion of the company's in-house censors, who can easily veer to the absurd—as when *Vogue* creative director Grace Coddington was temporarily banned from Instagram for posting a line-drawing cartoon of her topless self. These ridiculous situations helped inspire the "Free the Nipple Movement," a feminist movement meant to de-sexualize the female body that, coincidentally, had its birthplace in the country where I now live, Iceland.

In contrast to Instagram's prudishness, Tumblr, the Yahoo!-owned microblogging social media platform, has a more laissez-faire approach. That it also happens to be a vibrant platform for avant-garde artists and animators to collaborate and push the boundaries of creativity is probably no coincidence—nor that teens use it as a place to outwit each other with their irreverent memes. Instagram might serve the interests of established artists like Beyoncé who want to feed their fans an image of impossible, airbrushed perfection, but Tumblr's approach gives it a better chance of being an important incubator of the artistic ideas that will push our culture forward.

Now for Snapchat, a fascinating new phenomenon. The rapidly growing photo- and video-sharing app sets a time limit on each image for the designated recipient, usually a matter of seconds, an impermanence that in effect defeats censorship. Until very recently, the company claimed that its servers maintained no record of the communications so there was no archive from which to analyze the service's 100 million daily users' behavior. That policy was amended in the summer of 2016, when a new feature, called "Memories," was introduced to allow users to keep a selectively shareable archive of their own snaps. But in this new opt-in model, the power to commit images to the server-backed collection remained in the hands of the person taking the photo, not the receiver.

A 2014 poll of 127 users by the University of Washington offered some clues as to how people used what was then an entirely transitory experience—and it was not, as you might expect, mostly for "sexting." Some 60 percent said they primarily use it to share "funny content" and 30 percent said they use it to send selfies. Although 14 percent said they'd sent nude pictures over the service, only 1.6 percent did so regularly. The initial surge in popularity for Snapchat was in part about not wanting to produce a trail of behavior for others to later judge you by—whether it's your future employer or your future lover—but it was also about living in the moment. As Snapchat founder Evan Spiegel put it in an early blog post for the launch, "Snapchat isn't about capturing the traditional Kodak moment. It's about communicating with the full range of human emotion—not just what appears to be pretty or perfect. Like when I think I'm good at imitating the face of a star-nosed mole, or if I want to show my friend the girl I have a crush on (it would be awkward if that got around), and when I'm away at college and miss my Mom . . . er . . . my friends."

Snapchat represents carefree silliness and fleeting expressiveness. New filters allow for an endless stream of augmented human expression, which is why you can often spot some kid opening their mouth and raising their eyebrows to make silly faces at their cell phone. The model amounts to a very different value proposition from Facebook, and it appears to be gaining traction among the younger cohorts who will determine how the Social Organism functions in the future. A 2014 poll by Sparks & Honey showed a clear preference among Generation Z kids (those born after 1995) for Snapchat and other secrecy-enhancing services such as Whisper and Secret compared with more public platforms. That same study found that a quarter of that group had left Facebook in the preceding twelve months. In another 2014 poll, Defy Media found that 30 percent of people between the ages of eighteen and thirty-four—loosely conforming to Millennials—used Snapchat regularly. (In my adopted home of Iceland, a whopping 70 percent of its mere 320,000 citizens are connected on Snapchat. Let's just say a party travels fast.) It has been reported that Snapchat turned down a $3 billion offer from Facebook in 2013. Did they make the Friendster mistake? Time will tell. For the sake of open, competitive platforms for free expression, their refusal to sell was a good thing.

Then there's one of my favorites, Vine, owned by Twitter. This six-second video format, which forces creative self-expression into a narrow time window, has spawned an entirely new art form. One version: the "perfect loop," a six-second, repeating piece of music that merges so perfectly you can't tell where it begins and ends. Almost out of nowhere, Vine videos have become a vehicle for self-branded entertainment. It has turned a host of once-nobodies, many of them teenagers, into global marketing sensations. We'll meet some of these Vine stars in the next chapter, but for now it's worth pointing out that already many have audiences in the tens of millions, exceeding those of the world's biggest newspapers. As of November 2015, Vine itself boasted 200 million users.

We start to see even more digital biodiversity if we head overseas. Although Facebook dominates South and Southeastern Asia, local platforms are big in North Asia. And it's not just because of foreign website bans in China, where the most popular sites are Facebook-copy Renren and Twitter-like service Weibo. In more liberal South Korea, there is a preference for a local site called CyWorld, and in Taiwan many people use Wretch. Latin America, too, sports its own challenger, a site with 27 million registered users called Taringa! that uses bitcoin to share revenues with content providers. Life adapts to a given environment if it is to survive, and we see the Social Organism doing just that as it flourishes in different regions around the world.

Then, of course, there's Google. With the merely modest success of its community offerings such as Google+, the world's biggest Internet company has been less successful at founding social media networks—at least in terms of those services' narrowest definition. But it is in all other respects the uber-networker of our age. Google Chrome is the most popular Web browser; in 2016, Gmail surpassed more than 1 billion monthly active users, making it the most used email service; first, Google Maps and now, Google-owned Waze have become the community-populated navigation services of our age; YouTube looks after our videos; Google Hangout is a go-to video conferencing service; the same could be said for Google Drive and Google Docs in terms of storage and file sharing; Android claims more than 80 percent of the market for smartphone operating systems; and, of course, the Google search engine has a virtual monopoly, which means the entire World Wide Web is designed to cater to it. We are all, in effect, algorithmically tied to each other by Google.

For all the legitimate concerns people have about Google's immense power, its success is founded on the very principle of open platforms, interoperability and on an ingrained culture of open innovation. Yet the bigger question, one we will discuss at length later in the book, is whether its dominance—and that of Facebook and others like it—can remain compatible with the Social Organism's evolutionary process. Google and Facebook are themselves products of an underlying trend toward decentralization, an extension of the unraveling of power from the Catholic Church to CBS and News Corp. to social media. And with new ideas around distributed databases, decentralized cryptocurrencies, and anonymous information, these new giants of twenty-first-century media will also find themselves confronting the ruthless algorithm of evolution. If they can't adapt, they, too, will one day go the way of the dinosaurs and the newspapers.

* * *

Within the lifetime of a Millennial we have gone from online message boards and USENET groups to the communities attached to intranets like Prodigy and AOL, and from there to Friendster and Myspace and, eventually to Facebook and then Twitter, which together spawned Tumblr, Instagram, Snapchat, Vine, and others. Simultaneously, other decentralized models of human interaction are leveraging the Internet's ever-expanding global, multinode network: online marketplaces like eBay; peer-to-peer lending; crowdfunding networks such as Kickstarter; reputation-driven asset-sharing services like Uber and Airbnb; bitcoin and other digital currencies; online open-source code repositories like GitHub. While not technically part of the social media industry, these technologies are part of the same amorphous, organically evolving force that's shaping our culture and communities. They, too, define how the Social Organism lives.

As this new paradigm of hyper-competition grows, businesses designed around the old top-down model risk extinction unless they adapt. Centrally mandated corporate dogma and time-consuming chains of command are out of sync with the rapid demands of the Organism and the autonomous way in which it prioritizes how to occupy its limited attention quota. If brand managers, corporate PR teams, news organizations, politicians, and individuals want to get their message out, they, too, must move quickly. And that's not easy when authorization systems depend on approval from the top.

Some traditional brands are showing they can adapt. During Super Bowl XLVII, Oreo embedded its senior brand management team with the 360i ad agency for the duration of the game, allowing quick authorization for sending out real-time messages to consumers. When suddenly there was an unprecedented blackout in the stadium, Oreo sent out a brilliant "You can still dunk in the dark" tweet, which was retweeted more than 10,000 times and received more than 18,000 likes in one hour—and shifted the conversation around how to make messages go viral. By contrast, when Disney bought my company DigiSynd and hired me in 2008 as an "insurgent" to open up its content and its social media presence, the first Mickey Mouse image I tried to put on Facebook as a promotional strategy took thirty days to garner approval from the Disney brass. How in the world am I going to keep up with an audience whose social fabric changes in minutes, if I'm waiting for a month for each piece of content?

The problem facing pre–social media institutions can be expressed in terms of the link between information growth and the evolution of computational capacity that we described in reference to César Hidalgo's work. Whenever they process information to engineer products and services of value, individuals, firms, industries, and even entire economies will strive to gain more computing power. The competition for scarce resources demands it if they are to thrive and survive. Now that we have shifted information processing to a giant, interconnected network of human beings who are generating, sharing and processing ideas, that supercomputer's power has exploded. What it means is that new, nimble smaller entrants into the market can access it at very low cost—a prospect that, for the first time, gives the little guy an advantage over bigger players. In effect, these upstarts are tapping into what might be described as a universally accessible global brain.

To Howard Bloom, the brilliant but slightly mad music publicist–turned–evolutionary theorist, life itself has always been evolving toward the optimization of a global brain. In his ambitious book *The Global Brain: The Evolution of Mass Mind from the Big Bang to the 21st Century,* Bloom frames this idea around human beings' perennial battle with bacteria and other microbes—one we have occasionally come close to losing whenever pandemics like the black plague or AIDS arise. Bloom defines early-stage bacteria, which preceded all other forms of life on earth and took hold in the primal phase of our planet, as a giant data-sharing system. Devoid of the basic, membranous molecular form that most life would later assume and imbued with a capacity to share chemical signals across bacterial colonies, these microorganisms functioned, Bloom says, as a kind of network of computers. Together they collectively processed information about which version of their constantly morphing and adapting selves was the more superior and signaled that adoption of that structure. It seems as if this purpose—to process information and develop responses to it—is what got life started. Bacteria and viruses survived, even as more complex organisms started to arise out of the swamp. The microbes' survival meant that human beings, in their constant battle with these nemeses, had to formulate combinations of group power to enhance their own organizational and computing structure.

Bloom's idea might sound whacky when reduced to a few lines like this but it checks out with a lot of the research going into how microorganisms work as information-sharing networks. If he's right, it means that when we combine social media's organic interconnectivity of ever-expanding ideas with the powerful networks of supercomputers developing alongside it, we've arrived at a potentially transformative moment in our species' survivability. Ray Kurzweil, the famous futurist and Google engineering director, believes that by 2045 the "singularity" will be upon us. That's the point, according to his theory, at which computer-driven artificial intelligence reaches a kind of super intelligence that removes it from the control of inferior human beings and enters a process of rapidly reinforcing self-improvement cycles. If that A.I. machinery is designed to improve life for humans, it may well make us immortal, Kurzweil believes. More ominously, other Silicon Valley thought leaders, such as Elon Musk, worry that it could destroy us.

Bloom's explanation of how we arrived at the global brain departs somewhat from the favored version of evolution theory spawned by Richard Dawkins, the great zoologist and renowned atheist. Dawkins's notion of the selfish gene explained why much of the popular conception of Darwinism was wrong. To Dawkins—whose provocative take on memes will be addressed in chapter 4—the only reason group behavior emerged among animals, including humans, is because it suited the real architects of life, genes. He views both human flesh and the thought functions concocted by its biochemistry as mere vehicles for genes—he calls bodies "survival machines"—to raise the odds of their passage into the next survival machine once the current one reproduces. Everything, from altruism to social organizations like cities or corporations, is geared toward making that perpetuation more likely. Dawkins's take, published in his 1976 book, *The Selfish Gene,* was a rejection of the popular idea that selfless behavior among animals was an evolved trait intended to assure the perpetuation of the species. The group's interests have nothing to do with it, Dawkins argued; it's all about the genes' self-interest.

But now we have Bloom, with a powerful, long-arc theory that puts the idea of group interest back into the picture. To Bloom, the genome itself is a tightly coordinated group of units operating in concert for the common good. It sets the template for system designs that over time will show that the greater the diversity of organizational structure, the greater the survivability of the group—an idea that runs counter to the disturbing, exclusionary ideas of political figures like Donald Trump and Marine Le Pen and the British nationalists who successfully delivered "Brexit." On this point, it's not clear who's right between Dawkins and Bloom, but we can be hopeful that this current moment, where social media has taken the Social Organism's interconnected idea-processing power into overdrive, may bring us the answers.

In the chapters ahead, we'll delve into the fundamental question asked by these two theorists: Why do we do what we do? And we'll demonstrate how social media offers a laboratory to explore that.

CHAPTER THREE

THE AGE OF HOLARCHY

The Interconnected, Decentralized Cell Structure of Social Media

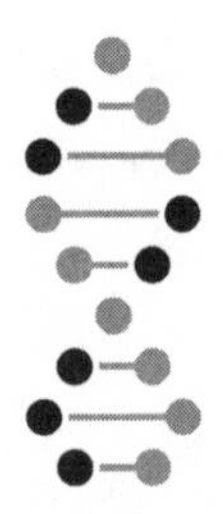

BACK WHEN I was a nerdy kid exploring life through my first Wolfe microscope—I still remember buying it from the Carolina Biological Supply catalog that Mrs. Franceschetti gave me—my favorite thing to find was a volvox, a green algae that forms spherical colonies inside pond water all around the world. Under the microscope a volvox was a beauty to behold: a perfectly spherical life form with tiny glowing green circles within it. In fact, although a volvox is classified as multicellular, it only took on this more complex form when, millions of years ago, its component single-cell organisms came together to form colonies. To this day, a volvox really functions as a group of fifty thousand unique organisms. They are connected to one another in a community matrix that forms a *holonic* structure—a state of interconnectedness in which unique entities exist in relation to one another. Each unit has the same basic form but differentiated purpose. Each is independent in its actions yet intrinsically part of a unified wider whole. In the case of the volvox, each organism develops different functions: some become photosynthetic receptors to generate energy for the community; some grow little flagella tails so they can carry out phototropic functions such as swimming toward the sunlight; some become daughter colonies to help reproduction.

That image of a volvox immediately sprang to mind when I saw the spectacular Opte Project's artistic visualization of the Internet, which hangs in New York's Museum of Modern Art. Created with a sophisticated program that produced images upon images of every network's relationship to each other in the online world, it makes for a striking juxtaposition when placed against a microscope-produced photo of a volvox.

In the Opte Project image, we see the decentralized interconnecting network of billions of nodes. It has become a template for many other visualizations produced for analyses of social media phenomena—for illustrating how a particular phrase or piece of news flows across the network, for example, or for how social networks of "followers" and "friends" tend to coalesce and form bridges. In all of such graphics, the bright spots, just like those in the Opte image, represent clusters of connectedness, the hubs from which our human connections emerge and interconnect. In a social media context, they are celebrities, brands, original thinkers, influencers, and anyone who's attracting a mass audience. Like the cells within the volvox, the clusters that form around them extend to make connections with the rest of the organism and thus to push out the message.

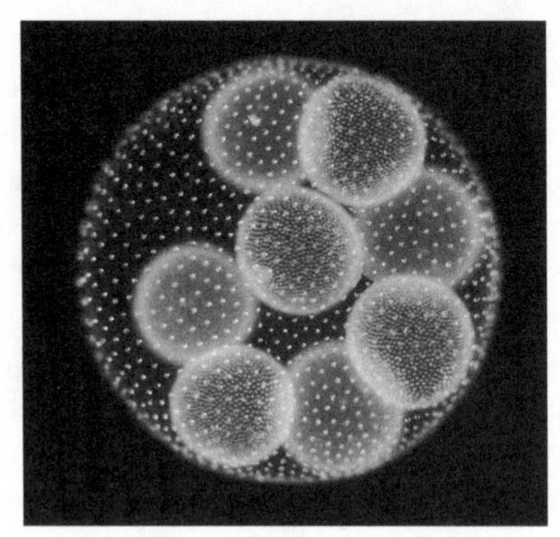

Volvox

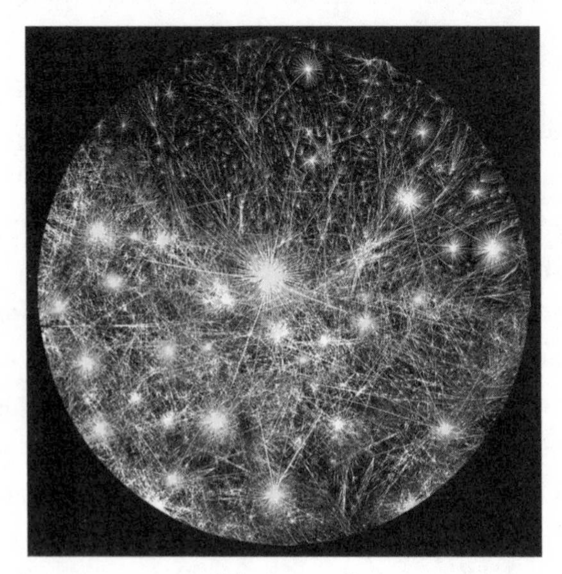

"The Internet"

It's consistent with the first defining characteristic of life, Life Rule number one: All living things have a cell structure. A corollary to this rule is that the more complex the organism, the more specialized and differentiated its cell types will be.

What does that mean when applied to the Social Organism? On the most simple level, the breakdown of the Social Organism's structure, roles can be split into influencers and followers. But in just a few short years, we've seen more complex and niche roles emerge. The classifications would also include artists and other creative types who turn existing ideas into new derivative versions of the art—which we can think of as hybrid memes—as well as trolls and other disruptive elements that challenge, redirect, and contain the flow of thoughts. Each depends on the others, and without their combined interactions the Organism could not live or sustain equilibrium.

In the following pages, I give a snapshot of some social media elites and their networks, which offer some key insights into the Social Organism's cell structure. Just like my beloved volvox, the relationships between the component cells in a social media network can be described as a *holonic* structure, where every entity is both an autonomous whole and part of a larger system of interdependent, self-regulating hierarchies. Holonics not only describes the order of the natural world, but an order that arises organically, without centralized control. Because such ideas are the antithesis of the vertical, command-and-control systems perpetuated by Western capitalism, they can seem contradictory to minds that are raised in that tradition, minds that imagine the absence of central authority as a recipe for chaos.

But make no bones about it, there *is* order in the Social Organism. And that creates opportunities for those who recognize it.

For while others see chaos in the social media universe, those with insights into this holonic structure are making a fortune by tailoring their networks to it.

Visualizations of social media clusters that follow the Opte image template shown on page 50 tend to mask the fact that the power relationships within this new communications architecture are in flux. As a function of the Organism's rapid, evolutionary state, the roles and status of influencers are always changing. When I founded theAudience in 2011, our first clients were people like Hugh Jackman, Charlize Theron, Mark Wahlberg, and Russell Brand—pre-established celebrities who were using social media platforms to maintain and build their brands. As my cofounder Sean Parker put it, these were the "digital immigrants," non-natives in the online marketing world who sometimes reluctantly dove into social media because their handlers told them it was necessary or because social media followings were becoming a measurement of worth.

Once the system for determining what content gets distributed shifts from one where it was decided by studios and record companies to that of a holonic structure in which autonomous individuals did so in concert with each other, big changes in the pecking order of the creative industries were inevitable. We're now seeing entirely new spheres of influence developing around networks of connected human beings, with an entirely new kind of celebrity sitting in the middle. They are people like Vine star Nash Grier, a prolific producer of silly, six-second video vignettes.

Grier's Vines project a lifestyle and way of being that taps into the imagination of a whole generation of digitally connected kids. He is witty, somewhat mischievous, irreverent, and moderately self-deprecating, yet also cool and, importantly, not too threatening. His jokey, slapstick clips exude a vision of carefree existence that's projected as if it belongs entirely to his generation; it's not a world that older folks can participate in. By connecting on that level he has accumulated millions of fans, many of them adoring females but also hordes of young men who want to be like him. By 2013, when he was just fifteen, Grier had amassed 6.8 million Vine followers. By mid-2016, that number had swelled to 12.7 million, encompassing a group of fans who had watched his clips a total of 3.4 billion times, as measured in "loops." Grier also had more than 5.5 million Twitter followers by then, a group that included numerous accounts set up purely to keep track and retweet everything he does or says—a network of sub-influencers working for a central influencer, an ecosystem within his own ecosystem. These sprawling tentacles of fans give him the same reach as most cable networks. Grier's currency is his digital persona.

Grier joins a host of Generation Z-ers and Millennials producing voyeuristic glimpses into their lives, a genre that's suited to short-form Vines and short-lived Snapchat messages. With their endless feed of vignettes—sometimes delivered as staged jokes and pranks, other times as brief windows into their "chill" existence—life emerges as a series of fleeting, transitory performances. Vine's jumpy, low-budget aesthetic, which eschews the brash glamor of Hollywood celebrities and instead contrives the star as an everyman, is the format's magic sauce. Despite the real-life mega-stardom that many of these leading "Viners" have attained, they convey a down-market image of lovable, knockabout kids. Beneath that anti-establishment image, however, these new celebrities are forming their own kind of organizational strategy, one in which they all feed off and reinforce each other's reach and influence.

The format has proven to be a winner among young followers and spawned an entire industry and subculture. Not surprisingly, it has also attracted some big advertisers. Coca-Cola, Hewlett-Packard, Procter & Gamble, and Warner Bros. have teamed up with Viners like Cody Johns and Greg Davis Jr. I routinely saw six-second spots with Nash Grier going for $25,000 to $35,000, and he's been known to attract as much as $100,000. Ritz Crackers got teen Vine star Lele Pons—the highest ranking female Viner, with more than 10 million followers and the largest number of total loops overall at 7.5 billion—to insert her prankster persona and slapstick style into an ad that involved her stealing unsuspecting people's crackers. The world's most successful Viner, Andrew Bachelor, better known as King Bach (15 million followers, 5.6 billion loops), has turned down loads of offers to do sponsored Vines but has nonetheless monetized his fame by landing lucrative TV and film roles from *Black Jesus* to *The Mindy Project*. In March 2013 King Bach posted a six-second "Ghetto Beat Down" derivative version of the Chainsmokers' #Selfie song, which theAudience had promoted. His video exposed a huge new digital audience to the song and pushed the daily views of the original #Selfie video from 800,000 to over 1.5 million during a sustained two-month period. It was a compelling example of how these uber-influencers have developed the capacity to tap this new organically interconnected network structure to rapidly spread information.

For its short content, Vine is also an oddly successful platform for music promotion. Husband-and-wife team Michael and Carissa began recording folk-pop music in 2011, but once they started putting six-second loops of themselves up on the platform, their career took off. A year later, they signed with Republic Records, marking what is thought to be the first ever deal spawned from Vine. Around the same time, Canadian singer-songwriter Shawn Mendes launched himself on Vine at the age of fifteen; two years later he had 4.5 million followers, had recorded two albums, had opened for Taylor Swift's world tour, and his "Stitches" single had reached number one on the Billboard charts. Jack & Jack (6 million followers, 1.8 billion loops)—high school buddies who became a comedic duo on Vine and with whom I worked to package content and advertising deals—have also topped the iTunes charts with songs like "Wild Life."

Then there are the YouTube millionaires, whose ranks include some very young stars. The most lucrative model: doing reviews of toys. By the age of eight, Evan of the YouTube channel EvanTubeHD, was earning an estimated $1.3 million in ad revenues for reviews filmed by his dad. Two Japanese children, Kan and Aki, appear to be even younger and were earning an estimated $3.2 million for their "reviews" in 2013. The biggest earner on YouTube is the unidentified owner of a site called DC Toy Collector, which never shows the face of the elaborately nail-painted hands of what appears to be a young girl opening and assembling Disney toys. The site earned $4.9 million in 2014, according to video data analytics firm OpenSlate—more than second-ranked YouTuber Taylor Swift earned for ads on her videos that same year. The third biggest YouTube earner is PewDiePie, a Swedish game commentator—a popular genre that involves recording a running commentary over the top of a filmed video game. With 40.9 million subscribers and over 11 billion views on his videos, he earned $4 million in 2014.

I'm going to guess that, perhaps with the exception of Taylor Swift and, maybe, Shawn Mendes, the names listed above are new to most of you reading this. They're not what most people of my generation or older would typically call "household names." Yet their ability to reach a targeted audience is more advanced than most established media outlets. Any brand or institution that wants to properly reach a major audience must come to grips with this new architecture and the powerful intermediation of these new, independent stars.

Social media's infrastructure of human networks is by no means an evenly distributed population of influence. If Twitter were a nation and follower numbers were dollars earned, it would look far more unequal than the American economy's notoriously skewed income distribution. A survey by O'Reilly Media in 2013 found that those Twitter accounts in the top 1 percent of follower tallies averaged 2,991 followers, a figure 50 times the average of those at the 50th percentile. (In terms of U.S. income, the top 1 percent has an estimated eight times those in the middle.) Go up to 0.1 percent of Twitter accounts and the difference with the median is a factor of 409. And that was in 2013, when that group averaged just 20,462 followers. What's more, it took no account of what we might see as the "Bill Gateses and Warren Buffetts" of Twitter's skewed influence distribution curve, the mega-influencers that claim more that 40 million followers, people like Lady Gaga, Justin Bieber, Katy Perry, and that uber-celebrity, President Obama.

It's worth also noting that the unequal influence distribution correlates with earnings. Only the elites, those at the very pinnacle of follower tallies, are killing it financially. Like brilliant footballers or basketballers who dominate college competitions but can't break into the professional leagues, YouTube, Vine, and other ad-earning platforms are filled with talented, almost-making-it types. People like Brittany Ashley, one of the biggest and best-known stars on BuzzFeed's four YouTube channels, which together account for 17 million subscribers. Ashley might have 70,000 Instagram followers but she still has to wait tables at a restaurant in West Hollywood to make ends meet. As Fusion writer Gaby Dunn noted in a piece about Ashley and other online personalities who get hounded by fans at their day jobs, "[m]any famous social media stars are too visible to have 'real' jobs, but too broke not to." Efforts to create mutual sharing agreements so that users can pool their follower networks, including that of the Shout! project by MIT Media Lab's Macro Connections group, might one day improve the economics of social media for little guys. But for now, when compared with more than a billion users worldwide, the winnings in social media appear to be extremely concentrated in the hands of a few.

Still, there's no denying there's been a major power shift toward the handful of newcomers who've fully mastered the art of social media marketing. Whether it's self-employed powerhouses like Grier or BuzzFeed's slightly more professionally produced YouTube channels, these people have something marketers and communicators want: command of a massive and directly targetable audience. How should we view this in terms of the evolution of mass media? In garnering such influence and audience, has this handful of instant millionaires simply converted themselves into a new oligopoly over cultural production? Are these teenage pranksters, with their often inane, mildly narcissistic statements on life's absurdities, the new commanders of our communication system? Are these zany kids now occupying roles that were, in times past, held by the church, newspapers, and TV networks?

Well, to a degree, yes. But this is key: These newcomers' grip on the fulcrum of power is tenuous. Their dominance of the market is not backed by economies of scale as it was for traditional media companies; they're not protected by the barriers to entry that old newspaper giants enjoyed when it was too costly for smaller competitors to invest in printing presses and delivery trucks. Rather, the social media influencers' power is instead founded on the trust and emotional connections they've built with their fans and friends. Social media stars are nothing without the cooperation of their followers and of the privately owned platforms where they distribute their content. In biological terms, these uber-users are what epidemiologists view as "super spreaders," those especially contagious types that play outsized roles in the dissemination of biological viruses. (Super spreaders typically account for about 20 percent of a population but have been shown to be responsible for 80 percent of all infections during epidemics.) Regardless of their mega-contagiousness, however, super spreaders' impact is only as strong as the receptiveness of others in the population to the virus they are spreading. To maintain influence, social media elites need their followers to consistently repeat, replicate, and share the ideas they generate. It's a distribution network that depends entirely on an ability to connect with other people who are willing to share the information you provide them.

These influencers' power lies in their ability to build networks. They do this not by laying out fiber-optic cable but by forging virtual personal bonds. The strategy is twofold: On the one hand, they cultivate a very large army of fans, focusing on delivering content that serves their viewers' emotional needs; on the other, they forge tight social ties with other strong networkers, partly by impressing them with their work but also through personal connections. By tapping this inner circle of uber-influencers with very large fan bases, they can launch messages into a gigantic network very quickly.

With Nash Grier and King Bach leading them, a Rat Pack for the digital age has arisen, including: Jack & Jack, Matthew Espinosa (6 million followers), Nash's own brother Hayes (4.2 million followers), Shawn Mendes, and, for a time, a young provocateur by the name of Carter Reynolds (4.4 million followers). They collaborate by doing cameos in each other's Vines, appearing in each other's music shows, and—most important—reposting each other's blogs. (At theAudience, we called this cross-popularization.) All of them moved to Hollywood to be able to coordinate their daily lives together. It's like a living reality show, playing out constantly on social media. And in a unique, social media way, they are building a kind of modern oligopoly in which celebrity and influence are the barriers to entry.

Yet those protective barriers aren't as formidable as those that monopolies in the brick-and-mortar world enjoy. The challenge confronting the Viners' Rat Pack oligopoly is that social networks that are founded on mutual interest can fall apart when someone acts counter to those interests. In the old media structure, the top-down hierarchy provides a check on what goes out: Material is carefully vetted to try to ensure that nothing is released if it could undermine the media company's market position. But in the holonic structure of the Social Organism, where both makers and distributors of content act autonomously, such calculated control over content isn't possible. And here's the thing: People, especially teenagers, make mistakes.

The speed with which Carter Reynolds lost control of his distribution system speaks to this problem. Reynolds was one of the biggest names on Vine until midway through 2015, when a hacker obtained and leaked a video of him pressuring his sixteen-year-old girlfriend and occasional Vine co-star, Maggie Lindemann, to have oral sex.

There followed a series of very public meltdowns, failed attempts at contrition, and a major Twitter war with Lindemann that earned its own trending hashtag, #MaggieandCarter. The defining moment was when Reynolds produced a long, rambling video, during which his phone beeped with what he told the audience was a threatening text from Maggie and then proceeded to explain how he'd been told that "she sucked Hayes Grier's dick." This was the same Hayes Grier who is the brother of Vine superstar (and devout Christian) Nash and with whom Reynolds had often worked. The whole sordid affair played out to millions of people. Not surprisingly, Reynolds's advertising dried up. Just as important, he was cut off from the Vine Pack. As of late 2015, Reynolds's Vine page still showed a following of more than 4 million and, with his notoriety sustaining some level of fascination, his post-scandal Vines still received just over a million views. But that figure was well below half of the multimillion loops he was clocking in the first half of that year. By 2016, his Vine output completely dried up, with his page showing just three "re-Vined" clips made by other Viners over the course of the first six months of the year. Without the shout-outs on Twitter, Instagram, and other platforms from his well-connected former buddies, he didn't have the same audience reach. In the Social Organism, those that giveth taketh away.

Social ties and networks are the very foundation of these young stars' fame. And they can break. People like Carter Reynolds can fall so rapidly out of the public eye, when even scandal-ridden celebrities from more traditional areas of entertainment often ride on their fame for longer: Tiger Woods, Mel Gibson, and so forth. The lesson here is not that social media influence can be both powerful and fleeting. It's that to be effective and sustainable, the social network needs to be constantly maintained and nurtured for the re-blogs, re-tweets, re-posts, and shares to keep going. Life Rule number four: To maintain this steady state of homeostasis, the Organism's metabolic pathways—in this case, social connections—need to be open and unbroken.

We learned a great deal at theAudience about maintaining ties with followers. Our relationship with the influencers we'd brought into our network was critical to its success. Through these well-defined bonds, a message could be fanned out to a global mass of hundreds of millions of people very quickly. But equally crucial, our influencers had to manage their own networks. They needed to keep their own followers actively engaged, with a steady stream of nourishing content that helped cultivate trust and loyalty. Doing so is what constitutes network maintenance in the social media age. Whereas network maintenance at a traditional TV channel refers to the upkeep of cameras, broadcast towers, and cables, in social media it's all about emotional maintenance. Viewers and readers are no longer just an audience; they are also a distribution mechanism.

In pop culture, Taylor Swift is the queen of network maintenance. She is arguably the most powerful woman in show business. (Eat your heart out, Oprah.) She alone stood up to Apple, the most successful consumer product maker in the world, and forced the company to change its artist royalties policy overnight, simply by publishing an open personal complaint letter to the company. The power of that letter was not based simply on the quality of her music but because she had an army of loyal followers behind her. With more than 50 million Instagram followers, the highest ranking on that site, and a Facebook page with 73 million likes, Swift commands the attention of a population bigger than France's.

But it's Tumblr that's become the singer's preferred stage for performing the character called "Taylor Swift." On Tumblr, Swift has cultivated a deep sense of trust, sincerity, and genuine affection with her young fans, a global community that self-identifies as "Swifties." She has done this by doing things like turning up on the doorsteps of some of them with personally delivered Christmas gifts and posting videos of the surprise visits. Alongside action shots of the singer strutting her long legs before stadiums filled with screaming fans, Swift's feed offers images and one-liners that, like the Vine stars, seek engagement through a common touch: selfies with her cats, shots of her hanging out in pajamas, hugs with her girlfriends.

To be sure, Swift's BFFs aren't exactly commoners. Her well-documented friendships with other influential young women include fellow singer Selena Gomez and fashion model Karlie Kloss, offering another reminder of how a powerful inner circle of fellow influencers can maximize clout. The star pull of the former child actor Gomez—who sits just two spots below Swift's number one spot in Instagram rankings—is impressive in its own right. She wins over the teen crowd with a persona that veers more toward the good-girl-gone-bad image (Miley Cyrus's forte) than does Swift's more wholesome self-portrayal. Many attributed the breakaway success in 2013 of *Spring Breakers*, the dark gangster romp from director Harmony Korine for which we at theAudience designed an unorthodox and highly successful marketing strategy, to the widely shared animated GIF, lifted from the movie, of Gomez smoking a bong. Her seductive self-branding is also fueled by her rocky former relationship with bad boy pop star Justin Bieber, the owner of the second-most followed Twitter account after Katy Perry and the fifth-most followed Instagram account.

But it's not just sex and close-knit celebrity partying that sells. Taylor Swift's careful strategy for fan management/network maintenance employs a much more personal touch. Just as Bill Clinton's capacity for empathy was key to his prodigious skills as a political networker, the twenty-five-year-old demonstrates how far humane gestures carry influence. When the hashtag #ShakeitupJalene alerted Swift to the fact that the final wish of Jalene Salinas, a four-year-old girl diagnosed with terminal brain cancer, was to dance with the star to "Shake It Off," the singer set up a Facetime call with her and her mother. Television cameras recorded the tear-jerking moment. Another time, she donated $50,000 to eleven-year-old Naomi Oakes, who was battling leukemia. A tearful Swift also gave a shout-out during a concert to the mother of another four-year-old who'd just died of cancer, sharing the fact that her own mother had been battling the disease.

Swift's charitable gestures may simply be contrived and self-serving. But even if they are, it's hard not to be impressed by the grand, international scale of her fan/follower management. It takes real talent to succeed in making someone feel like they are being spoken to personally when they are one of 75 million; these little acts of soft touch can create that illusion. Taylor Swift's fans feel a very deep bond with her—arguably more so than the "Rihanna Navy" population feels with their idol, Rihanna, whose social media image (primarily on Instagram) depends more on glamour and sex appeal than on personal connections with fans.

Swift is clearly a talented and hardworking performer. But the rest of it—the empathetic, big-hearted, all-around-nice-person image that she presents on social media—is also important. They form two parts of the same, combined package. Together, they demonstrate how the mechanics of fame work in this new era, where communication networks are managed with emotions. Since social media occupies a holonic structure in which the autonomous members of the network represent both the target audience and the distribution system, emotions are now the primary tool for spreading ideas and artistic works.

Nature does not have a dictator, benevolent or otherwise, telling it what to do—notwithstanding the millennia-old debates over the existence of a God. Neither do social media networks. This holonic structure offers not just a useful way to think about the Social Organism, but a satisfying, all-encompassing explanation for life itself.

Holonics can be described as a field of biological philosophy, though it also draws from physics and systems design. Developed by Arthur Koestler in the 1960s and furthered by the likes of Ken Wilber, the notion has fallen back into favor as the online economy has rekindled network theory. Holonics recognizes that the world comprises interdependent hierarchies and sub-hierarchies known as holons. (The word "holon," like "holistic," stems from the Greek word "holos," meaning "whole, entire complete.") Each holon is an autonomous whole in its own right and at the same time is a part of, and dependent on, an even wider whole, which in turn constitutes another, higher-level holon. A holon's status is inherently dualistic; whether it is a whole or a part depends on how you look at it. Together, holons form a progression of interdependency like an ever-growing stack of Russian matryoshka dolls.

The idea builds out to what is, in effect, a theory of everything. It's the kind of all-encompassing idea that could only take root in the broadmindedness of someone like Koestler, a brilliant polyglot intellectual of Jewish-Hungarian roots who lived all over Europe and flipped between left- and right-wing philosophies throughout a life that defied categorization. Koestler was born in Budapest, educated in Austria, and spent his early adulthood on a kibbutz in Palestine. He joined the German Communist Party in the 1930s right when Germans were warming to Hitler's Nazism and then worked as an anti-Franco spy on behalf of the loyalists in the Spanish Civil War. But later, after becoming thoroughly disillusioned with Stalin, he converted into a hardline anti-communist crusader from his adopted home in London. He was a prolific journalist, essayist, and novelist, writing articles and books of fiction and nonfiction that covered the gamut of biography, philosophy, physics, biology, and religious studies. In 1983, suffering with Parkinson's disease and newly diagnosed with cancer, Koestler and his wife, Cynthia, jointly committed suicide by overdosing on barbiturates and alcohol.

Holonics, the concept that arose from the holon theory that Koestler first expounded in his 1967 book *The Ghost in the Machine,* is perhaps his greatest contribution to Western thought. In a sweeping critique of the centuries-old prevailing human belief that the universe is defined by some centralized authority that established human domination, a model that gave birth to the horrors of the Holocaust and Stalinist authoritarianism, he offered the holon as an alternative construct from which to understand the nature of existence. To introduce this idea, Koestler retold the parable of two watchmakers that Nobel Prize–winning scientist Herbert A. Simon used to explain how complex systems form out of simple systems. In Simon's story, two watchmakers both make fine watches out of a thousand tiny parts. While they work, both must field frequent phone calls that interrupt their work. One watchmaker succeeds while the other fails. Why? Every time the unsuccessful watchmaker put down his unfinished watch to answer the phone it would fall apart, requiring him to build it from scratch. By contrast, the successful watchmaker built his watches from parts that were assembled into sub-assemblies of ten parts each, a modular arrangement that would hold together when it was put down. This basic idea—that stable, intermediate forms provide intermittent foundations upon which complex systems develop from simple systems—leads to the overarching concept of the holarchy. It's an idea that speaks broadly to how life takes form, how ideas develop, and how, in this seemingly chaotic world of social media, billions of autonomous nodes somehow, despite themselves, follow a degree of order and structure.

If you look at the picture of the volvox, with its spherical components comprising arrays of smaller spheres, you'll see how Koestler's model fits with microorganisms. But holonics equally describes more complex organisms, and even the ecosystems in which they exist, spreading out from the tiniest molecule to the structure of the entire universe (or multiverse, if you prefer). If we take the concept of "sheep," we can see that holonic hierarchies exist at each stage of the progression from biochemical compound, to cell, to organ, to the sheep's body, to the flock of the farm in which it lives, to its breed (Merino, say), to the species *Ovis aries*, and so on until these increasingly wide collections of units incorporate the biodiversity of the entire world. Each unit (holon)—be it the cell, the multicell organism of the sheep itself, or the flock to which it belongs—is simultaneously independent of and dependent on the wider group to which it belongs. As per the two diagrams below by Flemming Funch, a futurologist, philosopher, and systems designer, we can use this structure to describe a biological holarchy or that of a universal holarchy that lays out the overall dominions of life.

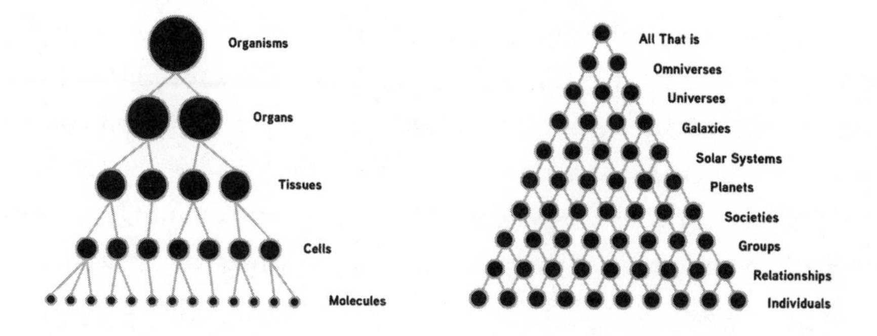

In fact, the beauty of Koestler's model is that we can apply it to any reference of existence, including social media networks. It explains the relationships between influencers, their inner circles of co-influencers, their combined clusters of followers, the wider platforms for sharing information, and the much, much wider ecosystem of the entire Social Organism. As with the holarchies of the natural world, the Social Organism has no formal leader, whether democratically elected or self-appointed. Instead, it's founded on a digital framework of interdependent relations that facilitates the system's own evolution and expansion.

To be sure, the Social Organism is currently not a very well structured holarchy, not in the idealistic terms of how well it serves the public interest, but understanding its organization will help us improve upon it—in fact, it's crucial to the technological future. In biology, holonics describes how social insects such as bees, termites, and ants work together. There's no central controller inside the mound dishing out orders to the termites; rather, each termite is genetically "programmed"—in its case by the great evolutionary algorithm of time—to respond to what it senses from its peers in a way that optimizes the group's interest and is influenced by biological signals. Now imagine a Google engineer who is designing self-driving cars that will interact with a fleet of similarly designed cars—all intended to optimize the traveling experience for the full community of passengers. There will be no super-command computer at Google headquarters directing all the cars like an airport control tower; rather the system will work because each car is individually programmed to respond to what it senses the others are doing and will adjust its "behavior" accordingly. This approach allows Google's engineers to design a holonic, leaderless transport system that can deliver all passengers to their destination more quickly and safely than in the current world of human-driven cars.

And while they might bristle at a comparison to termites, the Vine Rat Pack and Taylor Swift's BFF team are also "workers" in a holonic structure of creation. They're not constructing a termite mound or an efficient traffic pattern, but with their collaborations they are creating personas. Each influencer is autonomous in their creativity but at the same time works within the common whole of a set of shared values or patterns of thought. These shared values allow them to relate consistently to their audiences and become the basis upon which their followers engage in emotion sharing. When a single Vine, Twitter, or Instagram user relates to another within the Social Organism, they express themselves through the borrowed persona of one of these influencers. This then in turn becomes *their* persona. (Here we're talking about a much more fluid concept of the self than traditional liberal Western ideas of identity and personality. It's a concept we'll get to in chapter 5.)

As the Social Organism evolves and our means of communication move further away from a traditional, equipment-heavy media distribution model toward one founded on the holonic relationships between autonomous minds, the rest of society is going to have to reorganize, too. A good place to start is with that mainstay of capitalism: the company. We've already discussed how old style media companies' top-down authorization protocols and proprietary obsessions prevent them from keeping up with the rapid demands of social media. Similar problems are also arising in other pre–social media firms.

The most important objective of any organizational design is to facilitate efficient communication flow—internally among employees, work groups, managers, and shareholders, and externally with suppliers, contractors, customers, and the public—in order to optimize decision making and maintain a competitive edge. But now incumbent businesses that have relied on top-down communication are losing their edge, because social media and other online technologies let smaller, more nimble start-ups process information more efficiently. Instead of relying on their own narrow pool of thought capacity, these newcomers are leveraging the Social Organism's global brain, where ideas, content, and products are seamlessly shared without heed to geographical, national, or cultural boundaries. They're tapping a universally accessible system for creativity and computational capacity, a giant pool of potentiality that renders the old monopolies over information obsolete. The only way for incumbents to compete with this is to reorganize. To do so, they'll have to learn from the newcomers.

Salim Ismail and a team from Singularity University have a word for the most successful of these newcomers: exponential organizations. As they argued in a bestselling book of the same name, rapid, globally scaled growth is now possible if firms are willing to tap resources outside of their organization rather than depend on proprietary idea generation and implementation. This is not merely an outsourcing concept aimed at reducing costs; it's that external partnerships are the only way to rapidly build massive transformative networks, the only way to properly unleash new ideas and build new markets. To achieve this, firms must also be reorganized internally, with horizontal command structures that give greater autonomy to employees and encourage cooperation within and across self-organizing work groups. An exponential organization is one that favors symbiotic partnerships and collaborative projects over top-down, vertical control of the means of production. In such a firm, ownership and control are shared concepts.

One example is Chinese smartphone-maker Xiaomi, which relies on a fan base of 10 million "Mi Fen" followers to help steer product improvement. Non-employee users developed all but three of the programming languages available on Xiaomi's smartphone operating system; they also run the company's support system via a peer-to-peer advice platform and help keep the company's marketing costs low by voluntarily promoting its products over social media. What do these fans get in return? They get to engage in the development of an ever-improving and highly affordable line of smartphones that has in three years come from nowhere to become one of the five biggest in the world and is lapping at the heels of Apple and Samsung. That's emotionally satisfying.

Xiaomi is also a great example of how organizations need to restructure *internally* if they are to keep up with the fast-changing world of the Social Organism. Its work teams are conceived of much like clans or tribes, without strict lines of control. Emphasis is placed on mentoring, collaboration, and adhocracy, with profit sharing as a key incentive. Job rotation is encouraged. Worker autonomy is a key goal, so, too, is loyalty to the group. In that way it captures the parts-to-whole duality that's central to the concept of holonics.

Few have gone as far in formulating a defined management strategy around holonics as consultant Brian Robinson. He calls the ideal organizational design a "holacracy," a name that draws directly from Koestler and which Robinson's firm, HolacracyOne, has registered as a trademark. Rather than a pyramid structure based on authority, subordination, and control, Robinson's holacracy involves "circles" in which individuals are defined by their "roles" rather than by their titles. Such people have autonomy over decision making pertaining to their role, but they are compelled to address "tensions" within their circle before deciding on action and have no control over any other role.

Shoemaker Zappos.com is the poster child for the HolacracyOne model. CEO and founder Tony Hsieh, who is worth almost $1 billion but lives in a 240-square-foot Airstream camper in a communal trailer park in Las Vegas because he "really like[s] the unpredictability and randomness of it," has become a passionate believer. Hsieh wants to rearrange his firm so that it no longer has him, or anyone, at the helm. On its website, Zappos describes holacracy this way: "It replaces today's top-down predict-and-control paradigm with a new way of achieving control by distributing power. It is a new 'operating system' that instills rapid evolution in the core processes of an organization." Hsieh says he wants to emulate what happens in big cities, where innovation and productivity per resident increase 15 percent every time an urban area doubles in size, rather than accept the declining productivity that has traditionally hindered companies as they expand.

Implementing a holacracy is not easy, especially not in a firm like Zappos, which had operated since 1999 under a more traditional structure until Hsieh started to mix things up in 2012. When, in March 2015, he wrote an email to the company's 1,500 staff and offered severance for those who couldn't embrace the new culture, a surprisingly large 14 percent of the staff accepted it. Still, it's way too early to suggest that Zappos' experiment has been a failure; in fact, removing those who resist change may be exactly what's needed for success.

The exciting thing about these kinds of ideas is that, when taken to their highest level, we could reimagine an entire new societal arrangement, one that's less oppressive, more egalitarian, and more capable of unlocking the best in people. These are extremely lofty goals, the kind that have dogged philosophers and political scientists for centuries. How, though, might these ideas help us attain these goals in the era of social media?

Mihaela Ulieru, a researcher in intelligent systems design from Carleton University, offers a roadmap—and, perhaps not surprisingly, it comes down to how we treat each other, to the social mores of our culture. A necessary element of holarchic organizational design, she says, is that it unquestioningly recognizes the fundamental duality of a holon: that an individual is defined both by their independent sovereignty *and* by their membership of a wider collective group. She says this requires that people simultaneously embrace two different ways of perceiving the world. One of those is the "subject/object way of knowing," which she describes with the example of a bag of groceries that all individuals (subjects) can *objectively* agree weighs twelve pounds. The other is the "subject/subject way of knowing," an approach that's "rooted in an individual's subjective [and private, internal] experiences of the world." The latter perspective would recognize that the "bag of groceries that objectively weighs twelve pounds may feel subjectively lighter to an athlete but heavy to a frail, older person." Western societies have overly emphasized the first perspective, Ulieru says, but have typically downplayed the subjective differences between how people perceive the world. Incorporating the latter into our decision-making framework—an exercise that she says requires *empathy*—is thus the biggest challenge we face in designing holarchic systems.

Imagine now what Ulieru's schema might look like if applied to an optimal social media world. For now, it's hard to see much room in social media for the subject/subject perception model. All the mudslinging and quick-to-conclude responses of trolls and shit-stirrers on Twitter suggest a widespread inability to appreciate other people's subjectivities. Congregations of like-minded follower groups, where echo chambers of shared ideas objectify the identity of outsiders into catchall classifications—"Muslim extremists," "Christians," "liberals," "conservatives"—don't help, either. Will the Social Organism naturally evolve toward a more balanced and mutually beneficial set of relations? Or do we risk having it overrun by parasitic influences that skew the perspectives in their favor? Are empathy and a subject/subject system of sensory engagement part of its predestined progression, or will getting to that future require deliberate policy action? Is that even possible?

In chapter 6, we'll discuss how social media can be used to inspire empathy through emotive words and images. My hope is that we can collectively help the Social Organism to evolve into what I'd like to see it become: a body of shared humanity that's not only more creative, innovative, and prosperous but also more accepting of its own wondrous diversity. But before we discuss that meta-project, we must first delve more deeply into the workings of the Organism itself. It's time to explore the memetic code.

CHAPTER FOUR

CRACKING THE MEMETIC CODE

How Ideas Spread Like Viruses

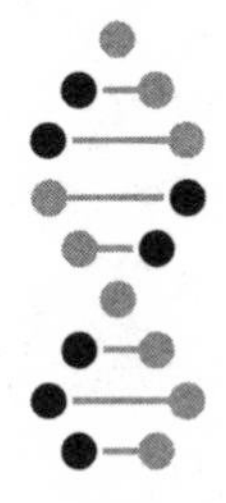

If someone asked you to explain what the word "Watergate" refers to, what would you say?

The majority of people would likely cite the political scandal that forced Richard Nixon from office in 1974. A smaller number would explain that the name attached to those tumultuous political events derives from the Washington hotel and office complex, where the Nixon-ordered 1972 break-in and burglary of the Democratic National Committee's headquarters took place. Only the biggest historical trivia junkies will know that the hotel's name itself refers to a nineteenth-century water gate that regulated the nearby Potomac River and the Chesapeake and Ohio Canal.

The rather functional historical origins of the term "Watergate" allow us to appreciate the interesting journey it has had at various junctures in the ensuing century, as it struck off on different paths of meaning. Then consider the powerful semiotic role that the suffix "-gate" has assumed since the Nixon scandal. When attached to a chosen noun, "-gate" now functions as a catchall signifier for anything possessing a whiff of scandal, conspiracy, or cover-up. I'd hazard a guess that plenty of political history-challenged Generation Z-ers recognize that "-gate" carries this meaning, but know nothing about the 1974 scandal. A Wikipedia entry on the topic lists 128 different scandals that have been given the "-gate" tag. Some of the better known ones: "Billygate" (President Jimmy Carter's failure to control his erratic brother), "Nipplegate" (for which Janet Jackson might be better known than her music), "Monicagate" (White House, cigar, etc.), and "Deflategate" (Tom Brady, football air pressure). What's most noteworthy is that only seventeen events on that list predate the Netscape browser (1995) and only a further twenty-one occurred between then and 2004, when Facebook was launched. The Internet did wonders for the "-gate" signifier. Now, social media has taken it into overdrive.

The "-gate" suffix is a great example of a meme—a unit or packet of information that conveys an idea and which, when shared with others, is mimicked, copied, and replicated and then, quite often, applied in new and creative ways to help forge culture. Memes aren't limited to words and language but are manifest in all manner of modes of expression—in pictures and other art forms, in photos, in songs or even parts of songs, in forms of dress, in body language, in inventions for new products, parts of products, or work processes. Infinitesimal in number—or at least approaching infinity—these conceptual packets are the basic building blocks of our culture, our social DNA. It's critical that we get our heads around this idea if we are to understand the Social Organism.

A meme, to quote Richard Dawkins, the zoologist, evolutionary theorist, and social commentator who brought us the idea, is "a unit of cultural transmission," which propagates by passing from brain to brain through a process of imitation. In coming up with the term, Dawkins borrowed from the Greek word "mememe," meaning "an imitated thing," and deliberately shortened it to something that sounded more like "gene." When he introduced the idea in a later chapter of his 1976 classic of evolutionary theory, *The Selfish Gene,* Dawkins highlighted the similarity between memes and genes: They are both entities whose essence lies in the fact that they self-replicate. Rejecting the popular "survival of the species" explanation for reproduction and evolution, *The Selfish Gene* argued that both processes reflect genes competing with each other to replicate themselves into the future. (The idea was that each gene dictates attributes to its host organism that give it a better chance at surviving until it can reproduce—Dawkins called human bodies "survival machines" for genes—which, by extension, gives the resident gene better odds of being replicated inside that organism's offspring.) Memes, Dawkins now said, functioned with this same innate need to replicate. And if genes were the basic autonomous replicators whose interactions drive the evolution of biological life, memes, he decided, were the auto-replicators determining the evolution of human culture.

It's a brilliant theory, one that's helped me forge a career around comprehending social media. The concept of memes gave me the framework I needed to comprehend how the Social Organism grows and evolves and to understand how the power of a popular (contagious) idea can be boiled down to a core memetic essence that facilitates its transmission from one person to another. I came to recognize how memes forge our complex thoughts into a digestible form so that others can absorb them, rework them, retransmit them, and broaden their reach. The further you dig into this idea, and compare it to what we know about genes, the more compelling it becomes.

We know that genes link up with each other to form strands of DNA, that beautiful double helix containing all the instructions that make each of us who we are, otherwise known as our *genetic code.* They also transcribe the proteins from which our complex bodies are built, both our hardware and our software. Well, memes do something similar. They come together to build ideas on top of other ideas—forming a series of holonic foundations. The process follows that of the successful watchmaker's modular assembly method, whose story Koestler used to explain his hierarchy of autonomous/dependent duality—as per the account in chapter 3. These tiny building blocks are the layers upon which bodies of knowledge and modes of understanding are constructed. They comprise a *memetic code*, one that the Social Organism, through the interconnections of its component "cells"—our brains—is constantly decoding in an ongoing process of cultural production.

We "inherit" this code from others as culture. And because its transmission occurs between people who share the same base cultural code—a necessary prerequisite to interpret and incorporate each new meme—this process of cultural adoption will create differences in the ways that groups of people see and comprehend the world. Aspects of the code might define one American as a fan of country music and another as a lover of seventies disco. Yet both are codified to prefer music in the polyphonic format of chord progressions that dominate the Western world, rather than, say, the monophonic Eastern form in which the structure hinges on the singular notes of melody. Our memetic code determines our nature as distinct agents of free thought with individual tastes, preferences, and worldviews. But it also establishes all the subjectivities we hold in common with others, thus forging broader cultures and subcultures. This is consistent with the role played by our genetic code, which both defines who we are as individuals and identifies and determines that we belong to wider groups of biological classification: human, mammal, animal, and so forth. Our memetic codes place our individuality into the wider context of cultural belonging.

Before we delve into what this means for social media, let's examine how the Social Organism determines what goes into the memetic code and what doesn't. Here Dawkins's broader evolutionary theory is useful. Just as genes, by his account, are constantly competing to survive and replicate, so, too, are memes competing with each other. In the memes' case, the competition is for the limited "computing" resources with which each brain is imbued: memory, information-processing capacity, and time. As we'll discuss later, successful memes are those that latch on to receptors in our brains—much as viruses parasitize a biological cell. And the memes that emerge as the most popular are those that can attach to receptors over and over again, jumping from brain to brain. Some do so with such lasting persistence that they grant an almost eternal cultural power to the owner of the first human brain in which they took root, a power that can long outlive the body in which the brain resided. (Beethoven's musical compositions gave his "memeplex" an immortality that the composer could never have.) Yet even those that are less resonant and long-lasting will play some role, however small, in forging the culture of the Social Organism.

Memes can be described as contagious ideas, another reason why it's extremely useful to view their expansion through the lens of biological contagion. Without that contagion, knowledge would not spread, information would remain static and unused, and cultures would not evolve. "The world around you is built from memes," writes social media marketing adviser Dan Zarrella. "Everything you see, touch or do is a contagious idea. The chair you sit in, the computer you're reading this on and the job that pays your bills all would not exist if someone did not have the idea to create it and that idea caught on and spread. This is true for the good things, as well as the bad things. The history of mankind is the history of contagious ideas."

So, ideas that catch on are pretty damn important. But what about those that don't? What about those packets of information that arise within someone's thought processes but are never successfully transmitted—and thus don't graduate to meme status—or those that fail to get beyond a few rounds of replication. Beethoven himself discarded countless bars of potentially moving music before the surviving memes found the right combination to cohabit his Ninth Symphony. Those lost musical segments were but a few of the overwhelming number of wannabe memes that our culture's evolutionary algorithm—the self-programmed director of an eternal movie that gives meaning to human existence—has left on the cutting-room floor over the millennia. It's mind-blowing to think of how different our sense of who we are would be if these lost memes had made it into the movie.

Just like biological evolution, there is nothing inherently purposeful or progressive about the selection process for memes. A meme need not be a practically good idea to catch on. The world is full of them—bacon doughnuts; stilettos; fascism. Likewise, lots of really good, useful memes never make it. It is worth keeping this in mind when we explore both the positive and negative cultural effects of social media.

Memes, like genes, also undergo mutation-like transformations every time they are transmitted or shared. Sometimes the change is minuscule, other times significant, but overall the rate of memetic mutation is generally much faster than the biological equivalent in genes. These alterations and adaptations help memes survive and adapt to alterations in their "environment," in this case the historical context in which they exist. In this way, old memes beget new memes and so on. As a result, our culture changes and evolves. For the Social Organism, this process of propagation and change reflects numbers six and seven of our biological rule book: respectively, that living things reproduce and that they adapt and evolve.

Let's return to Watergate for a moment. If we apply this evolutionary concept to our opening example, we can see how "Watergate" survived, adapted, and perpetuated itself as a meme. Much like biological evolution, it went through various changes because of accidents and coincidences, rather than by some grand design. In early nineteenth-century Washington, the words "water" and "gate" were merely conjoined descriptors of a common technology for controlling water. As city dwellers found it necessary to give a name to a geographic location in which that technology was deployed, the word combination won the competition for their limited mindshare. And so "water gate" the thing-meme became "Watergate" the place-meme. Then, in 1960, "The Watergate" successfully attached itself to receptors in the brains of some Italian property developers, who saw it as a fitting name for the hotel they planned to build in D.C., partly because it had an attractive ring to it but mainly because it matched the site of the development. Fourteen years later, "The Watergate" meme mutated into "The Watergate scandal" as the name of the hotel, the site of the break-in that prompted the legendary *Washington Post* investigation, lodged itself in the minds of the paper's reporters, editors, and readers. From there, "The Watergate scandal" would give birth to the "-gate" meme, in part because *New York Times* columnist William Safire kept affixing it to other words, such as "Vietnam," to describe new scandals.* His columns were effective in propagating this new meme partly because he was so widely read—think of him as a pre–social media "influencer"—and partly because the recent scandal resonated so strongly in the minds of his readers. At that time, the "Watergate" meme was so deeply embedded in Americans' collective consciousness that a single syllable from it contained enormous semiotic power.

In the forty years since Dawkins gave us the idea—more or less as an afterthought tacked on to the broader thesis of *The Selfish Gene*—it has spawned an entire field of study within the realm of cultural evolution. Naturally enough, it's called memetics. The idea is that by studying memes as genetic scientists study genes, we crack the code of culture.

Despite some serious consideration by sociologists and anthropologists, memetics has largely struggled to attain the unquestioned legitimacy that its adherents seek. Elegant as Dawkins's theory might be, the concept of a meme is not a clear-cut one. Unlike genes, which can be identified and isolated within strands of physical DNA, memes lack physical properties. They lack precision. There's simply no proof they exist. The ability to objectify a gene—to clearly

* Safire, who was formerly a Nixon speechwriter, has admitted that his discussion of a host of other "-gates" was partly motivated by his desire to dilute the attention on the Watergate scandal.

identify it as a "thing"—made it easier to embrace the main, radical idea in *The Selfish Gene*: that genes, preprogrammed to pursue the single goal of replication, are the driving force in the evolution of life. But it's harder to think of memes, these self-contained nuggets of information, having the same kind of autonomous agency outside of the human brains from which they spring.

It might be, though, that Dawkins, like Darwin, was ahead of his time. It wasn't until the twentieth century, when microscopes improved and scientists could study how DNA moved and subtly changed from organism to organism over time, that the great botanist was fully vindicated. (Even now, Creationists and Intelligent Design theorists try their darnedest to discredit him.) By the same token, what will happen when—possibly very soon—the capacity to view changes in neurological chemistry reaches a point that scientists can pinpoint the passage of thoughts and ideas from one person's brain to another? New developments in neuroimaging are pointing in this direction. In 2015, a team of researchers from Indiana University and Switzerland's University Hospital Lausanne unveiled a study showing how social network–generated information sets off unique responses within the human brain. We may be getting closer to a scientific definition of a meme.

I don't have that high-tech brainwave monitor at the ready, but we do have powerful tools to study how ideas are shared among humans. I'm talking about the billions of computers through which social media networks are connected and which are constantly accumulating data on how they interact. This giant pool of information can give rise to charts and graphic representations of how ideas, represented as packages of digital content, are replicated and shared among communities of interacting brains. These new data maps show memes functioning very much as Dawkins said they would.

Social media software platforms have been designed to facilitate this idea-sharing function in the smoothest fashion possible. The so-called "frictionless sharing" tools—the "share," "retweet," and "reblog" buttons—simply make meme replication that much easier and instinctive. Those additions seem like a natural response to market demand. Data suggest that people really like sharing meme-like packages of content. Every second, 7,000 new tweets are posted to Twitter, 1,000 new images are uploaded to Instagram, and 700 new blog items are posted to Tumblr.

It's no coincidence that the word "meme" has taken on new meaning in the social media age. Millennials and Generation Z-ers have embraced it to describe the humorous meldings of images and words that, when the formula is right, unleash an almost addictive effect on users to reproduce and share them. Some have become as iconic in our age as any movie or pop stars were in the pre-Internet era. Sometimes they come in standardized format with text typically added above and below a certain photo—for examples, see "Grumpy Cat," "Success Kid," or "Bad Luck Brian." I view such meme-making as the first real mass collaborative art form, with the organism driving their evolution as the underlying memetic code mutates.

These memes are new life forms defined by the particular environment in which they live, which in this case are the rules of the particular medium—from GIF, to picture, to YouTube videos. Other times there are pure text memes, such as that which arose from the revival of the World War II–era British poster "Keep Calm and Carry On" to spawn countless knockoff jokes. Some take the form of either static or moving (GIF) images—Pepe the Frog or, the original Internet meme sensation, the Dancing Baby. Still more defy categorization—case in point: The image of a Shiba Inu dog that someone labeled "Doge" in an homage to an episode of the Web puppet show *Homestar Runner* and to which a community of fans attach incongruous but upbeat sayings with purposefully bad grammar, Photoshopped Twinkie images, and the iconography of a bitcoin-like cryptocurrency, dogecoin. What's *that* about?*

As pointless as these exercises in communal mirth might seem, there's something undeniably impressive about the global flood of human creativity they unleash. And because of the trail of history that the Internet provides, a new field of pop science has emerged. The site Knowyourmeme contains detailed analyses of the history of different Internet memes; Tumblr employs its own meme librarian. The focus is typically on the kinds of memes that start after some jokester somewhere feels inspired by a certain photo or image and decides to devise a witty saying to accompany it. He or she then posts the combination onto a social media platform and from there it takes off. The most successful go beyond simple sharing to inspire new sayings that riff off the base memetic concept. It's crowd-sourced humor, aided by an entire industry of apps, including those of QuickMeme and MemeGenerator that allow users to quickly "memify" a photo.

In nearly all cases, there is a core artistic form that functions as the standardized foundation upon which the ongoing process of creative imagination is based. It can be viewed as the essence of the meme. In what's become known as the classic "advice animal" structure, a stage-setting line of text appears above a photo followed by the punch line underneath. Like a haiku or sonnet, or—for a social

---

* For the vast majority of these and many more of the Internet memes and other images mentioned in the book, simple Google searches will uncover them.

media comparative—a 140-character Tweet or a six-second Vine, this confining structure has given rise to a specific art form that becomes an avenue for creativity. But even when there's no such strict text-and-picture format, the idea of repetition and iteration of a core motif are central elements of the Internet meme phenomenon. New jokes often become the reference points for subsequent jokes, such that the process starts to look a little bit like the mutating of genes that leads to different lines of species and biodiversity in biological evolution.

To illustrate, let's look at the lifecycle of one of our favorites: the Ermahgerd meme, also known as Gersberms or Berks, which began in a Reddit post in 2012. The meme started with a decade-old photo of a preteen girl—later identified by *Vanity Fair* as Maggie Goldenberger, now a nurse in Phoenix—holding three books from R. L. Stines's *Goosebumps* series, her excitedly agape mouth showing a full set of braces. A Reddit user responded with a Quickmeme-generated take, adding the words "GERSBERMS…MAH FRAVRIT BERKS" to the picture (translation: "Goosebumps…my favorite books"), establishing what would become the meme's core motif: the notion of a speech impediment presumably brought on by the orthodontic work on the girl's teeth.

The gag took off, transitioning through multiple forms and morphing with other memes, almost like a mutating virus leaping from host to host. The line "ERMAHGERD" (Oh My God) was especially fertile, generating multiple new jokes as the meme jumped from its original "host" (the photo of Maggie) to photos of cats, dogs, babies, and athletes in identifiable contexts, each bearing a seemingly startled expression: "Ermahgerd…shertpert (shotput)"; "Ermahgerd…merlkbehrns (Milk-bones)"; "Ermahgerd…brehst merlk (breast milk)." Other jokes took their inspiration from the word itself: the image of a thumbs-up Jesus saying "Ermahgerd... Gerd!!!" and, naturally, "Ermahgerdden," signified by placing Maggie's face over that of Bruce Willis in the promotional poster for an apocalyptic film of (almost) the same name. The replication of this gag was amplified by the Web designer J. Miller's online ermahgerd translator app, which allowed the user to convert any phrase into ermahgerd speech. So mercurial was the meme that it fostered commercial ventures. There was a T-shirt showing Maggie's likeness inside the Starbucks logo encircled by the words "Sterberks Kerfer." The Nerdist YouTube channel produced a music video by Hard 'n Phirm singing, with total speech impediment, "Gerl, yer girven mah gersberms." Gersberms Halloween costumes were made in the same style that Maggie had worn in that now legendary photo. Below, our own artistic rendering of Ermahgerd's evolutionary process, shows how it fostered new forks of creative thought. I think it looks a bit like those taxonomy charts that illustrate how, over millennia, biological evolution has created new lineages of evolved life, with different *species* sharing common traits with others that belong to the same *genus*, these in turn being part of a common *family* that belongs to a wider *order* and so forth.

Unlocking all this crowdsourced creation and artistic output could, in theory, pose a problem for people who've made a living from this stuff—the elite few we've traditionally called "artists." They're no longer just competing with each other for attention—and for the financial patronage and advertising dollars that attention generates. They're competing with the entire world. Moreover, it can seem like we're all getting dragged down to the lowest common

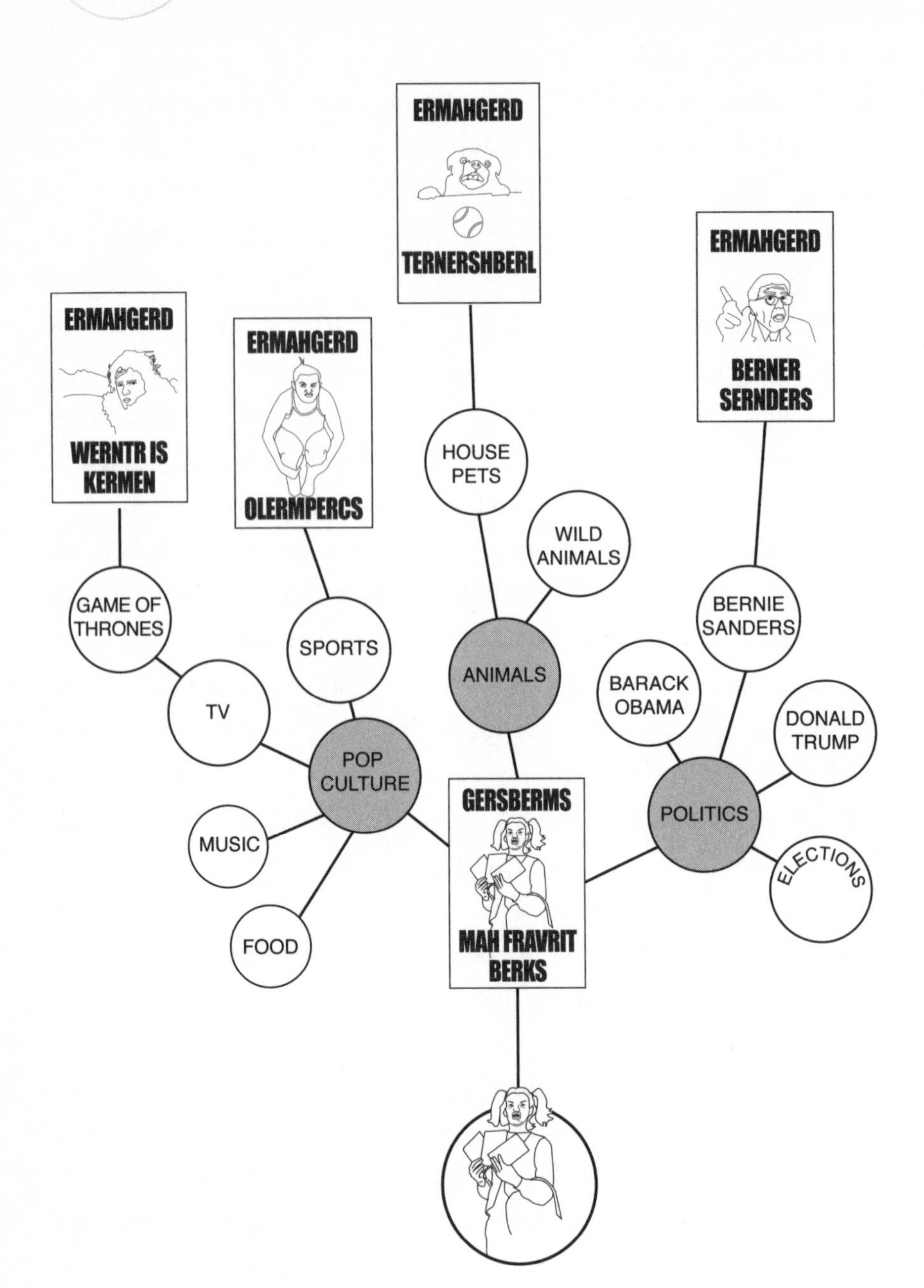
ERMAHGERD
TERNERSHBERL
ERMAHGERD
BERNER
SERNDERS
ERMAHGERD
WERNTR IS
KERMEN
ERMAHGERD
OLERMPERCS
HOUSE
PETS
WILD
ANIMALS
GAME OF
THRONES
SPORTS
ANIMALS
BERNIE
SANDERS
BARACK
OBAMA
TV
DONALD
TRUMP
POP
CULTURE
GERSBERMS
MAH FRAVRIT
BERKS
POLITICS
MUSIC
ELECTIONS
FOOD

denominator—a society obsessed with cat videos and embarrassing "nip slip" photos. There's no shortage of experts telling us that art and creativity are being destroyed by the distractions of social media, that we're all being dumbed down by constant notifications and bleeping alerts telling us to look at some must-see banality that our preferred site's algorithm has picked out for us. When Michael appeared on an NPR program to promote his last book, he was preceded by author Gary Shteyngart, who lamented to Leonard Lopate's listeners how Twitter's constant demands for instant gratification had killed his productivity. Ever since the Congressional hearings into the supposed threat posed by file-sharing renegade Napster, musicians like Sheryl Crow and the band members from Metallica have complained that file-sharing technology and unpaid replication of their work is killing the incentive system that encourages creativity in their industry.

This doomsaying doesn't hold up to close scrutiny. While life might be tougher for big-name acts accustomed to a captive (and patient) market, it's the opposite for everyone else who's never had such easy access to an audience. And although on an individual basis, some of us *feel* like our creativity is crimped by social media, if you look at the totality of human cultural production, there's clearly a more abundant stream of works than ever before—in quantity, variety, *and* quality. As an incessant collector of fine art, but also as a promoter and producer of films, music videos, and songs, I've been in the front row of what I can only describe as an era of unprecedented creative vibrancy. Even if the 76 million viewers who've watched YouTube user Rozzafly's "Surprised Kitty" video *are* detracting from the views, and dollars, that might otherwise go to a classical cellist or a documentary filmmaker, there's no evidence that the Chicken Littles' end-of-art thesis is anything more than a whiny canard. In fact, I believe we are living in a renaissance of boundless human expression.

Don't just take my word for it. Author Steven Johnson tested the thesis that social media was destroying artistic endeavor in 2015. In a well-researched *New York Times Magazine* article entitled "The Creative Apocalypse That Wasn't," he found that it was based on anecdotes originating from biased and interested parties, not facts. He reviewed the U.S. Bureau of Labor Statistics data on employment in the category of "Arts, Design, Entertainment, Sports and Media Occupations"—a category that includes the many journalists who've been laid off in a consolidation of traditional media—and found its numbers had increased by 1.8 million jobs, outstripping the wider economy's 1.5 million-job gain. Meanwhile, the category's earnings had risen by 40 percent, whereas the rest of the economy was up 38 percent. The data also showed that the number of people who self-identified as "musicians" had risen by 15 percent over the same period. Since the wider category excluded self-employed freelancers, Johnson also tapped the five-year Census data and found that between 2002 and 2012, the number of businesses that identify as or employ "independent artists, writers and performers" grew by almost 40 percent to post revenue gains of 60 percent and found that their revenues had grown, like the rest of the economy, in line with inflation. Artists continue to earn far less than the obscene incomes of, say, investment bankers and other rent-seekers who earn more than they contribute to society. Still, Johnson cannot help but conclude that "the turbulence of the last 15 years seems to have created an economy in which more people than ever are writing and performing songs for a living." After demonstrating similar trends in the movie and book industries, he concludes, "Contrary to [Metallica drummer] Lars Ulrich's fear in 2000, the 'diverse voices of the artists' are still with us, and they seem to be multiplying." I always chuckle at people like Lars whose art was supposed to reject "the man." He and others ended up as corporate stiffs, hiding behind and vehemently defending an archaic system when instead they could have embraced their fans, reaching them through new channels of distribution and connection.

It's worth noting, too, that Johnson's analysis focused on employment and income derived from creative output. It said nothing about the vast amount of content that people are now producing, replicating, and sharing without any attempt to make a living from it. Add to that the 12 million Vines uploaded daily, all the quirky videography on YouTube, the creative art on Tumblr blogs, and the army of meme generators on Reddit, and you get a picture of creative power unleashed like never before.

To get a sense of the great variety of artistic innovation taking place, go for a wander through the DeviantArt website, which boasts 323 million original works of art, 38 million members, and around 2.5 billion page views a month. Or consider that the majority of the more than 4 million e-book titles available in Amazon's Kindle store are now self-published books, some of which manage to break through and become bestsellers with the aid of the company's algorithm-driven promotional tools. Meanwhile, Hollywood is no longer the monopoly it was. EMI and other record labels, the behemoths of the music industry, are now competing directly with artists who record, produce, distribute, and market their own songs. (As I like to tell music artists today, your beloved record label's distribution system is no longer worth 75 percent of your income, but it is worth a flat fee of $10—that's what it takes to ubiquitously distribute a song on platforms like TuneCore or CD Baby. In effect, record companies are just bad payday lenders with usury fees, broken models, and silly, counterintuitive group restrictions on music rights.) But even those trends don't accurately represent how much art is being produced, its quality, or the diversity of "artistic voices" in our society.

Artistic expression is the natural extension of memetic expression. As societies have shown through the ages, art is the machine that drives cultural growth and evolution. And artistic memes are the foundation of that machinery. We have now exponentially expanded access to that machinery and prodigiously increased its power to reach people. This is helping to spawn new genres of artistic output, such as visual novels, which incorporate the multimedia facilities of video game settings, allowing readers to interact with characters while they progress through the plot. Or new works like Beyoncé's visual album, *Lemonade.* Connectedness has also added far more collaboration to the artistic process, with "fan art" increasingly integrated with proprietary content to expand the offerings associated with a particular artist or character. Complete strangers will work with each other and with the developers of the software behind the branded art form, creating an ecosystem of cooperation that's tied together by networked computers and a common love of the particular art form.

A stunning representation of this is found in the work of "vocaloid" enthusiasts. They will access trademarked voice synthesizer software to produce songs that are sung in the particular computer-generated singing character's distinctive voice and then submit them for the world—including the company behind the software—to listen to and share. Such contributions make up the bulk of the songs sung by Hatsune Miku, the immensely popular, (forever) sixteen-year-old vocaloid who appears as a hologram backed by a live band before screaming fans in sell-out shows around the world. Crypton, the Japanese company that created "Miku" in 2007, says this fan-based effort has resulted in the formal release of over 100,000 released songs, 170,000 uploaded YouTube videos, and 1 million Miku-inspired artworks. Human singers could never hope to match such prolific output, of course—nor the high-pitched notes or rapidly blurted-out lyrics that Miku is capable of. In effect, Miku is a new form of volvox, a colony-based holonic life form.

These examples help show how far the system of artistic production has traveled in a few hundred years. When the Church ran its top-down network, there was a limited number of sanctioned artists and the mediums available to them—the painter's canvas, the writer's book, the sculptor's stone—were not designed for rapid or wide distribution of their messages. Art was for elites, which meant its impact on cultural change was slow. Later, print, television, and other pre-Internet mass media outlets accelerated the process—the Beatles could go on *The Ed Sullivan Show* and quickly affect the fashion and social mores of American youth. But still, it was all mediated through gatekeepers, the powers-that-be at the top of the networks, magazines, and newspapers. It took social media to put the production and transmission of artistic expression into exponential growth.

Although my partner Scott and I have collected hundreds of pieces of art works from around the world, we have a visceral reaction to the cozy oligarchy of this old "art world." We detest the gallery scene and the art-as-an-investment crowd. The idea that I need someone to tell me what is hip or artful completely negates the idea of art as a moving form of human expression. So many people ask me, "What should I buy?" My answer is, "Buy something that moves you." And it's not only in the snobbish arbitration of taste that art elitism warps our thinking. It also restricts people's definitions of what constitutes "art." They tend to think of it as the product of an especially exclusive "industry," one that's run by a set of especially talented people who provide their creative output in the service of the rest of us non-artistic types. But in social media that us-and-them dichotomy doesn't hold up. We are all now, in some respects, artists. This is not to say that talent is evenly distributed—there can only be so many Hieronymus Boschs, Flannery O'Connors, and Talking Heads, to cite my trinity of favorites from the art, literature, and musical worlds. But it is to say that the total body of public-facing artistic work is now much larger. In posting Photoshopped meme gags, silly videos, and heartfelt commentaries on our experiences, we've become part of this industry. By extension, the world of art has gotten so much bigger, as has the opportunity that artists now have to forge direct relationships with their collectors and audiences.

Just as the "art" industry is getting harder to define, so, too, is its distinction from the "marketing," "politics," or "news" industries. Within the Organism, all are increasingly handled as one blended whole. We, the cells of that organism, the autonomous messengers who decide whether a message will be relayed to others or not, have become the conduits of all marketing efforts, political campaigns, and artistic expressions. And we don't distinguish one task from the other. If the core idea behind a piece of content resonates with us in some way—that is, if it fits with the way we are choosing to publicly *perform* our selfhood—we will choose to interact with it, irrespective of the purpose of the person who initiated the content or funded it. We might "like" it or share it with others, or we might do neither. In so doing, we get to decide what gets distributed—obviously, some of us with significantly more influence than the others.

This brings us to a question of paramount importance to marketers, politicians, journalists, writers, and artists alike: what kinds of content do we, the conduits of memetic replication, choose to spread? Brands, politicians, and artists are all competing to gain access to the receptors in the Organism's cells, but our brains have evolved to discard information that uses up scarce processing resources needed to address more appealing or pertinent information, putting up defenses that create a challenge for would-be memes. Only the fittest performances of a message will get through those defenses and reach the objective of replication and propagation. The question is, what are the qualities that give a meme the best chance of doing that? What makes a message spread? What defines contagious content? Figuring out the answer to those questions is what I've built my businesses on. I'll soon share those insights with you. But to properly grasp them we must first take a trip into the microscopic world of cells and viruses, from which now clichéd phrases like "going viral" or "viral content" are derived.

Viruses have a singular purpose: They coopt the resources and genetic material of living cells within host organisms in order to self-replicate. This hostile attacker role is not easy to play, as most organisms have evolved immunity protections against outside invasions. In order take over a host cell, a virus must pass through four distinct phases before it can spread to other cells—attachment, entry, replication, and shedding—with no guarantee it will get through each one. This has notable parallels to the tough process that memes go through before they successfully replicate and propagate.

The viral life cycle starts inside microscopic vehicles known as capsids, essentially an outer shell housing the virus's genetic material. The capsid will enter an organism and then seek to attach itself to one of the host's cells, using special receptors on its outer shell to try to bind to susceptible affinity receptors on the outside membrane of the targeted cell. That's easier said than done, as it requires compatibilities in the protein structures of each entity's receptors. But it happens. It's how we catch a cold.

If the capsid attaches, the virus then tries to enter the cell so that it can insert its genetic material. To do this, it uses a variety of protein-based signals aimed at tricking its deceived host into believing the virus is a harmless molecule with nutritional or other value. Then begins the replication phase, which also relies upon deception, as the virus overtakes the host cell's protein production process—its "programming" function—and tricks it into listening to the instructions of the viral genome instead of those of the cell's genetic code. (It's analogous to when a hacker inserts a computer virus into your operating system, convincing your computer's programming function to follow the virus's instructions and not those of the original OS code.) Once in command, the virus instructs the cell to multiply its genome many times over. Eventually, the cell can no longer function and its membrane breaks open, shedding the multiplied viral progeny into the metabolic pathways of the organism on a hunt for new host cells. Thus the cycle begins anew. Once repeated enough, this four-phase process will foster exponential growth in the virus, at least until the immune system of the occupied organism can muster a counterattack and bring the attacker to a standstill. As we'll see later when we trace certain hashtagged ideas and other memes, they too can go through similarly explosive growth phases before rapidly falling off people's radar screens.

That's not the only similarity between viral and memetic behavior. There's also a memetic equivalent to the four-phase viral life cycle, in which a meme is constantly challenged to be naturally selected to pass to each subsequent phase as it tries to get its "hosts"—the brains of a targeted audience—to help it propagate. The first is what Belgian cyberneticist Francis Heylighen calls assimilation, which we can think of as the equivalent of viral attachment. The key point here is that there also needs to be some level of compatibility between the meme and the targeted person's "affinity receptors." To achieve assimilation, a meme's design must be coherent and consistent with the preexisting cognitive framework of a host individual. The brain is not a blank slate, and new information simply can't attach itself if it bears no connection to the host's existing worldview. Thus memes exploit the mind's capacity for pattern recognition. This is akin to a biological virus exploiting a cell's ability to recognize different types of proteins to trick the unwitting host into letting it enter through the outer membrane. Pattern recognition also happens to be an important strategy for how our bodies resist such attacks: so-called toll-like receptors in human cells are specifically tasked with recognizing patterns in pathogens to identify them as "foreign" and signal to the immune system that it must marshal its defenses.

There's also a parallel in software design: Pattern recognition is a vital element of the "machine learning" techniques that computer scientists are using to develop early forms of artificial intelligence. Their recognition skills are still far from perfect, however—which, ironically, is creating interesting new AI-based artistic opportunities. For kicks, go check out the "Deep Dreams" application from Google. This AI system creates amazing new visual art by presenting images based on what it "thinks" it recognizes as patterns in a host image that it compares against a dictionary of previously loaded images.

This pattern recognition-driven assimilation—we might call it "catching the attention" of the target recipient—is just the start of the memetic process. The meme's survivability will be tested again in three subsequent stages: retention, expression, and transmission, using Heylighen's nomenclature. Once a target's interest has been piqued and the core idea or concept assimilated, he or she must *retain* that meme, committing it to some kind of memorization. Next, they must actively *express* that concept—in other words, give it form, articulate it. And finally, they must *transmit* that newly expressed concept to others. It must be communicated. At that point, the newly replicated meme, much like a newly shed viral capsid, can go off in search of another host to attempt the sequence again.

As time progresses—and, along with it, the survival-of-the-fittest algorithm—a meme continually competes with other memes to capture its target audience's limited information-processing resources. But just like viruses, which are arguably among the cleverest adaptive entities in the natural world, memes have a trick up their sleeve: mutation. The core idea of a meme functions like the basic genome of an organism; it provides the foundational basis for its existence. But beyond that, it can change when it leaps from one host to another. And if you think influenza viruses mutate quickly, forcing doctors to develop new flu vaccines each year, it's nothing compared with the rapid-fire changes that social media can impose on memes—as we've already noted in the rapidly morphing lives of Ermahgerd, Success Kid, and other social media–spread gags.

It's worth noting that artist rights lawyers would call such adaptations "derivative" works, and whether or not it's manageable in the hurly-burly copying culture of the Internet, the concept comes with clear legal connotations around copyright. But in truth this is a rather constructed notion, because in the broader context of how ideas spread and cultures are iterated, this process of mimicking, borrowing, and reproducing is simply the ongoing reality of memetic replication. It is how knowledge is shared and developed. It is how we evolve as a society.

Heylighen has analyzed and categorized the kinds of qualities that favor a meme's chances of undergoing replication—in other words, of passing through his four phases of the memetic life cycle. Among those he cites as valuable in the assimilation phase are the qualities of *distinctiveness* and *novelty,* a reference to how objectively different or unique a piece of content—a promoted tweet, for example—is perceived to be. Yet Heylighen also reminds us that a meme's *coherence* with a host's preexisting cognitive framework is just as critical for both assimilation and retention, as is its *conformity* with the person's existing social mores. In summary, people tend to notice new, distinct ideas but they'll better absorb and retain them if the core ideas are familiar enough to be comprehensible and sit within their cultural comfort zones.

Other qualities that Heylighen identifies as giving a meme a better chance of assimilation and retention include *authority.* In other words, the source of the information should be viewed as trusted, truthful, reliable, or simply valuable. This need not be scientifically founded, of course; it merely matters that a large enough group of people perceives some sense of authority. Witness how basketball star LeBron James, who presumably has no greater automotive knowledge than you or I, and who could afford an entire fleet of top-range Lamborghinis and Bugattis, appears in Kia ads as the driver of a sensible K900 sedan. It's the content that matters from a person that matters.

For the expression and transmission phases, Heylighen refers to a trait he calls *expressivity*, which we can think of as a measure of how easily a meme or idea can be conveyed to others. A new idea that can be expressed in fairly simple terms with strong analogues to existing experience will be more easily replicated than a complex concept. This is why, despite serious journalists' complaints, sites like BuzzFeed and Huffington Post persist with the "listicle" formats for "clickbait" purposes—"18 Things Guys Need to Stop Wearing After College"; "The 27 Best Moments from the Golden Globe Awards"—and lay-up headlines to videos that say "X does Y... What Happens Next Will Blow Your Mind." These formulas create simple patterns, a predictable order that's easy to express and thus to replicate.*

Finally, there's the transmission phase. Whether a meme rises to that final task, Heylighen tells us, is a matter of *publicity*. In a traditional media environment, this would translate into the amount of ad time and column inches that a marketing manager buys or into the effectiveness of a public relations rep's outreach to journalists, and so on. But, in the social media age, as we discussed in chapter 3, transmission success is all about the human network: Reach is determined by the breadth, the connectedness, and the appeal of the influencers who are exposed to a new meme.

Once the meme is transmitted to a new host, the four-phase replication and propagation process starts again. And with each new target, the goal is to get into the person's consciousness in such a

* Gilad Lotan, chief data scientist of New York venture capital firm Betaworks, studied how much different BuzzFeed listicles were shared and found that the number 29 seemed, on average, to be the ideal "shareable" number of factoids.

way they will in turn send it off to get replicated by others. It's like a never-ending game of Chinese Whispers; the fittest, most memorable memes will persist through each transmission while the weakest ones won't stick in people's minds and will be lost in translation.

For a marketer, publicist, or brand manager working in social media, finding the distribution network is not the hardest part of their job. With the right connections, planning, and money, it's possible to build a social media distribution network to push content out to the masses. The challenge is coming up with the right content. How can you ensure that your messages pass through the memetic selection process and achieve viral replication? At theAudience, new clients would often hand me a half-baked video and say, "Here, make this ad go viral," wrongly assuming that our far-reaching distribution mechanism would automatically achieve that. I'm not an alchemist; if a piece of content doesn't have the right conceptual patterns to resonate with its audience, I can't magically make it spread. It's *the message* that's paramount, the content that will dictate whether a meme is fit enough to survive.

But how do you make it stick? How does it become a hit? Here, we need to look beyond the utilitarian mind-set with which we tend to view information and instead grapple with the more fuzzy lens of emotions and context—because, really, that's where the action happens in social media. Emotions are the key ingredient determining a meme's virality. The question is, which emotions are triggered and what role do they play in propagation?

A Wharton Business School study of seven thousand online *New York Times* articles and their propensity to appear in *The Times'* most-emailed list found that the emotional component impacted decisions to share in two ways. First, readers would put a binary emotional value on the content—whether it triggered positive or negative emotions—which would impact their willingness to share it. Second, the specific emotion that was triggered would have varying motivational effects, evoking different degrees of "physiological arousal or activation"—in this case, to feel inspired or compelled to email it to someone else.

In the first case, and contrary to the "if it bleeds, it leads" rule of journalism, the Wharton professors—Jonah Berger and Katherine L. Milkman—found that content was more likely to become viral if it was positive in nature. But in the second, they found that different emotion triggers had different impacts on the probability of an article being widely shared, and at the top of the list was a negative emotion: anger. As per the chart below, the authors found that among the other emotional triggers that help increase virality, some were positive or neutral (awe, interest, surprise) and at least one other, anxiety, was negative. Only sadness, clearly a negative emotion, was unambiguously a factor in making an article less likely to make it onto the most-emailed list.

Thanks to modern biochemistry, these ideas fit comfortably with the biological framework of the Social Organism. While emotional responses are triggered by outside stimuli, how they play out is now widely seen by psychologists and neuroscientists as a function of different chemical reactions inside the brain. Happiness and other positive emotions are regulated by the release of neurotransmitter chemicals such as dopamine, endorphins, oxytocin, and serotonin, which are produced by the pituitary gland and managed by the brain's emotion-controlling limbic system. They moderate pain and will counteract sadness—which is why

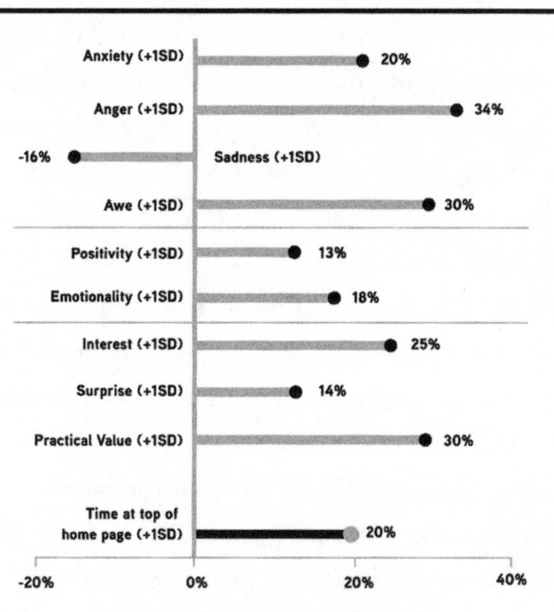

poor serotonin production is associated with depression. Depending on the complex balance between the production and depletion of these chemicals, they can induce feelings of outright euphoria or leave us in a deep funk.

Scientists have proposed that joy and other positive feelings are an evolutionary trait that emerged to encourage certain pro-survival behavior, and in the case of fear, sadness, and other negative emotions, to prevent us from doing harm to ourselves. But as human beings have become so uniquely defined by our social context, we are constantly confronted by modern-day stimuli that set off these emotions and the countervailing chemical reactions inside the body. In biochemical terms, we might rephrase Jefferson's immortal words about the "pursuit of happiness" in terms of an endless hunger for dopamine releases.

Social media means that a billion of these chemical-sensitive brains are now connected by a giant information-sharing network, each node with a limited capacity to process new information but at the same time instinctively inclined to let outside stimuli manipulate its internal hormonal chemistry. Seen in that context, the demand for meme jokes, for example, reflects the Social Organism's collective desire for positive hormonal releases—since smiling and laughter have been shown scientifically to trigger these neurotransmitters. Cute animal images might do the same. (Japanese research found that subjects who were shown such images worked more productively than a test group that wasn't shown the pictures. Maybe silly cat videos aren't such a time suck after all.)

What about anger? Why do people on social media spit out such an enormous amount of bile? Where do these virally spreading mushroom clouds of rage come from? Why are we so instinctively drawn to something so inherently destructive? Here we need to consider the overall management of our emotional life within the brain's limbic system, which, among other roles, regulates our fight-or-flight response system. Many of its functions have primordial roots; they release hormones such as adrenaline to prepare the body for battle against a predator. Adrenaline is addictive, and for good reason, albeit one that's of less relevance in our largely cocooned urban life in the twenty-first century. Since anger releases adrenaline, we are drawn to anger.

Let's just leave that thought hanging for now. It will be a critical consideration when we come to examine, how to best use social media in a constructive way in the following chapters.

* * *

In this chapter we've discussed how memes are the cultural equivalent of genes, the units of transmission, and replication upon which we build our shared ideas, tastes, mores, and artistic innovation. We've explored what makes one particular meme successfully outbid others for access to the limited pool of the Social Organism's human mindshare and achieve selection as one of the shared building blocks of our culture. We've looked at what happens as the endless inflow of external stimuli enters our brains in the form of social media content and reacts with the core biochemistry of our brains, and how, depending on its structure, it will set off certain emotions that either increase or decrease its likelihood of transmission.

Now, before we move on from this chapter, let's look at how the spread of some real-world biological viruses played out over time and line them up against the behavior of actual memes on social media. Recall the terrifying recent Ebola outbreak of the virus in West Africa. From the first reported case in Guinea in December 2013 to the World Health Organization's January 2016 declaration that West Africa was Ebola free, the caseload showed an initially gradual increase. But then it went exponential as it spread to Liberia, Sierra Leone, Senegal, Nigeria, Mali, and even showed up in the United States, United Kingdom, Spain, and other places, only to rapidly peter out in the second half of 2015.

Let's compare this with the trajectory of the hashtag #OutBoastKanye. On February 15, 2016, that meme went viral after an inane tweet from Kanye West—"Yes I am personally rich and I can buy furs and houses for my family"—led Twitter users into a contest of wit. From a starting trickle, the #OutBoastKanye joke soon became contagious, appearing in 28,227 tweets and retweets by the end of

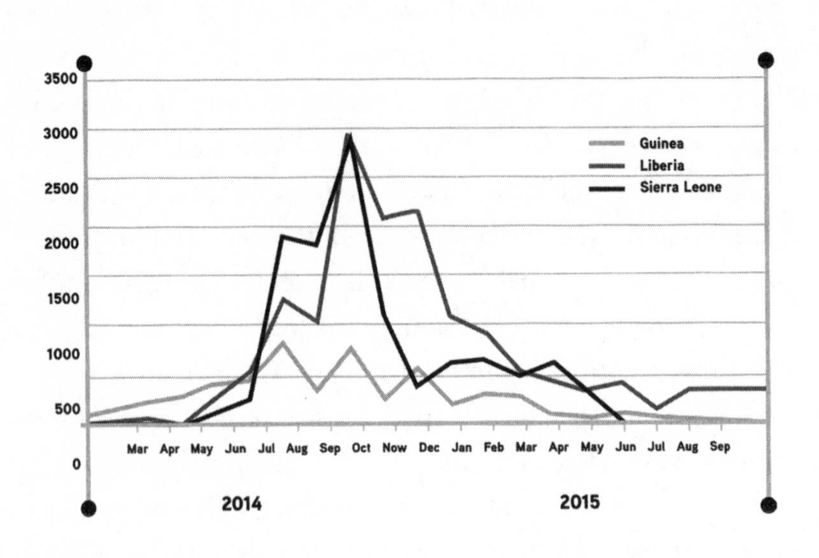

the day. Among the funniest: "#OutBoastKanye. I can cook minute rice in 57 seconds" from @DatOwlTwitch and "I sometimes don't even lick the yogurt lid, just put it straight in the bin" from @SadFaceOtter. The fun continued on February 16, when the hashtag notched up 20,726 tweets and retweets. But, much like Ebola, albeit even more quickly, the hashtag replications petered out in time. The next day, it tallied 2,152. Then it dropped to 591 on February 18, and then to 281 on the fifth day. The slide continued, such that by the end of the month, #OutBoastKanye's daily appearances were barely in single digits. Once the summer rolled around, it was making just an occasional appearance every second day or so. See the chart of its February 2016 performance below.

Those two examples follow the typical pattern of viral develop-

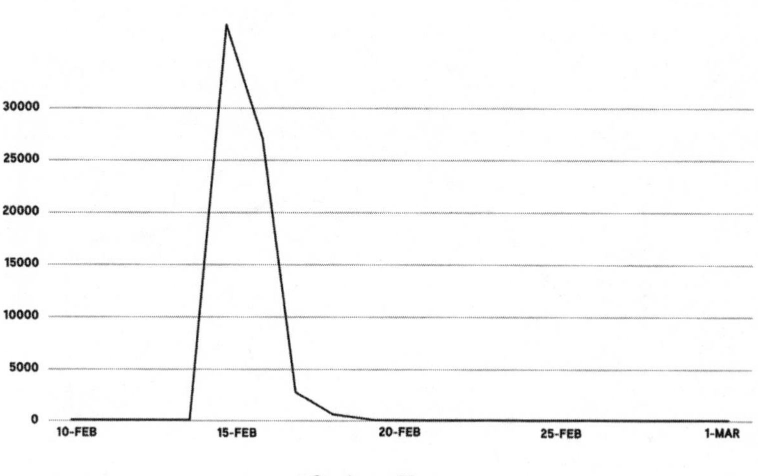

#OutboastKanye

ment in both biology and social media. But every now and then, an especially virulent virus comes along that defies this surge-then-burnout pattern—either in biological or memetic form. So let's look at examples of each. For the first, we'll chart the ultimate super-virus of the twentieth century, the one that has led to the deaths of more than 35 million people: the human-immunodeficiency virus, or HIV. It took a long time for the rate of new HIV infections to slow and, even now, the numbers of new cases remain very high.

There are social media memes that also show staying power. Let's return to the one with which we started this book. The #Black-LivesMatter hashtag began in 2013 with a surge of outrage over the acquittal of George Zimmerman for the killing of Trayvon Martin, but it really took off the following year with the killings of Michael Brown in Ferguson, Missouri, and that of Eric Garner in New York.

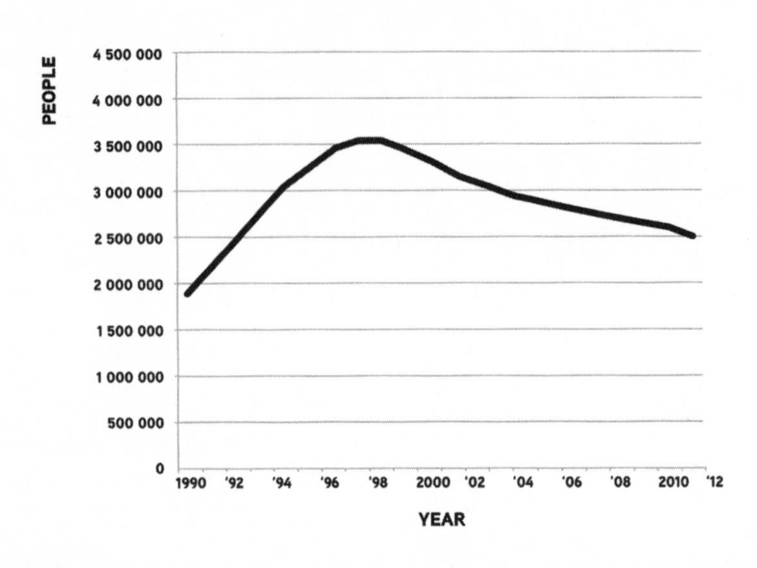

In its association with massive street protests, the hashtag spawned an entire movement, an ethos even. The death of Freddie Gray in Baltimore and the massive protests it spawned gave new impetus to the movement in the spring of 2015. It then gained traction and legitimacy as the U.S. election cycle cranked into gear and as the leading activists within the #BlackLivesMatter movement formed a well-organized campaign of protest and political advocacy. When prominent #BlackLivesMatter leader DeRay Mckesson filed his bid to become mayor of the troubled but iconic city of Baltimore, it marked a milestone in American democracy: the first political candidate born of a hashtag. Around the same time, in a fitting re-examination of the notion of personal identity in the social media era, *Time Magazine* named the Black Lives Matter movement as the runner up for its 2015 "Person of the Year" award.

Then, in the summer of 2016, we experienced the tragic deaths of Alton Sterling in Baton Rouge, Louisiana, and Philando Castile in Falcon Heights, Minnesota. These—along with the subsequent murders of eight police officers in Dallas and Baton Rouge, lone-wolf acts that, sadly, fed a false conservative narrative of the movement as "terrorists"—once again thrust #BlackLivesMatter into high public profile. Much of this is captured in an impressive report published by the Center for Media and Social Impact. Its three authors—academics from American University, New York University and the University of North Texas—dove into the frequent resurgences in social media activity around the Black Lives Matter movement, waves that I would call viral "outbreaks."*

To visualize all this activity, we added 2016 data provided by Soroush Vosoughi and Deb Roy of MIT's Laboratory for Social Machines to a chart in the CMSI report that shows the #BlackLivesMatter hashtag's mentions in 2014 and 2015. Far from petering out, it keeps resurging, and in a progressively stronger way. On one day in July 2016, the hashtag was tweeted and retweeted more than 1.1 million times.

* It will be clear to most readers, but given the sensitivity of the subject, we feel compelled to say that in comparing #BlackLivesMatter to patterns of behavior shown by viruses we are in no way suggesting that the latter is some kind of harmful disease. On the contrary, we see this new civil rights movement as a powerful, progressive force for cultural change. The viral analogy deals solely with the mechanics of how an idea spreads, to illustrate how an agent of cultural change can, in certain circumstances, experience the same kind of impressive life cycle as a super-virus. In fact, it's our hope that the #BlackLivesMatter meme infects the social fabric of America so deeply that it gets into people's psyche and promotes a long-overdue awakening to the injustices that pervade it.

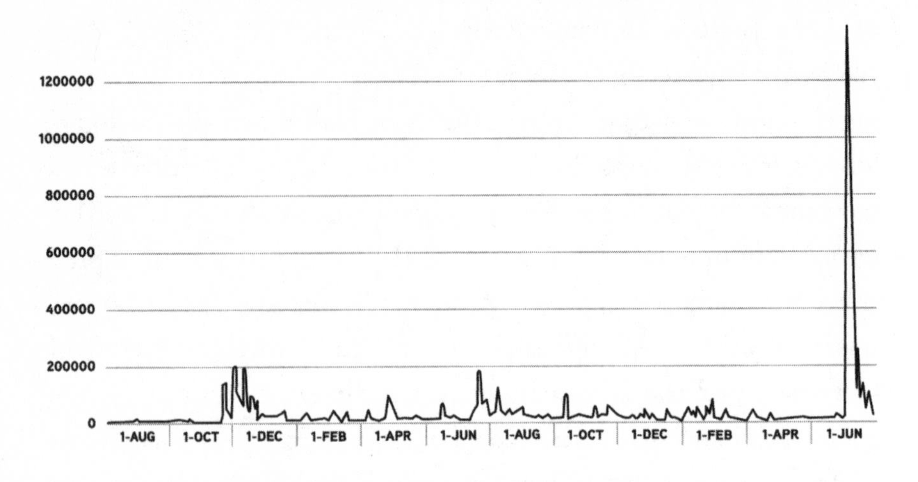

Tweets and retweets of #BlackLivesMatter

In analyzing and comparing these phenomena, the first thing to note with HIV is the virus's MO. It launches a total attack on the body's defenses against disease. Not content to simply occupy any old host cell for replication purposes, HIV latches on to CD4 receptors located on our all-important T-helper cells, a type of white blood cell whose role is to activate all the other white blood cells within our immunity system in response to a foreign invader. In taking over those cells, the virus doesn't just disable the body's defenses against HIV; it destroys the immune system's ability to defend against *any* attack. Once it has completed this nefarious role and its victim is riddled with AIDS, it's not HIV that kills them but something else: cancer, meningitis, pneumonia, you name it.

Now, think of the words "black lives matter" as a similar broad-based attack on an entire system—and by that I mean as a *shock* to a flawed, anachronistic system that has not yet evolved to an optimal state of race-blind inclusion and fairness. Could there be a more powerful, foundational call to action? This movement—and the meme associated with it—isn't merely defined around a narrowly expressed political idea of, say, police brutality versus young black men, or of access to services for poor minority communities, or of affirmative action. It's not promoting a particular solution to a particular problem; it's demanding that society as a whole adhere to a fundamental principle of life itself. It's an all-out attack on the system. And it does so in the most dramatic, emotion-triggering way. It does so with language whose power derives directly from its unambiguous simplicity and from its implicit reference to the lasting stories and images (prior memes) that have forged the imbedded memories of a nation's painful past into its collective consciousness. Black. Lives. Matter.

The other similarity is the mutation cycle. The RNA within HIV mutates at a faster rate than anything ever seen in a living entity, which means that its evolutionary algorithm runs faster than the R&D teams of drug companies can keep up with. To contain HIV's impact, it took a heavy combination of antiretroviral drugs—which block the process through which the viral RNA takes over the infected T-helper cell's DNA and so curb its replication—along with extensive education campaigns over the use of condoms and needles, which in that case blocks the wider transmission mechanism. But even then, no real, comprehensively available cure has yet been found—though in chapter 7, we'll look into one of only two cases of a cured AIDS sufferer and at the lessons it might hold for how social media could "cure" society of its cultural ills.

With #BlackLivesMatter, various "mutated" spinoff expressions emerged but held true to the original statement's sweeping demand for justice. In those we find the power of a strong meme, one that's capable of evolving and adapting on a grand scale. There was the "Hands Up, Don't Shoot" saying and gesture that was displayed en masse during protests at Michael Brown's killing in Ferguson—a sub-meme that was even replicated in Hong Kong during that city's concurrent pro-democracy protests—and the "I Can't Breathe" slogan, along with a chokehold gesture, which was aimed at New York police for their handling of Eric Garner's death. These gave rise to hashtags such as #Ferguson, #MikeBrown and #EricGarner. As we discussed in the introduction, there was also the #TakeIt-Down hashtag and others, such as #JeSuisBree, that were associated with the removal of the Confederate flag after the Charleston killings. (In an indication of how much content was generated around these themes, the three researchers who compiled the CMSI social media study of the Black Lives Matter movement analyzed a whopping 41 million tweets through 2014 and 2015.) All of these added to the indignation people felt about the second-class treatment of African Americans in U.S. society while re-emphasizing the values expressed in the #BlackLivesMatter core meme. They all empowered the original message and gave it even greater saliency.

One clear demonstration of the lasting and even expanding power of #BlackLivesMatter came when Beyoncé, backed by dancing girls dressed in Black Panther garb, joined Coldplay on stage at the 2016 Super Bowl's halftime show and belted out her highly charged, just released song, "Formation." The video, replete with images of post-Katrina New Orleans and references to the singer's own roots from a racially divided South, was released just in time to stir up a social media frenzy before the big event. It was a direct embrace of the #BlackLivesMatter movement, an anthem of black anger in the making, by a black woman who is also pop culture royalty. It was all the more significant that she made this statement at the biggest TV event of the year, hosted by the NFL, an all-American institution where the racial divide in the hierarchies of its football teams remains a blatant but rarely discussed matter. Three years on from its founding, #BlackLivesMatter was not only alive and kicking, it was taking center stage. If HIV is a super-virus, then this is surely a super-meme. And, much like a powerful virus, that super-meme now has the capacity to infect the out-of-date, racist cultural legacy that hate-mongers like Donald Trump appeal to.

Although not everyone with a message can make the same impact on our memetic code as #BlackLivesMatter, the lessons from genetics and biological viruses are valuable for all of us. We are all grappling with how to make ourselves heard in social media's complex new communications architecture. But these lessons are far from all there is to learn about the inner workings of the Social Organism. It's time to explore how its metabolism functions, how it grows, and how it maintains internal stability, or homeostasis—rules two, three, and four from the seven features of life.

CHAPTER FIVE

BALANCED DIET

The Organism Must Be Fed Healthy Content

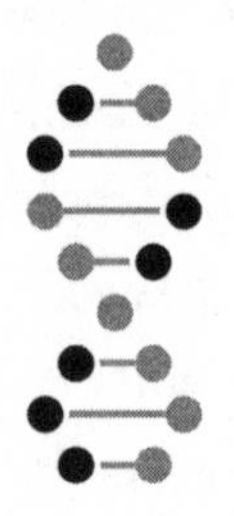

David Bowie's death in January 2016 left people in Michael's and my cohort in a state of angst. Tributes to the brilliant musician–actor–performance artist poured in over Facebook as Generation Xers reminisced about Bowie—and what he represented in terms of their own youth. We, old friends and online strangers alike, engaged in a global ritual of nostalgic embrace and shared heartache. Bowie may not have achieved the same dominant influence as the Beatles, but in some ways his death was to our generation what John Lennon's was to Baby Boomers. There was a "The Day the Music Died" feel to it all.

It wasn't until he'd gone that we could understand Bowie's true genius. In the final act of a life filled with character shifts, multiple personas, and mercurial plot lines, Bowie showed us in death why he mattered in life: He had, almost singlehandedly, taken the postmodern notion of a fluid, category-defying identity and made it mainstream. For tens of millions of young men and women who struggled to fit into a world that wanted to pigeonhole them according to their gender, sexuality, color, and other rigid definitions, Bowie showed that it was okay to be different, that it could in fact be cool to be weird. For me, a young man coming to terms with his homosexuality within the rigid confines of American Southern society, that was a powerful message. For his embrace of music, sexuality, and expression, I now see Bowie as a "mutant." He added reams of new DNA to our culture, reshaping our preconceived ideas of who we were. He redrew the boundaries of our immunity, expanding our freedom of imagination.

Bowie's message was not only liberating, it was prescient. His life, with its multiple personas from Ziggy Stardust to the Thin White Duke to Aladdin Sane, and with his deliberately ambiguous sexuality—he variously described himself as gay, bisexual, and a "closet heterosexual"—was a bellwether to our new, social media–fueled existence. The anonymity of the Internet—where, as *New Yorker* cartoonist Peter Steiner put it, "nobody knows you're a dog"—has given a powerful new outlet to what anthropologists call "performativity," the idea that we are constantly performing different versions of our "self" depending on the social context. Social media had brought out the inner Bowie in all of us.

Given that we are developing a biological analogy for our new social media–driven communication system, it's appropriate that the most common metaphor applied to Bowie's ever-changing persona comes from the natural world. He is frequently referred to as a chameleon, which, not coincidentally, was the title of an Australia-only Bowie compilation album from 1979, a treasured item in Michael's early vinyl collection. Chameleons, of course, are the most fabulously versatile of animals, able to change their coloration at the drop of a hat. With four differently pigmented layers of skin, they can shift from bright green to dull brown to vibrant, multicolored patterns of the rainbow. Sometimes they change colors for camouflage, opting for a hue that blends into their environment; at other times the color expresses the chameleon's mood or its eagerness to mate. It's as if the chameleon is playing out different versions of its self depending on the "social" context in which it finds itself—whether it's seeking to ward off competitors, attract a mate, or discourage a competing chameleon from going after whatever scarce resource it needs.

Chameleons are merely one particularly striking example of mimesis, a form of behavior that's found across the animal and plant world. (Mimesis, which describes the act of mimicry, derives from the same Greek root as "mimeme," from which Richard Dawkins came up with "meme.") Mimicry is a fundamental aspect of life. Cuttlefish—sometimes called the "chameleons of the sea"—will change not only their color but also the pattern, texture, and shape of their skin to communicate with other cuttlefish, camouflage themselves, or scare off predators. Cats mimic the impression of a larger, more threatening attacker when they haunch their back to ward off unwanted challengers. Peacocks' fluff up their hind feathers to give the impression of majesty when they seek a mate. Toads in Central American jungles make themselves look like leaves on the forest floor to hide from predators. Mexican milk snakes are harmless, but by mimicking the red, black, and white rings that mark the deadly Texas coral snake they scare off would-be predators. To avoid being ripped out by a farmer, various species of weed have evolved to look like the crops within which they mingle, including *Echinochloa oryzoides*, a species of grass that looks like rice (*Oryza sativa*). (In fact, rye was initially an unwanted impostor of wheat.)

Mimesis is the art of deception. It relies on the same tricks that illusionists use to deceive their audiences: by preying on the fact that the visual, auditory, and olfactory abilities of any organism are limited. We living things have a pre-programmed capacity for pattern recognition, which means our senses will struggle to perceive anything that falls outside of it. We are constantly looking for a certain order, seeking to recognize consistent, predictable patterns; that way we can make sense of the signals in our environment and respond accordingly. But we tend not to see—or smell, or hear, or feel, or taste—differently ordered patterns. Our narrowly proscribed perceptive ability is derived from both genetically inherited traits and, for more sophisticated organisms such as humans, from an ongoing learning process. Accordingly, our brains can be easily fooled by alternative, but no less true, versions of reality when the sensory signals fall outside those patterns. Essentially, mimesis is pattern mimicry. It confuses the readout that our internal computers conduct in surveying their surroundings.

Another way to think about these acts of mimicry in the natural world is as "stories." They represent a particular *version* of reality, by no means a false one, that's told—or, better put, performed—by one organism about the state of the world to influence the perception of other organisms. And it's fair to say that no species has perfected this talent anywhere near as comprehensively as humans. As Yuval Harari points out in *Sapiens*, his sweeping explanation of the roots of civilization, the human arts of persuasion, storytelling, and myth creation were vital to the development of social organization and thus to our dominance of the planet. With our unique cognitive powers, we have taken the art of representation and description to a new level and have changed the world in the process. We've created societies in which millions of complete strangers convince themselves to join together to go off to fight and kill millions of other strangers. They do so because of a narrative that appeals to the "common values" they supposedly share as a result of their membership of an ambiguously defined idea called a "nation." Religions, nationalisms, political allegiances, even schoolyard friends and enemies are formed around the stories we tell each other.

There's something innately human about needing stories. Without them, could we even imagine life has a purpose? In a popular NPR Radiolab episode, Tom French, who read Harry Potter books to his very prematurely born daughter while she clung to life in an incubator, observed that her vital signs would pick up when he read to her. He took it as her sign that they should keep the machine on, that she wanted to keep up the struggle for life regardless of the risk that she might end up living a highly institutionalized life. Whether there's a scientific explanation for her body's response to hearing the passages, or whether it was just coincidence, the important thing was that it conveyed to this father who craved to "do something" an essential insight into who we are. "She didn't know what a chapter is, but she was in her own way very eagerly waiting for the next chapter. And I don't know a better way to describe wanting to be alive than that you want to find out what happens next," French told his interviewers. Juniper is now a healthy, rambunctious toddler.

The rise of the Internet and in particular social media has dramatically changed the context in which this storytelling takes place, mostly by massively widening the audience for it. As publishers of information over social media we are all engaged, often subconsciously, in acts of mimesis, mimicking and expropriating others' behavior and images to create new ideas, concepts, and memes that we want, in some way, to reflect back on us. We social media users, especially the younger ones among us, will frequently shift between different avatars and online monikers; we'll create a variety of Twitter and Tumblr accounts, sometimes role-playing alternative characters and doing so in ways that can blur the lines between our "real" and "fake" online identities.

With an ever-present audience listening to us, we experience feedback that reflexively triggers ever more of these "stories." I like to think of this new fabric of storytelling as a "cultural agar," a "flat" place connected without time and distance in which new ideas bloom. (Agar is the concoction that scientists put into a petri dish to cultivate bacteria.) Office water coolers were once the proverbial place where employees came together to swap their stories from the day or night before. Now we have millions of virtual water coolers that come together to transcend location.

This global explosion of mimesis can be confusing, revealing the limits of our pattern recognition skills for understanding the world. Social media frequently demonstrates that what we think is an indisputable comprehension of reality is actually dependent on subjectivities formed by the patterns of our shared experiences. When that happens, we are fascinated by how our eyes and minds seem to play tricks on us. Witness the obsession with #TheDress, when millions worldwide debated whether a posted photo showed a dress that was white and gold or blue and black, or with #Findthesheep, in which it was impossible to see five hundred sheep in a photograph until the camera zoomed in on them.

More important than these quirky examples of the eye failing to "see," the Social Organism's memetic process of cultural change is also challenging the long-established patterns with which we understand markers of social order. The gender, sexuality, and racial identifiers through which we have traditionally classified people were always nothing more than social constructs, albeit powerful and long-standing ones. Individuals have always existed who felt that they belonged outside those categories, but society—like the prisoners in Plato's Cave—could not see them for what they were. Their unique forms of self-identification lay outside those that society had constructed and, as such, lacked social legitimacy. But now social media has made it easier for such people to form groups of solidarity.

As the father of middle- and high-school-age kids, Michael is noticing that so many more LGBTQ teenagers from their generation are coming to terms with their sexuality at an earlier age than those of previous generations. In part, that's because of the support they find in online communities that transcend their immediate neighborhood. These social media friendships give them confidence to be who they truly are. I can only imagine how my life, growing up as a closeted gay boy in Mississippi, would have been different if I'd had the same tools. My mom would put me in corduroy pants, never jeans, to go to school, and that simple feature of my dress made me a schoolyard pariah. Non-conformity was viewed as devilish and queer, something with which to feed the circus show of freaks that Katherine Dunn so wonderfully allegorized in her novel *Geek Love*, a story set in a context where "specialness" defined your value to the crew. We grow up with the imposition of our environments. But now the connectedness of the social Internet allows us to build tribes around value affinities instead of geo-locations.

One way to think about all this is that we are developing the social equivalent of biodiversity. Nature doesn't care whether the tiny pink fairy armadillo of South America looks almost nothing like its more common cousin, the nine-banded, or long-nosed, armadillo found in the United States. It seems to be part mouse, part mole, and—only thanks solely to the rippled, armor-like dorsal shell on its back—part armadillo. Nothing prevents it from burrowing, feeding, and mating with other pink fairy armadillos. The platypus is a furry mammal, but it lays eggs, swims, and has a duck's bill. It does just fine despite its defiance of classification. At its most broad and heterogeneous level, the Social Organism treats people with the same level of indifferent acceptance and creates room for them. It's not a moral consideration; it's a function of its organic, holonic architecture. That architecture is founded upon the subjective relationships between each member's stories, not on an "objective," pre-classified order to which all must conform.

The Social Organism might contain many divisions—which we'll discuss in the next chapter—but within it there are opportunities for inclusion that never existed before.

Within this open space of possibilities, and amid the massive, chaotic, global interchange of images and text, people are exploring different identities and personas, just as the trailblazing David Bowie did. Simultaneously with this growing experimentation in self-expression, we are discovering that the rules with which we identify others are no longer as clear as we thought they were. The very process by which we define who we are is changing. That can be very disorienting. To make sense of it, we're going to need to understand something that Shakespeare recognized centuries ago: All the world's a stage.

Performativity theory, which dates back to the writings of the sociologist Erving Goffman in the fifties, holds that human communication via speech, images, gestures, and other tools is not merely carried out to convey information but also to construct notions of selfhood, as if we are performing different roles. Goffman argued that we adjust these performances—and thus the various "selves" we present to the world—according to different "frameworks," or contexts, defined by the audience, the circumstance, and the ways in which our words and actions might be construed. The idea is that the self we perform when we are out drinking with our old school friends is different from that which we perform in the bedroom or that we present in a résumé for a prospective employer. In the nineties, the philosopher Judith Butler gave the theory a provocative turn when she argued that gender is not some prima facie fact of material sexual difference but a function of the roles that boys, girls, men, and women perform for the world at large, all in response to constructed social contexts.

Now, in the age of Twitter, Instagram, and Facebook, these ideas are drawing attention all over again. The fact that these social media platforms offer a giant global stage whose audience composition is unpredictable creates an entirely different framework and encourages a new type of performance. The feedback from the audience isn't always constructive—I think one reason Justin Bieber has sometimes acted with recklessness and impunity is because his tweets and Instagram posts get immediate "likes." His fans enable him. Other times the feedback is a brutal check on our behavior, as victims of the overreaching efforts of social media's "morals police" can attest. Yet because mimesis and self-performance is biologically ingrained in our makeup, we just keep on doing it—listening as we go to the Organism's signals.

The most blatant performative act in the social media realm is arguably the selfie. Whatever one thinks of this self-infatuation phenomenon, its ubiquity speaks to an innate human desire to present an appealing face to the world. Much as Facebook's and Twitter's creation of the "share" and "retweet" buttons were a response to their users' ingrained desire to spread content, an industry of tools has evolved to feed what seems to be a market demand for this unique form of self-performance. In the pre-smartphone days of 2003, Sony Ericsson figured out that people would want a front-facing camera to take shots of themselves, in addition to an outward-facing camera to take photos of others, and so installed one in its Z1010 mobile phone. Soon, selfies were an obsession—in the immortal words of Paris Hilton, the camera phone became "the autograph of the twenty-first century." Since then, the tools of the trade have become even more sophisticated, allowing people to touch up their photos and present their most preferred image. And with the spectacularly successful selfie stick—known to more cynical types as the Wand of Narcissus or the Narcisstick—people can take the performance to a new level by capturing their surroundings. *Look at me. Here I am at Times Square. Here I am in front of the Eiffel Tower. Here I am at a Beyoncé concert.* The selfie has become a restrained art form, one that falls within the rules of a certain genre, a memetic code that we all instantly recognize.

We can't all be like Kim Kardashian and turn our selfies into a money-spinning brand. But that's not stopping many teens from striving to attain the Kardashian-like "it" factor that their favorite social media stars seem to have. The currency of uniqueness—or at least the appearance, or performance of uniqueness—is now extremely valuable for acquiring like-minded followers. The starting point for all of that is getting the right "face" out there.

All of us, in some way, are Kardashianists. (I've been dying to use that word.) Think of how much time many of us spend selecting our social media profile images. Clearly, my own choices for my various offbeat publicity photos (one with tongue out; one that looks upward into an agape mouth and nostrils that I call the "O-face"; one in which I'm flippin' the bird, etc.) are a form of performance. But so, too, are Michael's, if a touch more restrained: his daughter's anime sketch of his face for Twitter; the pic with requisite quasi-intellectual expression for speaking engagements; the front profile half-torso photo with a sufficiently welcoming smile for LinkedIn and other "professional" situations. Our profile image is an integral part of the modern-day performance of selfhood.

The selfie and profile pic are merely two of the most obvious ways in which we perform on social media. Every word we utter in a Facebook post, every Tweet we make to score a political point, every time we choose to repost something witty or make a pertinent comment on someone else's post, every photo of our holidays, family portraits, or pets that we offer to the world—all of it is performance. And we are performing not just one, but multiple personas. The digital era has turned all of us into chameleons.

As ardently as we go about this process of identity formation and reformation, total control of our online personas will inevitably elude us. While we might present images and impressions that we want the world to associate with us, the world will come up with its own interpretations. The lesson learned from people who've seen their image turned into an Internet meme—Ermahgerd!—is that, ultimately, we may have little choice but to embrace the process and accept what the social media world projects back onto us.

After Laney Griner's 2007 photo of her fist-clenched baby son, Sammy, started getting replicated on MySpace, Reddit, and numerous other platforms as the widely shared—and, frankly, hilarious—"Success Kid" meme, her first response was dismay. "This picture has been stolen over and over. It makes me very unhappy, as this is my baby boy," she lamented in the comments thread to the original Flickr post. But further down the same thread four years later, she wrote, "Thanks everyone! I'm happy about this little internet celebrity. It doesn't bother me anymore. I love that so many people know this photo and like it. He's an awesome little boy." Another three years later, she used her "little internet celebrity" to raise $100,000 for her husband's kidney transplant in an online crowdfunding campaign, declaring that "Justin 'Success Dad' Griner got his long awaited kidney transplant just one week ago. Such wonderful, life changing news for the Griners. Thank you all for your support. #successkidney."

The appropriation of Leon Mitchell II's image for the "Meth Curry" meme in late 2015 was more problematic. The joke, which paired NBA star Steph Curry's face with that of Mitchell's significantly more gaunt likeness to suggest that he would be Curry's doppelganger if the basketball player were a methamphetamine addict, fostered mirth across Twitter and Instagram. But a week later, an Instagram post from Mitchell wiped the smile from everyone's faces. After explaining that his appearance was the result of years of cancer treatment, he ended the post by saying, "If we are going to allow something like this to go viral, let's do it for the right reasons! I am more than a meme, I am a father, husband, survivor, mentor, community advocate, and Positive motivational speaker. Proud to have endured and conquered everything I have!!!!" Within a week, his post had 90,000 "likes" and almost 7,500 comments filled with words of encouragement and admiration. Mitchell's Instagram account leaped to 20,000 followers. Social media users who had shared the original meme contacted him to apologize. The publicity was a boon for his K.N.O.E. Clothing line, whose name stands for "Knot Now or Ever," a play on the phrase that he and his wife used when he was battling cancer. Whether Mitchell's case gets many social media users to think twice before leaping to conclusions remains to be seen. But it's hard not to conclude that the episode ended on a higher note for humanity than where it started.

These examples remind us that in the dynamic world of social media the ever-changing definition of the "self"—a "story" attached to our persona—is a two-way street. Partly it's constructed out of the singular performance we alone present to the world, but it's equally dependent on what the community pushes back in response to that. Audience feedback helps propagate new ideas. It also dictates the algorithmic system with which Google ranks pages in search results, an extremely powerful determinant of status in the online world.

This two-way process is a kind of negotiation. Or, to stick with the thespian metaphor, it's as if the consumers of our content aren't so much the audience but fellow cast members in the performance of "me." We are the protagonists; they can either be sympathetic minor characters in the play, or full-blown antagonists. Either way, our interactions with them are what round out the story; they make the impression complete.

One person who has demonstrated complete mastery of this interaction with the audience/fellow cast members is Banksy, the mysterious, unidentified graffiti artist whose provocative work has captured the public imagination like no other practitioner of this renegade art. Not only is Banksy a shape-shifting icon of this social media era, he has adeptly used the technology to accentuate the performance of his craft. In a one-month New York "residency" in October 2013, the artist managed to surreptitiously produce a provocative new mural in a different part of the city on each of thirty consecutive days. Just as important, every morning after his illegal artwork had been completed overnight he (who is widely assumed to be male) would post an image of the work on a website, complete with an audio recording describing the work's relevance as social commentary, all done by mimicking the voice of a museum guide. The hunt for each new Banksy became an obsession for many New Yorkers. Once it was found, word would go out on social media and a horde would descend on the site, their smartphone cameras filming the chaos that ensued and massively amplifying the experience to the wider world. We might not know what the artist looks like or the name he was given at birth, but he has figured out how to use the giant audience of social media to *perform* the persona known as "Banksy" and in so doing turn it into a larger-than-life artist-hero.

Very few people have Banksy's ability to mold the views of the social media crowd so completely to their needs. (Based on his effective use of the @RealDonaldTrump Twitter account during the 2016 electoral campaign, Donald Trump seems to also share such talents.) The rest of us should be wary. While we can and should take care in how we express our identity in the public domain, we can't control the fact that the Social Organism will do its own work constructing (or reconstructing) *its* interpretation of our identity. We have no choice but to work with it, rather than against it.

This isn't easy, or fair. Some people have been truly hurt by the arbitrary and overpowering way in which social media pitchfork mobs can engage in mass character assassination against targeted individuals, responding to flimsily established evidence of antisocial behavior that's often based on information taken out of context. In coming chapters, we'll discuss how we might as a society manage the mob-like tendencies in social media. For now, it's simply worth remembering one maxim: Engage positively with social media, not negatively, for the latter will only fuel kneejerk, countervailing responses, which can escalate into full-blown ill will.

To my celebrity clients, I've always said: "Don't feed the trolls." If you ignore those whose comments and tweets seem designed solely to provoke anger, thus starving them of the attention they crave, they will cease their infuriating behavior. (I always say a troll is like a quantum particle: It only exists when you acknowledge it through observation.) This lesson was very painfully learned in the summer of 2016 by the comedian Leslie Jones when an online argument with the misogynist "alt-right" leader Milo Yiannopoulos—an openly gay right-wing media commentator—stirred a mob of his fans to deliver a barrage of racist, sexist abuse on her. In engaging with her attackers, Jones fed them into a frenzy. Twitter only made it worse when it shut off Yiannopoulos's account, turning him into a martyr and spurring his fans to start a #FreeMilo movement. Some of these low-lifes went so far as to hijack a proxy for Jones's Twitter account to make it seem as if she herself was putting out homophobic, bigoted commentary. When her publicist called on me for advice, I responded with my standard line about simply ignoring, about not feeding the trolls. Jones took a two-day break from Twitter and then came back with the perfect response, tweeting out this quote from an anonymous social media philosopher: "Don't try to explain yourself to idiots. You're not the fuckface whisperer."

We can also use this food metaphor for the opposite lesson: that if you want to create an appealing persona and a positive impression among certain people or target markets, then the content you feed them should convey that positivity. As per Life Rule number two: the Social Organism *needs to be fed.* Like all living things, in order to grow—to create new nodes and cells—the organism's metabolism takes in sources of energy, processes it, and then purges itself of waste. For this to work optimally, it needs to be fed a healthy diet of content. The more it is fed, the more it grows.

Much as Laney Griner learned that she was better off feeding the Social Organism what it wanted with the "Success Kid" persona that meme jokesters had imposed on her baby son, I've learned from working with companies that a similar, nourishing approach is the best way to develop their own effective identity—or brand—on social media. I first learned this at my video content start-up Revver, where we discovered and monetized the famous "Diet Coke + Mentos" video for the crazy "scientists" at Eepy Bird. (If you're not familiar, do yourself a favor and go YouTube it now.) Their now legendary choreographed display of exploding Diet Coke geysers infused with Mentos mints has been seen at least 50 million times across various platforms. Mentos immediately saw the value of associating with a viral hit and sponsored some of the versions. In other words, it chose to feed the Organism. And in a rapid affirmation of that decision, the company's iconic brand of mints started reappearing at checkout counters shortly afterward. By contrast, Coca-Cola first distanced itself, reckoning that it was an unauthorized message, inconsistent with their in-house brand definition. "We would hope people want to drink [Diet Coke] more than try experiments with it," a company spokeswoman told *The Wall Street Journal.* "The craziness with Mentos...doesn't fit with the brand personality of Diet Coke." Coke's stance denied the soft-drink maker an opportunity to convert the fun, widely inclusive conversation into a stronger brand awareness strategy. In fact, I was later vindicated when Coke, seeing that the phenomenon had raised Diet Coke sales in North America over 5 percent, changed its tune. The company has since worked with the Eepy Bird duo on various Diet Coke and Zero Coke "experiments."

In the ten years since the first Diet Coke and Mentos performances, countless brands have learned a lesson on the importance of engaging, rather than opposing, the social media feeding frenzy. Even a stodgy, conservative brand like Red Lobster knew that it had to do something constructive, however meek, after Beyoncé's bombshell "Formation" release included a racy shout-out to the restaurant chain, "When he fuck me good, I take his ass to Red Lobster." Eight hours after the song's release had social media in stitches about it, Red Lobster came back with its own tweet, in which it substituted the singer's nickname for the middle word in its trademarked Cheddar Bay Biscuits: "'Cheddar Bey Biscuits' has a nice ring to it, don't you think? #Formation @Beyonce." It wasn't exactly a zinger, and the long delay suggests that the marketing team agonized over how to respond to this unsolicited, explicit association with their brand. But in the end, it was the right response: Don't resist, roll with it. By staying out of the way, the collective genius and wit of social media delivered Red Lobster the best boost to its brand awareness that it has had in decades. Noting that its name had received 42,000 mentions on Twitter in just one hour, Red Lobster announced that sales on the weekend of the song release were up 33 percent from where they were a year earlier.

Even if traditionally structured companies now understand that they must work with social media, not against it, and are trying not to be overly controlling of what *they* think their brand's identity should be, vested interests inside these organizations can keep working against this organic process. There's still a prevailing mind-set, just like that of the broadcast news presenters, that their version of a story is the only one that can be presented. Sometimes it's the marketing guys refusing to feed the Social Organism. (As I like to say, passersby have no way to directly respond to billboards on Sunset Boulevard, which is why marketing teams keep using them: They're insulated from negative feedback.) Other times, the ones who are starving the Organism are the lawyers. In taking legal action, supposedly in the protection of proprietary interests, they're capable of totally cutting off the metabolic pathways of the Organism and breaking its flow dynamics. This speaks to the full aspect of rule two: To function well a living thing must take in food, transport that converted energy around the Organism, and trigger the chemical reactions needed for it to grow and regulate the body. In other words, the memetic process of content replication and mimicry needs to be left unimpeded. Censorship—which is what excessive trademark or copyright control ends up being—is like a blocked artery that's preventing oxygen and nutrients from circulating around a body. That means that for the Social Organism, proprietorial lawyers are like saturated fats. Their actions lead to the accumulation of bad cholesterol and impede healthy blood flow.

At theAudience we deliberately eschewed strict corporate controls over proprietary material, which meant we could move quickly as we avoided the lengthy approval processes that can impede a message from spreading. But even then, we'd still often run into corporate lawyers who couldn't help themselves. Case in point: We developed and released the hit song and video #Selfie by the Chainsmokers, tapping forty-six influencers to launch it into the network and exploit their armies of followers. The strategy was resoundingly successful, in large part because of the memetic mutations that we'd actively encouraged. We had learned from the accidental success of Baauer's "Harlem Shake" and used all the tricks of replication that we'd observed in that free-content explosion. We preloaded the music-posting site SoundCloud with six-second, fifteen-second, and thirty-one-second #Selfie "drops" so that people would use these seeds to make their own songs. We actively seeded the phenomenon, we put forth examples, and we used the power of influencers as distribution. The result: lots of riffs on the core refrain of "but first, lemme take a selfie," including edgy plays such as "but first, lemme drink a protein" or "but first, let me take a dick pic." For the core song, these riffs were a huge boost, helping make it go platinum in ten countries. But then, suddenly, it ended. The band sold the song to Universal, which immediately took on the draconian policy of shutting off all YouTube derivative works on mobile—and limiting video playback to only fourteen countries on VEVO. Immediately, the momentum stopped. The song's new owner had curtailed the Organism's memetic replication, in essence starving it to death.

As we've discussed, it takes more than simply pushing a message out to a broad number of influencers to make it grow. To harness the Social Organism's global distribution system for maximum impact, the message must possess the right content, too. We know from history that artworks that become powerful memes are those that tap into deep-seated emotions: the uplifting celebration in Beethoven's "Ode to Joy"; the rousing "I have a dream" speeches of Martin Luther King Jr.; the patriotic stirrings that Americans found in the Iwo Jima flag-raising image; or the resolute determination that Alberto Korda's portrait of Che Guevara inspired in generations of would-be revolutionaries. Now in the social media era, the ability to stir up emotion is as important as ever to the success of any piece of content.

Remember the Wharton business school study of the differing impact that a variety of emotional triggers would have on people's propensity to share news stories on social media? It showed that our responses to a piece of online content will fluctuate depending on the type of emotion that it elicits. The researchers showed that the response was determined first by a binary question of the *feeling* generated—whether it was emotionally positive or negative—and second by a more nuanced matter of whether the particular emotion elicited was more or less likely to motivate action. But there's a third way to break this down: What kind of a response do we want to generate? Just because an image or a piece of text is shared doesn't mean the memetic replication will automatically confirm to the positive image, persona, or brand management we intend to cultivate. We might think we're "performing" certain desirable versions of ourselves, but there's no guarantee the audience will see it that way. Their responses to our performance, the choices they make in how to portray it, can do as much to determine the public persona that emerges out of this interaction as we can. A social media audience in this sense is also composed of cast members engaged in the performance of "you."

Let's return to the biological analogy. If we examine different types of emotion-inducing content as a biologist might study the impact of consuming different sources of nutrition, we can think of the various types of published messages as food types. Each will have unique, distinct effects on the Social Organism's well-being. What the Organism's metabolism needs, I like to say, is a balanced diet. So while a message with an angry tone, with its capacity for adrenaline release, might be an especially strong motivator for someone to hit the retweet button, it's not a healthy source of sustenance over the long term. It breeds negativity on a wider scale, which as the Wharton study suggests, would, over the longer term, tend toward the contradictory impact of lessening people's desire to share content. Much like Big Macs, anger releases endorphins that give a transitory sense of satisfaction. But most of us know we should limit our consumption of cheeseburgers.

The kind of content that best succeeds within the social media architecture is not based in fear, sadness, or fury. What works is optimal, positive emotional resonance. At theAudience, we made it our business to figure out what that was. Before we decided on what content we would release to our network of influencers and nodes, we had to decide on the just-right emotional tone. The content varied tremendously, and the mood for each message contained plenty of nuances. But we always, always went for positivity. We asked ourselves, does the piece of content seek to inspire? Does it uplift? Amuse? It had to pass a positive emotion litmus test.

To trigger these optimal emotional responses, the food also needs to be properly packaged. Specifically, content needs to be delivered in a nonlinear object-based narrative form, a lesson that—despite its basis in millennia of human communication and storytelling—seems to be lost among the senior marketing managers of our world. Traditionally, stories have followed formulas. Remember pattern recognition, the memetic coding structure with which the receptors in our brains engage with incoming information? If the narrative follows a pattern that's familiar, the recipient's brain can process it. In that way content pierces the defenses of the host and begins to replicate itself. It becomes a meme.

* * *

I like to give clients a piece of advice I learned from John Lasseter at Pixar: To write a successful story that conveys an intended message, you need a narrative that centers on a lovable character that keeps you on the edge of your seat but that also lives by a set of rules. But in the Social Organism even the best scripted narratives become a living, iterative story over which we do not have complete control. The script will change, depending on how it is received by the Organism.

Getting this right is as much art as science. Social media is still very much in its infancy. I use the example of breaking apart the story into photos, images, videos, and spreading them as ubiquitously as possible through multiple channels and then using hashtags and search engines to weave them back together in narrative threads. It's hard to predict how content will be received and treated. Often what seems like a harmless, open-minded message can prompt an unexpectedly negative backlash. But this *is* an art that can be learned. The starting point for figuring out how not to inadvertently foster negativity around your brand must be an understanding that social media is a living, breathing organism. It is the antithesis of a static, one-way distribution mechanism; it's a complicated, multiplayer dialogue over which content creators have limited control.

J.P. Morgan Chase's social media strategists were given a hard lesson in this when they decided to use the hashtag #AskJPM to invite Twitter users to an online Q&A session with the soon-to-be-named new leader of the investment banking division. These poor, misguided banking flaks seemed to forget that Twitter was not like a confidential helpline for the firm's customers. Twitter is a public forum in which participants will take your content and reinterpret and manipulate it in whatever way they choose for their own self-expression and identity performance. The other thing the mega-bank's publicity mavens forgot was that it was November 2013, just five years on from the worst financial crisis in eighty years, a tragedy that left millions out of work and millions more stripped of their homes, and which was widely blamed on the greed and recklessness of senior bankers at firms like J.P. Morgan. In the two previous months, the bank had been forced to sign a $13 billion settlement with the Justice Department for peddling bad mortgage loans and was hit with a $920 million fine over a London trader who'd manipulated the derivatives market.

When the tweet went out with its #AskJPM invitation, it immediately elicited questions like these:

> "Did you have a specific number of people's lives you needed to ruin before you considered your business model a success?"
>
> "What section of the poor & disenfranchised have you yet to exploit for profit, & how are you working to address that?"
>
> "When [CEO] Jamie Dimon eats babies are they served rare? I understand anything above medium-rare is considered gauche."

Hours later, with more than a thousand retweets on the clock, this tweet was posted by the @jpmorgan account: "Tomorrow's Q&A is cancelled. Bad Idea. Back to the drawing board." To this day, #AskJPM is used as shorthand both for bad social media PR decisions generally and by activists looking to attract anti-bank sentiment to their cause. It's pretty much the epitome of a hashtag fail. Still, given the post-crisis context in which it operates, it's hard to imagine how J.P. Morgan could have used social media to prompt *any* open questions from the public. If it had properly understood the beast it was dealing with, perhaps its publicists would have concluded that they shouldn't have tried in the first place.

Most companies aren't as hamstrung by negative public opinion as J.P. Morgan. And if they're willing to relinquish some control, social media can be a resoundingly effective way to reach a mass audience and positively shape a brand. But once we recognize it as a living organism that needs nourishment, there are definite dos and don'ts when it comes to choosing what to feed it. Here's one rule of thumb: Let the Social Organism think for itself.

I first learned these lessons after I was hired to take over Disney's social media strategy. I was tasked with promoting the new *Toy Story 3* movie in 2010. It had been eleven years since *Toy Story 2*. So the six-, seven-, and eight-year-olds who'd fallen in love with the toy characters Buzz Lightyear and Woody in the first two versions were now in high school and college. TV advertisers—focused, misguidedly as always, on women and young kids—were ignoring these Millennials, who in any case weren't even watching TV because they'd discovered a unique new form of entertainment: Facebook. So when confronted with the challenge of connecting with these young adults, of trying to get them back for a third go-round, we decided that Facebook was the right medium. (We called them the Andy-ites—Andy of course being the central boy character who, like our target audience, goes off to college in *Toy Story 3* and must decide what to do with his old toys.)

I went to the marketing team and they said, "Congratulations, here's our new movie poster; go make it viral." There were two problems: (1) the poster, which was simply a yellow number three against a black background, and (2) the copy that they insisted I use with it: "Hey kids, here's the new *Toy Story 3* poster. Isn't it great?" Within five minutes of that being up on Facebook it had generated five hundred responses, most of them with varying uses of the word "fuck": "No, it's not fucking great; it's a three on a fucking black background" or, the one that really hit home, "Fuck you, Disney, you ruined my childhood." I went to the guy who made the poster and I asked him why he thought these kids hated it so much, and he replied, "Oliver, it's not the poster that they hate, it's your tone, because you were telling them, in the rhetorical voice, what to think." So, we just put it up again with the straightforward statement of "Here's the new *Toy Story 3* poster." The response was 100 percent positive. I'd never seen such a 180-degree turn in public opinion. On social media you can't tell people what to think. Dogma invites negativity.

So that's a cautionary tale on what *not* to do. But what about more constructive uses of emotional content? Well, a subsequent experience during the *Toy Story 3* marketing effort would teach me that if we tapped the right emotional triggers on social media, we could reach an enormous audience and have far more influence than anything we could ever hope to achieve over traditional media outlets. A few months after the Facebook release of the first movie poster, I gained access to Pixar's rich archive of artwork. The archivists found a wonderful image, a gouache painting from the original storyboards, of Buzz and Woody arm in arm. We posted that one on Facebook, too, with the caption, "You've got a friend in me"—a line from Randy Newman's popular song of the same name, which was featured in the first and second movies. I was simply unprepared for the impact that it had. That post was shared a quarter of a million times, which because of the effects of friend networks on Facebook meant it appeared on about 200 million people's newsfeeds.

When *Toy Story 3* was released on June 12, 2010, it earned an astonishing $41 million at the box office before the day was over. It would go on to gross more than $1 billion, a figure that, until *Frozen* overtook it in 2014, set the record for the highest grossing animated film of all time. What drove all those people to the theater? Market research revealed something that the ad agencies had refused to believe: that a staggering 42 percent of those who attended the movie were motivated not by some expensively produced ads they'd seen on TV, or even by the word-of-mouth advice of their friends, but by Disney's virtually costless direct postings on Facebook. This was a fundamental shift in movie marketing. And this had all happened because of the unique power of the "You've got a friend in me" meme to have an emotional influence on our target audience. With that one piece of social media magic, we helped turn *Toy Story 3* into a bonanza. By unlocking a bundle of positive feelings—nostalgia, warmth, and the loyalty of true friends—we'd gotten these eighteen- to twenty-four-year-olds to fall back in love with the story of Woody, Buzz, and Andy.

I took those lessons to theAudience, where I saw, again and again, how tapping feelings of love and warmth proved the most effective way to spread a message on social media. For example, in the social media research we undertook for a promotional campaign for the singer Usher, we tested the resonance of various images that might best characterize the pop icon's public persona. Our options included instantly recognizable images of Usher as a sexy, shirtless performer, Usher the ladies' man, and Usher the philanthropist, but the one that got by far the most likes and shares was Usher and his two beautiful children. "Daddy Swag," as this image was later coined, connected intrinsically with the middle-aged mother of two into which his fan base had matured. The image of Usher as a doting father was viral gold.

One of my all-time favorite campaigns at theAudience was for the skin and hair care product maker Dove, which took a stand against the poisonous tactics that cosmetics companies use to make women feel anxious about their looks and scare them into buying their products. Dove made the "Real Beauty Sketches" video, which became the most watched online video advertisement ever. (At last count it was viewed 66.7 million times on YouTube.) In the video, a professional forensic artist sketches unseen women based on their own descriptions of their facial features. Later the artist draws the same women's faces based on descriptions from other women whom they'd just met. The magic happens when the subjects of the drawing are shown the two versions and discover that the other women consistently describe them in more flattering terms than they described themselves. For the "Real Beauty Sketches" project, we generated over a thousand pieces of ancillary content in seventeen languages, each of which was tied to a unique moment in a woman's life. It won numerous Golden Lion Awards at Cannes. Later we also worked on Dove's follow-up "Beauty Patches" campaign, which showed the tearful, positive reactions of volunteer women after they were told that the supposedly scientific "RB-X patch" that they thought was making them feel better about their looks contained no active ingredients at all. It was a placebo effect, designed to show that beauty is a state of mind. Last count, the video hits for that one stood at 21 million.

I know what you're thinking. If social media responds so well to life-affirming messages of love and warmth, then why is it filled with so much hate? How do we cope with this seeming contradiction? Well, just like the human body, the Social Organism has a functioning immune system to ward off such negative invaders and dangers. We need to keep it in good shape. That's the topic of the next chapter.

CHAPTER SIX

THE IMMUNE SYSTEM

How Social Media Responds to Unwelcome Threats

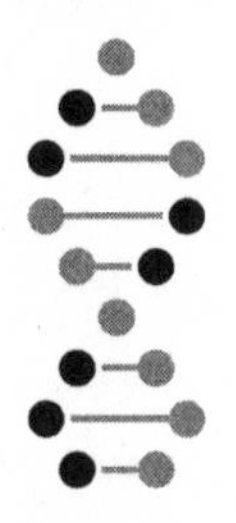

IT'S HARD to imagine greater grief than that of a parent who finds a three-year-old daughter's bed empty in the middle of the night and then never sees her again. But it *can* get worse. Social media trolls made sure that Gerry and Kate McCann's actual nightmare wasn't limited to the anguish of being unable to find their daughter Madeleine and whoever abducted her from their Portuguese hotel room in 2007. Those digital vigilantes perpetuated the conspiracy theories that bubbled up in the initial aftermath of what is now recognized as a deeply flawed initial forensic report. The British tabloid press, which first floated some of those theories—that the McCanns killed their daughter or that she'd died of an accident and they'd hidden the body for fear of retribution—have long since reined themselves in, forced by a libel case to pay damages and apologize. But on social media, the drumbeat of accusations just grew and grew, even as a new investigation exposed the deep flaws in the first one and fell heavily in support of the abduction theory. For years afterward, millions of viewers and vitriolic commentators were drawn to YouTube posts that showed photos of the middle-class British couple smiling—suggesting it as evidence of their guilt—complained of the articulate Dr. Gerry McCann's access to politicians, and hashed together armchair detective theories on the real "truth." Then as Twitter, which was founded the year before Madeleine's disappearance, evolved into a global town square of relentless heckling, the cacophony of harassment just grew louder. So much so that the family closed the official @FindMadeleine account in 2015 because of what they termed the "toxic" postings of their accusers.

Yet the McCanns are not the only victims in this Salem-like rush to judgment that social media seemed to encourage. In some respects, their critics have also suffered—perhaps their failure to filter their own instincts is to blame, but they are victims nonetheless. Take Kerry Needham, the working-class mother of Ben Needham, who disappeared at the age of twenty-one months on the Greek island of Kos in 2001. She was heavily critical of the disproportional attention and UK government resources dedicated to the McCann case and made her point known on social media. Because the McCanns blocked her @FindBenNeedham Twitter account from posting on theirs, she felt they were unfairly implicating her in the circle of "toxic" attackers and went public to say so. Two grieving families were now slinging mud at each other in what amounted to a classic British class war. Then there's the case of Brenda Leyland, the owner of the Twitter account @sweepyface, on which had appeared tweets calling for the McCanns to "burn in hell" with the promise to "supply the petrol." In October 2014, with Gerry McCann calling on police to target "vile" trolls like @sweepyface, Sky News outed Leyland as the Twitter account's author and confronted her near her Leicestershire home, later broadcasting the exchange on air. A week later, the sixty-three-year-old mother committed suicide. As Emma Barnett, a columnist at *The Telegraph*, wrote of the whole tragic affair, it should be a "wake up call" for everyone, a lesson that "we must confront this uncomfortable dichotomy between our real lives and our online ones."

How did it come to this? Why is there such a relentless outpouring of fear, anger, and vengefulness in Reddit threads and the accounts of Twitter trolls? Why are there so many virtual pitchfork mobs attacking strangers for their perceived wrongs, often resulting in "punishments" like destroyed careers that far outstrip the original "crimes"?" Why do extremist organizations like ISIS succeed in using social media to recruit young people to their barbaric causes and stoke fear into the minds of Westerners?

I *might* respond by stating that to focus on the ugly side of social media is missing the forest for the trees. I *could* say that the problem is simply that the most alarming, negative posts tend to grab your attention, drowning out the silent majority of reasonable people and distorting the overall picture of positive change. I could tell you to instead focus on all the powerful, progressive stuff: social media's role in helping foment the Arab Spring, its capacity to rapidly disseminate vital information during natural disasters, how Parisians used it to share secure information about safe houses amid the ISIS-led terrorist attacks of November 2015. But those answers aren't satisfying: The fact is that social media *can* be an extremely effective tool for doing social harm, especially because of the virtual mimesis concept we outlined above. People who hide behind anonymous avatars and alternative online personas feel less retribution for being hateful and abusive than they would if people knew who they were. There's no negative feedback mechanism to stop them.

The Social Organism covers a wide breadth of humanity, which in theory should create a market that inherently demands inclusiveness. The problem is that the network's overarching heterogeneity is broken down into isolated pools of homogeneity. The all-powerful social media platforms offer tools to tailor newsfeeds to content we (or they) perceive to be the content we want. We've carved up this big universe of diversity into narrower subgroups of like-minded "friends" and "followers," forming echo chambers that subject our creativity to the corrosive influence of groupthink. This birds-of-a-feather instinct, which sociologists call "homophily," is not new. But social media is amplifying the process. And it has gotten more intense as platform managers have unleashed algorithms that control the reading habits of their audiences so that they can package up target markets of supposedly similarly minded people to advertisers and political pitchmen. (Check out a recent *Wall Street Journal* online graphic entitled "Blue Feed, Red Feed" for a startling demonstration of how Facebook was amplifying the homophily experience of Conservatives and Liberals during the 2016 election campaign.) Many of these divided groups are now constantly attacking each other. Humans have been waging such battles for centuries, of course. But now they are played out in ceaseless dialogue across our segregated newsfeeds.

In the last chapter I showed that the Social Organism responds positively to content that elicits feelings of love and warmth. But what one group "loves" can differ diametrically from another group. One man's terrorist is another's freedom fighter. In the 1930s Hitler was loved by millions of Germans, their hearts filled with Teutonic pride by the emotion-stirring images of swastikas and goose-stepping Nazis. He was hardly lovable to the rest of humanity.

It's important, too, that the "love" people feel for their fellow ideologues can now be expressed with the click of a button. On social media platforms the "like" buttons and emoticon response options offered to readers are nearly always limited to positive expressions. For a long time it was impossible to do anything but "like" a Facebook post. Now, there's a wider array of response options, but still no way to "dislike" a post. You can express anger, laughter, awe, and sadness with cartoon faces, but these tend more toward solidarity with the post's point of view than critique. We can, of course, express opposition in comments, but the basic architecture of social media tends to promote like-mindedness.

Segregation in social media is by no means democratic. Due to disparities in digital education and access, the censorship structure of social media platforms (which we'll discuss later in the book), and the pre-existing biases and inequalities imported from the physical world, some online groups have more clout than others even when their ideas are anathema to a wider humanity. It can be a question of how loud your voice is and how many influencers you have in your circle.

The #Gamergate scandal of 2014–2015 helps illuminate this phenomenon. In that case, men in the online gaming community—many hiding behind anonymous identities—attacked female game developers such as Zoe Quinn in what seemed like a concerted effort to inculcate gaming culture as a bastion of masculinity. Theirs was a nineteenth-century mind-set applied to a twenty-first-century, high-tech setting. Yet as regressive as their views were, the trolls' waves of attacks overwhelmed Quinn and her supporters, some of whom had to go into hiding because of rape and death threats. A year later, despite the disgust that #Gamergate elicited in wider society, it was hard not to conclude that the misogynists had won. In the male-dominant online gaming subculture, the most antisocial voices were sufficiently numerous, vocal, and tech savvy to hijack the debate and turn it to their advantage. It was a discouraging challenge to the rosy Silicon Valley narrative that online technology breeds inclusiveness.

Sometimes warring social media factions will reach a kind of equilibrium in which neither side wins, leaving a cacophony of vitriol with no room for constructive dialogue. Consider the U.S. political sphere, where conservatives and liberals are locked in a quasi-permanent but restless impasse. Twitter feeds, news sites' comment sections, and Facebook discussion groups reveal a world of perpetually uncompromising positions by Republicans and Democrats. This stalemate, which is directly manifest in Congress's policy gridlock, is rooted in the disruption of broadcast news by cable TV in the 1980s. An early contributor to this failure to interact and negotiate was CNN's *Crossfire* show, which decided that the public's interest in "objectivity" was somehow served by having two egomaniacal personalities from either side of the political divide yell at each other across a table. Now, we see the same character attacks and petulant fights occurring right inside the two political parties; during the 2016 Republican primaries, standards got so low that when Donald Trump boasted about the size of his penis in a televised debate, the general reaction was a collective "of course he did" shrug.

If this inclination toward permanent conflict is frustrating, it is nonetheless a useful foundation for understanding how the Social Organism deals with stress. That understanding will help us design messages and mechanisms that encourage people to dial down the anger and hate and instead promote compassion and love. Not surprisingly, what we find is that this tendency toward equilibrium is consistent with how nature works. All living things—as per our rule number four—are constantly working to ensure that their internal environment maintains homeostasis, or balance. They need stability, not entropy. And often that means finding the point where each of two competing forces is unable to overwhelm the other.

YouTuber C. G. P. Grey offered an explanation for this dysfunctional aspect of social media in a video entitled "This Video Will Make You Angry." Grey, whose real name is widely believed to be Colin Gregory Palmer Grey, drew heavily on biological analogies to describe how anger, that adrenaline-releasing motivator of action, can have a viral impact on like-minded thinkers. He started by describing ideas posted on social media as "thought germs"—he might not have recognized it, but he was talking about memes—that latch on to the receptors of people (cells) who sympathize with the idea. The most powerful thought germs, he argues, are "anger germs," since—as the Wharton study showed—ideas that provoke ire are especially capable of spurring sympathizers to share them on social media. As these anger germs encounter new sets of like-minded people, they lead to a viral-like explosion of replicated anger. Soon enough, though, this burst of fury across social media is spotted by people from groups holding opposing viewpoints, which prompts a countervailing, equally angry response. As each group succumbs to a constant, reinforcing feedback loop, they plunge into a fierce competition. "Each group breeds thought germs about the other, and the most enraging, but not necessarily the most accurate, spread the fastest." Often, this competitive process ends up at "symbiosis," he adds, a point in which "a super successful symbiotic pair of anger germs [reaches] ecological stability." It's a version of homeostasis.

Not all anger-inducing ideas reach equipoise with their antithesis on social media, however. Some ideas are so unacceptable to the bilateral status quo that the Social Organism swiftly responds to dispel or neutralize them. It's as if they are foreign intruders from outside the organism, a threat to what it currently defines as its homeostatic steady state—which in this sense we might define as some kind of cultural benchmark of acceptable norm of behavior. Ideas outside the acceptable range are treated as a threat, like a disease-carrying bacteria or parasite, and prompt the Organism's cells to unleash a defensive response. At these moments we see how rule number five applies to social media: The Organism responds to outside stimuli to adapt and or protect itself.

We saw this in 2015, when the Social Organism responded to news that Minneapolis dentist Walter Palmer had shot and killed Cecil, a beloved lion that lived in Zimbabwe's Hwange National Park. Hordes of people took to social media to express their disapproval of what he'd done, which in turn spilled over into his offline life with sweeping effect. Palmer's vacation home was sprayed with the words "lion killer." The Yelp page for his dental practice was inundated with negative reviews that, despite Yelp deleting hundreds that it deemed motivated by politics rather than dentistry, left him with an ongoing one-star rating. Most tellingly, dozens of airlines from the U.S. and other countries responded by banning the transport of trophies from game hunting experiences.

In our bodies, the immune system is triggered when antigens carried by parasites, bacteria, or other unwelcome substances make contact with the protective antibodies we've built up through evolution and from our own past experience. It is as if the Social Organism recognized Walter Palmer's behavior as a harmful foreign substance, a threat that needed to be expelled, akin to the racist Confederate flag. Much like the all-encompassing immune system in human bodies, the Social Organism has a collective subconsciously evolved networked system for defending the status quo of cultural norms. When the antigens contained in a toxic, antithetical idea make contact with receptors in the human brains that comprise the Social Organism, they encounter the cultural "antibodies" that have developed within our culture against offensive concepts. These unwelcome parasites, along with the human cells associated with them, are swiftly rejected and purged.

This kind of group policing on social media, however, does not always hew to the prevailing standards of our wider society. Walter Palmer's problem was not necessarily that his behavior was outside such norms—though killing lions is now pretty widely frowned upon—rather that it was antithetical to the particular homeostatic balance that existed within social media. #Gamergate misogynists don't represent the existing state of Western thinking on gender equality, but at that moment in the evolution of social media and its power dynamic, they had sufficient numbers to control the debate. If there was a similarly well-organized community of highly motivated, strong-minded safari hunters to come to Palmer's defense on social media, his case may have played out much differently. While the Social Organism's immune system is acting as an arbiter of its own cultural norms, it does not fully capture those of society as a whole. Social media still has a lot of growing up to do. We are seeing this played out to great fervor on the issue of gun control in America. It seems with every passing day, a new mass killing happens, and at some point, the American society is going to overturn the boundless notions of the Second Amendment and the NRA, and do something about this toxic influence in our culture.

Interestingly the debate still rages on about the Orlando massacre that left fifty gay men dead. The killer mixed so many metaphors: a disenfranchised mental health patient, a self-loathing homophobe, or an ISIS member and Islamic terrorist. Each group of social media pundits and activists locked on to their version of the story for their agenda.

The social media purging process can go too far, too. In *So You've Been Publicly Shamed*, journalist Jon Ronson details many cases in which hordes of social media users have taken a person's actions or utterances out of context and responded by attacking them with devastating effect. There's the case of Justine Sacco, who boarded a plane in Heathrow and made the fatal mistake of sending what she says was meant to be a sarcastic joke on Twitter: "Going to Africa. Hope I don't get AIDS. Just kidding. I'm white!" She'd been sending a number of tweets employing racial stereotypes that, taken together, make it seem like she was really poking fun at racists and, perhaps, at her own privileged position. But social media doesn't handle irony very well. So, unbeknownst to Sacco, while she was unplugged from the world during the eleven-hour flight, her tweet unleashed a deluge of opprobrium. Tens of thousands of indignant replies were thrown back at her, calling her racist and insensitive. While she was in the air, #HasJustineLandedYet became one of the top trending hashtags. Upon disembarking at Cape Town she discovered an overwhelmed Twitter account and a receiving line of journalists, both professional and hobbyist, waiting to document her arrival. Within hours, she was fired from her job, her career in tatters. Sacco's joke was certainly ill-conceived and reflected an ignorance of the Social Organism. But did she deserve all this?

The same question could be asked by Tim Hunt, the Nobel Prize–winning biochemist and molecular physiologist (my kind of scientist). He was famously fired from an honorary professorship at University College London after he joked before a gathering in Seoul that the problem with having women in a lab is that "they fall in love with you and when you criticize them they cry." A comprehensive analysis of the events from former UK member of Parliament Louise Mensch later revealed that a journalist whose coverage of Hunt's remarks sparked outrage and mockery on social media had overlooked clear signs that Hunt was being ironic and self-deprecating. He spoke before an audience of female scientists and women journalists—a setting in which it's almost inconceivable that someone of his caliber could say something so blatantly sexist unless he was being ironic. An audiotape of the event released one month later, which revealed a laughing audience's response to his joke, contradicted the reporter's claim that his comment had met with silence and seemed to confirm Hunt's assertion that he'd simply made a rather ham-fisted joke about his own less-than-perfect looks and love life. Eventually, Hunt was reappointed to some of his posts, in part because UCL's overreaction prompted a separate backlash against the university. But the damage was done.

One way to think about these mob-driven overreactions is to contemplate the failings of our biological immune system, which can also take things too far. If you have allergies, you may dread springtime, when your immune system reads false antigen signals from otherwise harmless pollen and, viewing it as a threat, produces mucus and unlocks your tear ducts to dispel it. After all, antigens are just another "pattern" that the body has learned to recognize, and it can misinterpret those patterns. Whether immune systems do or don't overreact in this way is a function of genetics. The same principle might apply to memetics with the Social Organism. We need to evolve a more sophisticated memetic code, one that allows people to use context both to interpret others' comments and to recognize the outsized harm that their own kneejerk responses can have when they're unleashed on social media. This technology, and the online society that has built around it, are young and underdeveloped. Nuance is often absent. Perhaps the answer is a more multisensory world within our social media experiences, one that virtual reality technology might eventually bring us. For now, we must grapple with an imperfect evolutionary state. We must figure how to encourage its healthy, progressive evolution.

Other examples of tension within social media have less to do with swiftly purging a threat and the pursuit of homeostasis and more to do with how competing memes within the Organism battle for ascendancy over time. Yet in these cases, too, responses and counter-responses look very much like the behavior of an immune system. The street protests and mass actions that the #BlackLivesMatter movement coordinates via social media seem like a concerted attempt to purge racist ideas and institutions. Because they face stiff resistance from anti-BLM forces, the movement doesn't consistently succeed in immediate expulsion. Few cops, for example, have been charged with murder in these police brutality cases, let alone convicted. On the other hand, as we've documented, the accumulation of actions from the #BlackLivesMatter and other social media–led activist movements are nonetheless driving evolutionary change within the Organism. Over time, they have developed ever-wider support from a large subsection of the population. In time, I believe they will change the entire Organism for the better.

#BlackLivesMatters was a constructive idea that inserted itself into the Organism from outside. But destructive memes can also enter the same way, using the Organism's cell structure and metabolic pathways to sow hate and torment. We've mentioned ISIS, but there are many others that we should be concerned about, too.

Consider simply the coldheartedness with which some people denigrate appearances, whether in reference to complete strangers or to public figures like tennis star Serena Williams, who has been frequently subjected to racist and sexist comments on social media about her muscular body shape. Such cases are examples of the least compassionate aspects of human behavior.

I think of these unadulterated blasts of hate as social cancers. Like cancer, they use the Organism's own system to nourish abnormal growth, creating tumors that can outpace the growth of normal cells. Typically, our immune system is adept enough to stop carcinogens from triggering tumors. Other times, that same system might fail to stop the advent of a tumor, but it will curtail its growth and prevent it from metastasizing. Often, however, the cancer wins—often enough to put the various diseases that come under this category in the crosshairs of medical researchers the world over. By stealing nutrients away from healthy non-cancerous cells, a malignant tumor will starve the organism to the point of death unless chemotherapy or radiation is successfully administered. (Here, too, failed pattern recognition is to blame: The most deadly cancers are those that disguise themselves so that the immune system fails to recognize the mutated cell growth as a foreign invader.) We can think similarly about memes that do harm to the inclusive, wider body of the Social Organism. While I believe that the Social Organism will eventually mount the defenses required to overcome these diseases, they are undoubtedly working against the constructive value of social media.

How to stop these cancers? For solutions, we should look—you guessed it—at the study of human biology, specifically at how it informs cancer treatment. A key word here is "mutagen," which doctors use to describe an agent, either radiation or chemical, that induces genetic mutation. Many mutagens, like the chemicals in tobacco smoke, are unwelcome because by changing our DNA, they can provoke cancerous growth. But mutagens are also useful as weapons against cancer. Both radiation and chemotherapy (a chemical-based treatment) are used to force changes in the underlying cell structure of different types of cancer and stop or reverse their growth.

A related approach is immunotherapy, an exploding new medical field that my allergies-suffering partner at theAudience, Sean Parker, has aggressively supported with $600 million in funding. It aims to train the body how to better fight true enemies like cancer, and not substances like the peanuts and shellfish that Sean's body mistakenly sees as a threat. Whereas mutagen strategies involve altering the genetic mutation process, immunotherapy is about teaching the immune system to interpret information. In both cases, however, we see a type of "recoding" taking place, and that notion may be the key to strengthening the Social Organism's defenses against hate.

As we've been saying from the outset, there's no turning back the clock on the new communications architecture that social media represents. So, if we are to harness more of this new system's positive features and diminish its uglier, negative aspects, we must explore new strategies for fostering a more inclusive, empathetic society. We need to start thinking about how to mutate or rewrite parts of the Organism's memetic code to foment fundamental changes in our social mores and culture, to make them more resistant to the disease of hateful communication.

How might we deliberately alter the memetic code? We could start by simply expanding the meme pool with healthier memes. Just as the strength and resiliency of an organism is bolstered by the number of positive, strong genes from which its DNA is drawn and undermined by the weak ones that leave it susceptible to disease, so, too, the health of the Social Organism is determined by the right mix of memes. One way to build a healthier, more positively inclined social media environment, then, is simply to encourage a greater abundance of emotionally positive, uplifting content. We need to celebrate and promote the human spirit; encourage compassion, empathy, and respect; build bridges of tolerance and inclusion; provide sustainability for art and culture; and seek reconciliation and rapprochement between enemies.

That may sound like stating the obvious. Our poets and priests have been calling for more compassion for centuries. It might also sound a little naïve and idealistic seen through the lens of pre–social media communications history. But only now, in this new era of communication technology, do we have the data to test and measure the effectiveness of different strategies for spreading goodwill. Social media can be mapped, studied, and quantified—a living laboratory, hundreds of millions of interconnected nodes that powerful computers can analyze. To be sure, the astronomical fees that social media platforms like Twitter charge to access their core data will for now constrain our ability to learn from it. To me, that's an incentive to develop decentralized social media systems that no person or company owns, an idea we'll address in chapter 8. Still, with the right access to all this complex data, we really can start to study social interaction as a more precise science. One example of this being put into practice comes from the Kavli Foundation's HUMAN Project, an interdisciplinary analysis of an enormous, decades-long dataset lifted from the actions of ten thousand New Yorkers. In Kavli's words, it aims to "enable the development of new theories, therapeutics, and policy recommendations currently unattainable through traditional studies of human beings."

Much of our work at theAudience involved studying human socialization, albeit somewhat less rigorously than Kavli. In the interests of helping our clients to profit from making constructive messages go viral, we explored data to find the right methodology for spreading goodwill. Now, with Big Data, machine learning, and sophisticated analytics, we could similarly measure the efficacy of how different strategies play out across the social media universe. In the process, we could help to build a friendlier, healthier Social Organism.

Rather than studying how negative content breeds hurtful feedback loops, it might be more useful to start by looking at where social media is succeeding in promoting tolerance and inclusion. Many publishers are already demonstrating its enormous capacity to breed positive, uplifting sentiment. I noted in the previous chapter how we'd had viral success at theAudience with advertising shaped around life-affirming content. The same is occurring in new forms of journalism and non-commercial creative content. These are the people who will help us rid the Social Organism of its cancerous cynicism.

Brandon Stanton's hugely successful Humans of New York blog and Facebook page (17 million followers) are shining examples of how to harness social media to encourage compassion and pathos. Stanton's simple formula, coupling a daily photo of an ordinary person with a quote that captures their hopes and fears, routinely draws a flood of heartfelt, uplifting comments from readers. The photos aren't always exceptional; neither necessarily are the comments. But day after day, these posts form a uniquely humanizing story that can have an infectious effect on those who encounter it. Stanton's posts become powerful memes shared by millions around the world. "HONY" is a phenomenon, so much so that a photo of one kid from a poor Brooklyn neighborhood inspired a fund-raising drive that raised more than $1.4 million for his school and earned the photographer, student, and his school principal an invitation to the White House.

Some critics have charged that HONY's posts are superficial and breed sentimentality rather than real connections or knowledge. But based on how I see the evolution of the Social Organism and the importance of emotions and empathy within it, the very creation of positive vibes between people is a valuable contribution to society. I like to think of HONY as an empathy replicator. We need to build more of them. Activists, policymakers, educators, journalists, even corporate brands—anyone who wants to make a positive difference—could follow this model. It's the kind of healthy living the Organism needs to ward off its cancers, precisely because it encourages us to celebrate each other's presence on this earth. It is an example of what Ethan Zuckerman, a media theorist at MIT's

Media Lab, calls "digital cosmopolitanism," an inclusive model that breaks us free of our homophily-saturated newsfeeds and treats the viewpoints of others with respect and compassion.

Other examples of content providers taking a positive approach include Upworthy, whose posts over social media typically combine a video with a positive, humanistic message. Within months after it was founded in March 2013, the service's posts had surged to third place among the most shared and liked items on Facebook, hitting a combined tally of 14 million in November 2013. Upworthy's success has spawned a slew of imitators, including Distractify.com, ViraNova.com, Liftbump.com, FaithIt.com. Cynics will charge that these sites are all just "clickbait" ploys, and that may be the case. But clickbait that celebrates positivity is a good thing in my book.

Social media can also turn the inspiring acts that people carry out in the offline world into something with a viral, global impact. When the Make-A-Wish Foundation granted five-year-old cancer survivor Miles Scott his wish to play the role of "BatKid" and save Gotham (aka, the City of San Francisco), it staged an elaborate performance across the city that enlisted the help of professional actors, the city's mayor, and even a herogram Vine loop from President Obama. But it took the power of social media, which alerted a massive crowd to the prospect of attending as cheering onlookers and which was used to broadcast the events to millions of viewers worldwide, to turn this into an international celebration.

There's also the case of Liz Woodward, the waitress at a New Jersey diner who left a note for two firefighter customers, telling them that she'd personally paid their breakfast tab in gratitude for their service to the community. When Tim Young, one of the firefighters, posted a pic of the note on Facebook in which he called on his friends to frequent the diner and "tip big," his post about her thoughtful gesture went viral. When it passed over the feed of Lorraine Hatcher, she sent a message back to Tim pointing out that Woodward had been trying to raise money to buy a wheelchair-accessible van for her invalid father. The firefighters seized the opportunity and launched their own campaign in support of the Woodward family's online GoFundMe campaign and turned the whole thing into an even bigger good-news story. Donations started flooding in from around the world. In short order the fund had reached $86,000, enough to buy the van and then some. The story went national, including an appearance on *The Ellen DeGeneres Show*, and played out for months on Woodward's own infectiously uplifting Facebook page, where she posted about the positive turn her life had taken. In her re-affirmed worldview, she saw how good deeds beget good deeds. "Look for those opportunities because they are everywhere," Woodward wrote in one post. "You can make a difference—it doesn't always have to be an elaborate production or effort—it's always the little things that have the greatest impact."

This kind of good-vibe contagion was not possible in the pre–social media world.

Even so, against a relentless stream of articles about humanity's capacity for cruelty, and faced with depressing clickbait headlines—it's hard not to take a jaded view. The feel-good stories discussed above can seem tokenistic against this overwhelming flood of gloom.

Michael and I believe that social media is a major contributor to positive change. Like all technology, it has its negative side effects. But it helps us in so many ways we already take for granted and which bring convenience and security to our everyday lives: We're able to crowdsource knowledge and ask questions that get answered in seconds, whether in a neighborhood Facebook group or a forum for people with common interests. Information-sharing apps in which each node on the network contributes seamlessly to the overall good of the system are changing the face of cities, exemplified by Google's traffic info service Waze, tweet analysis is being used to send early warning signals for everything from earthquakes and disease outbreaks to market behavior.

But it's more than just utility. It's the possibility that individuals can broadcast powerful statements about our shared humanity that makes this technology so important. In the days following the 2015 terrorist attacks in Paris, a blindfolded man appeared in Place de la Republique with a sign that read, "I'm a Muslim, but I'm told that I'm a terrorist" and "I trust you, do you trust me? If yes, hug me." As people constantly came up to hug him, word spread on social media of the opportunity to be there and videos and photos of the exchanges were shared around the world, often with a hashtag that expressed the solidarity that people felt for the city at that time: #JeSuisParis. A work of performance art became a powerful contributor to reconciliation.

As we'll discuss in the next chapter, there's strong evidence that, with the rise of the Internet and social media, society has become more tolerant and less violent—despite what might seem like appearances to the contrary. If we use this technology well, it should help us to transcend our social fragmentation and push this new digital society toward a more inclusive future. More than a billion people from all walks of life, cultures, religions, and political perspectives use platforms like Facebook, Twitter, and Tumblr. And because of its holonic structure, no one interest group can ever truly wield power over all others. We might hide in groups of common interest but with just one mouse click we can reach across those divides and find a common humanity with someone from a different background.

Still, we *do* have the capacity to screw this up. Look no further than how Donald Trump used this technology to bring racists and xenophobes from out of the woodwork during the 2016 election campaign. We can hope that the positive forces of cultural change described above will have a self-correcting effect to reverse these worrying throwbacks to exclusion and bigotry. But there's no guarantee that this will occur on its own. By definition, evolution is not something we can micromanage. What we can do instead is establish the right preconditions to encourage positive, progressive evolution—or, even more important, avoid those that would steer the Organism's evolutionary direction into something nastier. We don't want to be like the cotton farmers who tried to poison the boll weevils only to find that they'd created a more virulent, resistant strain. And to carry that analogy further, I would say that censorship, both by governments and from the social media platforms themselves, is the equivalent of the USDA scientists' DDT dumps on the cotton fields of the South.

When we see the kind of sexual harassment that Caroline Criado-Perez endured on Twitter in response to her feminist activism in the United Kingdom, the instinct is to create rules that curb such hateful expression. But as understandable as that impulse might be, the secondary effects of such draconian responses always do more harm than good over time. It's why I worry about the European Union's move in 2016 to force social media platforms like Facebook and Twitter to censor hate speech—the line could get fuzzy very quickly, and such bans are open to abuse and poor discretion.

One big problem is that censorship sets a precedent, giving de facto license to information gatekeepers—be they governments, traditional media companies, or the corporate owners of our social media platforms—to use these sanctioned speech curbs to pursue and protect their own interests. In the pages ahead, we'll discuss the prospect of inserting certain software algorithms into social media platforms that create incentives for people to engage in positive speech. This is a softer, carrot-like approach and whether it's successful or whether it also creates unwelcome distortions remains to be seen. But I do know from years in this business that the stick approach definitely doesn't work. People will still be shitheads.

The other big problem, as we'll discuss in the next chapter, is that by explicitly limiting our exposure to even the most hateful of speech, we constrain the Social Organism's ability to evolve in a way that positively influences our culture. The last thing we want to do is turn the hatemongers of social media into super-mutant, indestructible boll weevils.

CHAPTER SEVEN

CONFRONTING OUR PATHOGENS

Bolstering the Cultural Immune System

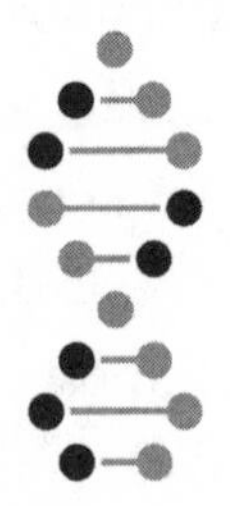

Like Darwinian evolution, the evolution of the Social Organism isn't without pain and struggle. Europe's ongoing refugee crisis, for instance, has unleashed xenophobia and brought out the worst of human reactions—again, played out in social media. This was encapsulated by the #wearefull hashtag that emerged in 2015 in Britain, a mutation of a more profane meme that appeared in Australia in association with that country's draconian refugee policy: #FOWF for "Fuck off, we're full." It later fed into Britain's massive and successful #Brexit campaign. Amid this vitriol, however, a single, heartbreaking photo had a dramatic sobering effect on public debate. Nilufur Demir's photo of three-year-old Syrian boy Aylan Kurdi's lifeless body lying facedown on a beach went viral on Facebook and Twitter.

In the days that followed, dozens of people staged a performance on a Moroccan beach, where they dressed in the same colored clothes of the boy and adopted the pose of his lifeless body in the sand. In both Gaza and India, giant sand castles were built in the shape and colors of Aylan's body to pay tribute to the boy and appeal to people's compassion for the fleeing refuges. Artists around the world began making poetic renderings of it, giving it an almost spiritual quality. These included a giant mural aligning Frankfurt's Main River near the headquarters of the European Central Bank. It was one hell of a meme, joining the ranks of other iconic images of history—the naked girl fleeing napalm in Vietnam, the raising of the Stars & Stripes at Iwo Jima.

The greatest measure of the image's power came shortly afterward, as there was a clear, discernible change in the public discourse. A Scottish tabloid began a campaign that spawned the #wehaveroom meme. In Germany, where the government decided to open the door to incoming refugees from Hungary, thousands turned up at entry points to cheer and welcome the new arrivals. German soccer fans displayed welcome banners, an unexpected gesture from a group more infamously known for their hooliganism. Images of signs at matches saying "Refugees Welcome!" spread on social media, leading some brands to seize a chance to show their social conscience. The soccer club Bayern Munich quickly announced a 1-million-euro donation to the refugees, and English clubs followed suit by creating a day of solidarity. It didn't mean that the voices of exclusion such as France's Marine Le Pen didn't continue to milk people's fears, especially after the Paris attacks. But it did mean that empathy was given a seat at the table when previously it had been denied one. In the ongoing cultural struggle in which opposing viewpoints do battle to determine which meme is fit enough to survive, this one made a powerful bid at inserting a lasting, positive mutation into our social DNA.

To unpack what we mean by a positive social mutation, we'll first explore an example of a positive biological mutation. In this case, we'll talk about one with a high-profile beneficiary: Timothy Ray Brown, the famous "Berlin patient," the only known person to have been functionally cured of AIDS/HIV—distinguishing him from 10 million who live with the virus but have kept it dormant with expensive anti-retroviral drug therapy.

When Brown was treated for leukemia in 2007 he received a stem cell transplant bearing a unique genetic trait known as the CCR5 Delta-32 variant, an inherited feature that puts a protective seal over the carrier's T-cell receptors and thus prevents HIV from finding an entry point into a host cell. Some 10 percent of people with European ancestry are believed to share this condition, but it is very rare among other populations.

The Delta-32 mutation has been passed down over centuries, and scientists are now researching its origins by analyzing human genetic history. At first it appeared to have originated with survivors of the bubonic plague. Now, scientists are zeroing in on a confluence of seminal epidemiological events over two millennia: the Roman conquests of Europe during the fifth-century BC, the great Plague of Athens in 430 BC, and the resistance that certain European populations showed smallpox scourges up to the eighteenth century. What we do know is that over the course of European history, ethnic intermingling helped spread this valuable genetic trait, and that it gained greater presence within inheritance lineages whenever devastating disease breakouts amped up the natural selection process. Only now, in this more scientifically advanced era, do we have the potential to replicate the helpful mutation and pass it on to anyone who needs it.

While it's hard to imagine anything positive about HIV, smallpox, and Ebola outbreaks, scientists now know that viruses like these play a critical role in evolution. These maladies drive the mutation of genes, which in turn breeds resistance, much like that which the Delta-32 variant conferred on Timothy Brown. In fact, the human genome is riddled with genetic material from viruses that infected our ancestors. For example, blood tests of some AIDS patients, in whom HIV has disabled their immune system, have found traces of a reactivated virus that dates back 6 million years to the time when humans and chimps first parted ways. Much as a software engineer might describe a less-than-perfect piece of computer code as "buggy," we could say the same about our human DNA.

Our growing knowledge of the relationship between viral mutation and human evolution, and of how antigens and antibodies develop and evolve in tandem, is forging promising new disease treatments such as immunotherapy. By determining the causes and patterns of mutation in our genes and those of viruses, doctors can teach our immune systems new awareness and convert them into more effective defenders of our health. But there are also lessons in this process for understanding how the Social Organism undergoes cultural evolution via mutations in its memetic code. Recall rule seven: All living things adapt and evolve. If we want society to grow up, and if we want to turn social media into a constructive forum for improving human existence, then we must expose ourselves to the "diseases" of hate, intolerance, and intimidation that persist in our culture. It makes for a powerful case against censorship.

Many different measures show a dramatic improvement in the socializing tendencies of human beings since the rise of the Internet and social media in the early 1990s. While we can't definitively prove that technology was the cause of these results, they do convincingly challenge the view among many that social media does great harm to society. Critics complain that people are now exposed 24/7 to displays of human conflict across a much less sanitized and more globalized media landscape than that of the pre–social media world. But that's different from saying that society has become crueler. The evidence suggests quite the opposite has occurred.

Crime statistics are a good place to start. Police, coronary, and hospital data across the Western world all show that a decline in violent crime accelerated after 1993, when the Internet first made inroads into mainstream society. Most strikingly, data in the United States show that violent crimes for people between the ages of twelve and twenty-four—the cohort that has traditionally suffered the most violence—more than halved in the twenty years that followed. This generation, of course, comprised the first digital natives, with their lives defined in sweeping ways by online activities.

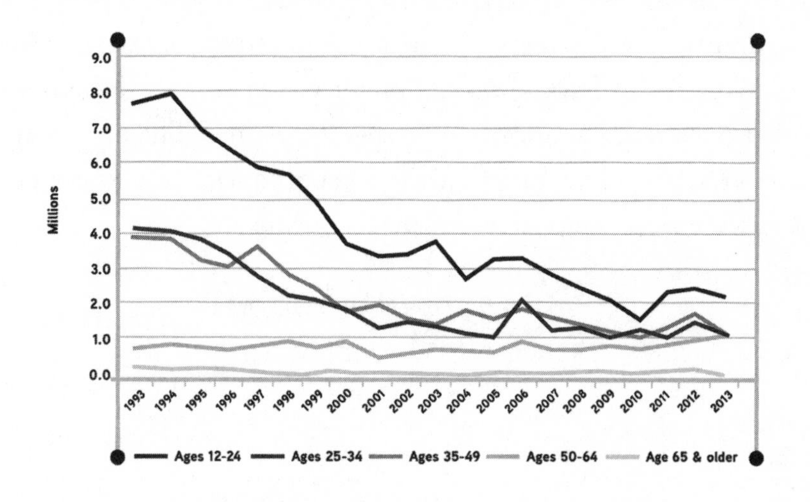

We see similarly striking evidence in Americans' views surrounding race, religion, gender, and sexual preference. Attitudes toward marriage are a good barometer. The non-partisan Pew Research Center's studies on same-sex marriage show that we've gone from only 35 percent in favor of such unions in 2001 to more than 55 percent in support by 2015. In that sense, the Supreme Court ruling legalizing same-sex marriage nationwide that same year was a case of the majority on its bench simply keeping up with society. Similarly, acceptance of interracial marriage has expanded rapidly, Pew results show: In 2012, two-thirds of Americans said they "would be fine" with a member of their family marrying someone of a different race. In 1986 the figure was only 33 percent. A more recent study of Millennials showed an even higher acceptance level, with nine in ten saying they'd be happy with a family member marrying outside their race.

Attitudes on such matters are changing at an accelerating pace.

A 2015 Bloomberg graphic showed that on the legality of five key social questions—interracial marriage, women's suffrage, prohibition, abortion, and same-sex marriage—the time between the first state to change its laws and the Supreme Court's eventual validation of that position dramatically shortened over time. The article suggested that a similarly rapid shift was about to happen with support for legalizing recreational marijuana use.

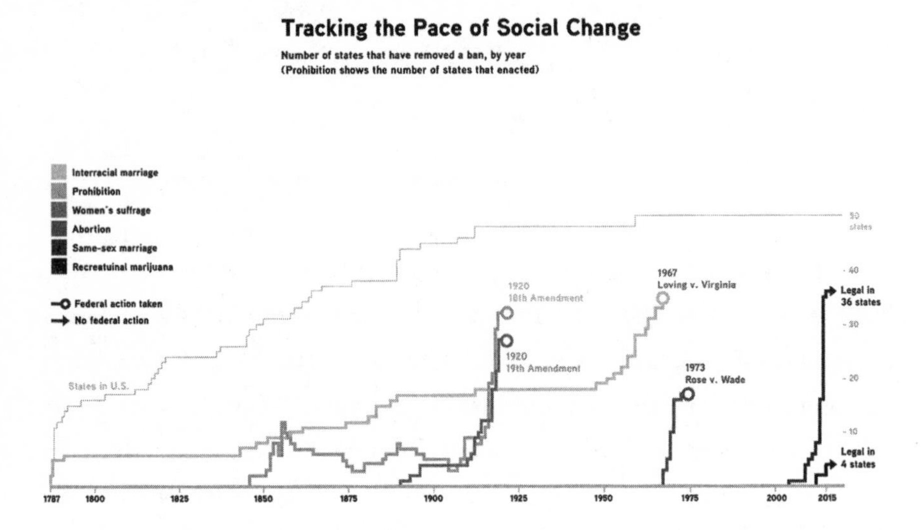

Our culture is evolving at a faster pace, and that acceleration, we contend, is a function of the comingling of thoughts and memes—first on the Internet generally and now, more specifically, within social media. Despite the impression given by the warring factions on social media, we have become more tolerant, more inclusive.

We can view this trend toward greater social inclusion as an acceleration in the mutation rate for the Social Organism's memetic code. Like the reproductive intermingling that imbedded the HIV-resistant CCR5 Delta-32 variant into some parts of the European population, this cultural change is encouraged by the interchange of ideas through memetic replication across the social organism. The process is incomplete, much as the spread of HIV-resistant genetic traits remains incomplete. But similarly to the role played by plagues and disease outbreaks, we can think of it as an evolutionary trend spurred by periods of epidemiological stress. These are the moments in which more highly evolved, inclusive ideas get most heavily tested and promoted through the machine of social media. We know that the strongest genes survive such stress tests; so, too, do the organism's strongest memes. Those memes that best promote the growth and advancement of its heterogeneous, holarchic makeup will replicate, and thus rise to prominence. Ultimately, as the evidence suggests, this process favors ideas that further social inclusion.

Some readers, particularly those of a more conservative political bent, may dispute our socially liberal interpretation of these changes as a positive development. Religious groups will see the expansion of rights around sexual preferences as a regressive step. And whereas we see the diminishment of the Confederate flag's presence in popular culture, cited at the outset of this book, as a progressive evolutionary leap, those who've held on to that symbol as a badge of Southern pride will see it as a retrograde move.

As we've stressed, evolution cannot be defined in moral terms. It doesn't necessarily imply "better." But it does typically mean stronger, more resistant to threats. From that perspective, we think there's a scientific argument to be made that cultural evolution should tend toward greater inclusion. We can address it with some of the laws of physics and ecology that have dictated the algorithm of biological evolution over time. These tell us that if you widen the gene pool, for example, or expand the number of possible variables in a set of molecular reactions, you raise the chances of a stronger, more resilient form or strain emerging from the survival-of-the-fittest competition. Similarly, if we expand the array of cultural mores and ideas that are input into the Social Organism—if we widen the "meme pool"—we end up with a stronger, more resilient culture. Add to that the Social Organism's natural instinct to grow, to expand, and you get a kind of mathematical logic calling for inclusion. Its antithesis, exclusion, goes directly against these instincts. This is why it is so alarming to see the rise of the Trumps, LePens, and movements like Brexit, which are all about building walls. Their approaches will narrow the pool of ideas.

It so happens that this fits with that long-held liberal intellectual tradition that defines history as a progressive march toward ever-greater individual liberty—from the absolute monarchies of feudal Europe to the Enlightenment to the Declaration of Independence to the civil rights movement. We can view this sequenced establishment of new freedoms as a record of society becoming progressively more accepting of difference. It's a chronicle of how the powers that be have been compelled by changes in society, including those fueled by technology, to widen the boundaries of inclusion. There are retrograde phases in this process—some might argue that pervasive state surveillance in the Internet era represents one—but modern history has clearly moved along a continuum of great openness and acceptance. At each step, there has been a struggle between the old and the new. There is no free lunch. We may not need violent revolution to force change these days, but if we want to evolve, the conflict generated by exposure to raw content is inevitable.

Social media facilitates this movement toward inclusion, precisely because it compels us to pay witness to conflict in our midst. By opening ourselves up to an always-on, ubiquitously connected media environment, we are exposing our culture to more and more antigens. Whether it's spam or hate messages, or the interjections of trolls, this otherwise ugly flow of antisocial communication is a necessary aspect of how we strengthen our immune system. Since we are only in the early days of this new reality, we are now going through the most difficult period in this process of cultural evolution. We have entered an unprecedented moment in the history of human socialization when the Organism has suddenly been exposed to a rash of different "diseases."

One of the scariest aspects of these diseases has been the rise of a new breed of populist fascism. In this case, it's a trend that readers on the more liberal side of the political aisle might use to counter our claim that social media is creating a more inclusive society. During the 2016 electoral campaign—still undecided at the time of writing—Donald Trump used his anti-immigrant and anti-Muslim rhetoric to bully his way to the Republican nomination and attract hordes of passionate supporters to rowdy rallies tinged with violence. This hardly looks like "progress." But as Dartmouth professor Brendan Nyhan noted in a nineteen-part "tweetstorm" after a clash between Trump supporters and protestors in Chicago fueled concerns about the state of American democracy, statistics about American attitudes toward others—like those we cite above—do not support the notion that the egomaniacal failed businessman's popularity reflects an overall rise in racial hatred. Rather, Nyhan argued, the Trump phenomenon stems from a failure of established political institutions to execute effective governance and balance out those destructive, exclusionary ideas that have always found a home in a large but otherwise disempowered minority of the population.

The old, vertical power structures in business, government, and mass media have been severely disrupted by our new communications paradigm, with its leaderless, holonic structure. As a result, their grip on power has waned, which is why they are proving to be impotent against an emotion-stirring personality cult like Trump's. It's also why UK political elites failed to dissuade a majority of Brits from voting with the "Leave" campaign, with its xenophobic undertones, when the "Brexit" referendum that they recklessly introduced on June 23, 2016 returned a decision that their country should depart the European Union. The big question is whether society can use the new media architecture, which follows the rules of biology more than those of Washington, to create a new system of mediation in place of those failed institutions. We think it can, and that the mechanism for doing so will come via the Social Organism's evolutionary algorithm. It's just that getting to that more comfortable, harmonious place is going to be a bit of a wild ride and will require thoughtful, open-minded policymaking along with pro-social civic action.

Is this social media moment in time the cultural equivalent of the black plague or whatever major historical epidemic gave rise to the CCR5 Delta-32 variant? Perhaps. The hope is that the accelerated rate of mutation set in motion by an unprecedented, worldwide memetic exchange will see us through this period of pain and discord relatively quickly. Already, people are learning what to do and what not to do on social media. The Social Organism is developing the antibodies it needs to survive.

Our bodies grow up stronger if we are exposed to more bacteria and viruses in childhood. When Michael and I were growing up, if word got out that someone in a school had chicken pox—a highly infectious disease that mostly just left kids covered in itchy scabs for a week or so—parents would bring their child to the home of the sick kid to deliberately expose them to the pox. The idea was that this would allow the child to create the antibodies early on to prevent them from ever catching it again. Given that it was far safer to catch this disease as a child than as a post-pubescent teen or adult—when the risk of more serious complications such as pneumonia or encephalitis is much higher—this seemingly reckless behavior was founded on sound reasoning, even if there were still some risks to your child's health. Since 1995 there's been a perfectly good chicken pox vaccine, offering a far safer way to build up the antibodies. Yet the concept of a vaccine, which of course is derived from the DNA of the threatening virus or bacteria, is based on the same core idea: Our genetic disposition is such that exposure to things that can ostensibly harm us also makes us stronger.

Unlike vaccines, which build up our immune system with antibodies so it can fight disease on its own, or immunotherapy, which effectively teaches that system to do the same, antibiotics are like an army of hired mercenaries. They directly attack infection-causing bacteria, killing these single-cell microorganisms on our behalf and preventing them from growing and reproducing. But once these mercenaries complete their job, they leave. They do not train the inhabitants of the previously occupied territory to fight on their own. What's more, antibiotics have generally been unable to fight viruses, which are much smaller than bacteria and don't have all of the features of full living organisms. (Recall that viruses are essentially just pieces of genetic material—either RNA or DNA—housed inside a molecule that can only replicate itself by entering the cell of a living organism and hijacking its internal reproductive machinery.) You can't "kill" something that isn't technically alive, which is why the only way to defeat a virus like the common cold is typically to wait for our immune system to figure out how to quell these constantly mutating diseases. But it also explains why the overuse of antibiotics poses a threat to public health. Like all living organisms, bacteria adapt and evolve, which means many are becoming resistant to antibiotics, a serious concern for the World Health Organization and Centers for Disease Control and Prevention. So as important as antibiotics have been to saving lives ever since Louis Pasteur discovered penicillin, it turns out that it's much better to teach our immune system to fight its pathogens—as it must do for viruses—than to rely on outsiders to do the work for it.

We can think of rules that curtail or censor antisocial speech, such as those that Twitter and Facebook are often being called upon to deploy, as a strategy akin to bringing in a disease-fighting mercenary service like an antibiotic. It might suppress the particular manifestation of the pathogen, but it won't destroy the root DNA and the Social Organism won't learn to fight back by itself. The memetic core of the offensive thought or idea—take, for example, the essential misogyny of the #Gamergate bigots—will live on and, with the aid of the cells that it has occupied (the supporters of that idea), it will fight back against this outside attack. Those supporters will, as they've always done, frame it as an attack on free speech. And, unfortunately, they will be right.

* * *

All social mores, the cultural norms that define who we are and how we interact with each other, have emerged out of these kinds of conflicts. In his book *The Better Angels of Our Nature: Why Violence Has Declined*, Steven Pinker cites sociologist Norbert Elias's theory on the "civilizing process," which deals with the development of social graces and etiquette, to explain how European society became more peaceable as it emerged from the Middle Ages. If you were invited to a banquet it was once commonplace to bring one's own knife, an instrument that was used both for killing your enemies and for eating food. Gathered around the food, you would carve off a piece of the carcass and bring it to your mouth on the same knife. The problem with all these unsheathed knives around was that there was always a risk someone might get stabbed over a disagreement. This was not a comfortable situation for either the host or the guests, but violence was a part of everyday life in early medieval society; what was there to do about it?

The solution came in the evolution of table manners, which eventually dictated that it was unacceptable to use your personal knife to eat food, an idea that went hand in hand with that of cutlery. The fork was invented and special, less lethal knives were set at the table so that guests would not have to unsheathe theirs in the presence of others. Rules about the proper use of cutlery emerged, mostly concerned with what not to do with the table knife—don't bring it to your mouth; don't stir ingredients with your knife. What began as a practical solution to the dangers of provoking a knife fight evolved into a set of ingrained culture rules that happened also to keep conflicts at bay. Over time, these kinds of subtle shifts helped develop a value system that saw it as unacceptable to act violently in an ever wider array of arenas. In Pinker's words, Elias's research showed how "Europeans increasingly inhibited their impulses, anticipated the long-term consequences of their actions, and took other people's thoughts and feelings into consideration. A culture of honor—the readiness to take revenge—gave way to a culture of dignity." This was moral evolution at work.

As our interactions with each other change and migrate to digital spaces, we are forced to reassess our norms. Society then does what it has always done: It "polices" the newly unacceptable behavior, mostly by conveying disapproval, shaming the wrongdoer. Not only is this response aimed at changing that one person's behavior; it also puts everyone else on notice that this is the new code. I think of it as a newly evolved immune response: Once the new antibodies are added to the immune system's police force, it responds with as much clout as it can muster, both to beat off the foreign intruder and to lay protections against any future incursions.

With social media, we have radically expanded the potential for these kinds of value clashes to occur and, as a result, the transition period for cultural change has been dramatically shortened. In this new, borderless, global communications architecture we are experiencing an explosion of previously impossible cross-cultural interactions. These at first provoke conflict, which can only be resolved if there is some kind of collective cultural shift that redefines the boundaries of what's acceptable. Just as important, once those new mores are established, social media provides a vast, open new platform for society's immune system to do its police work. Think of this new online communion of human beings as a massive dinner table for hundreds of millions of interacting guests and for which a new etiquette must be developed. Dramatic, frequent changes in values are necessary if we are to avoid "killing" each other. Breaches of this newly established cultural order can inspire quite a powerful shock-like response as the Social Organism's immune system kicks into gear.

Whether it's cases like the Charleston massacre or the killing of Cecil the lion, the social media–driven purging response reminds me of a coagulation cascade, the biochemical reaction behind blood clotting that I found so fascinating as a teenage lab rat. When tissue is damaged and blood escapes, a synchronized dance of enzymes and metabolic factors occurs along the arachidonic acid pathway that leads to and from the site of the wound. This causes an army of tiny platelets to bind together, then, subsequently contract to contain the hemorrhage. To the body of the Social Organism, with its evolving culture, sometimes breaches in social harmony can seem like a deep wound that demands a similar response.

There's another reason why cultural evolution is accelerating: We are now, in effect, crowdsourcing our mores. Etiquette and values were once dictated from above. In the Middle Ages, it was the aristocracy that led the way on table manners and the Church that told people what they could and couldn't believe. Even in twentieth-century, pre–social media America, it wasn't nearly as easy for those outside of the media and political establishment to argue for reforming social values. People could attend rallies, go on strike, and, if they had a way with words and access to a publisher, write a persuasive treatise. It was far better than nineteenth-century America, but it was nothing like what it is now, where with the mere click of a "like" or "retweet" button almost anyone can play a part in a movement that helps our culture evolve. Now it is the pool of society's collective ideas, not the exclusive opinions of a priest or a CEO, that determines how we should behave toward one another. Sometimes the collective goes off kilter; other times it inspires progressive change.

Most people don't grasp how this is happening. They see social media as something external to our culture, a distinct technology that can be isolated as a standalone phenomenon from the rest of our lives. They can't see it for the driving force that it is: the primary engine of cultural disruption, a paradigm shift that's changing us from within. Hashtag memes are still thought of as modes of expression that reside solely on social media, even though we are perpetually, if subconsciously, dragging them into the non-online world. The fact is that these memes and the stories that get attached to them are having a profound, far-reaching effect on our society generally, whether online or offline.

Let's once again consider the #BlackLivesMatter movement, which I see as a form of immunotherapy. It is training society to develop the pattern recognition it needs to "see" the latent, institutionalized racism that continues to pose subtle but real barriers for black people. It forces us to recognize that this is a fundamental human rights issue. Yes, it has fostered an inevitable backlash from those whose ill-formed pattern recognition, shaped by a life of white privilege that they wrongly assume to be a universal experience, denies them the ability to comprehend the reality of black Americans' lives. The first group sees what it believes to be a more-or-less non-discriminatory system; the latter *knows* that the state, in the form of armed policemen, systematically assigns less freedom of movement to their bodies than to those cloaked in white skin. This backlash engenders conflict and, in unpredictable ways that a leaderless movement like #BlackLivesMatter simply cannot control. We saw it in the summer of 2016 when the cities of Baton Rouge, Dallas, and Falcon Heights, Minnesota erupted in conflict amid the senseless loss of both black and "blue" lives. But while this conflict proceeds, so too does the evolution of our cultural immune system. #BlackLivesMatter has indeed shocked many whites out of their complacency. It is forcing all of us to see the different reality of others' lives. It is creating a capacity for empathy that was until now sadly lacking.

It's important to be clear about what we, in this context, mean by empathy—a critical emotional trait in the functioning of the Social Organism. Within individuals, scientists believe, empathy is both a learned behavior and genetically determined (people with Narcissistic Personality Disorder are thought to lack the empathy gene). Empathy is also a common element of the Social Organism's shared culture. In that case, where the goal is to progressively update our memetic code and expand our culture's empathetic reach across an ever-wider radius of living beings, the distinction between genetically acquired and learned empathy is moot. We should be constantly "teaching" our culture to be empathetic, and thus strengthening it, which is where the metaphor of immunotherapy is relevant.

Art, which has always played a fundamental role in getting people to recognize their common humanity, is as important as ever in this bid to foster empathy. I was exposed to its potential with a visit in 2011 to *You Me Bum Bum Train* in London, a unique theatrical experience in which you, as the sole audience member, become the central focus—the lead character, if you will—in a series of improvised scenes performed by over five hundred volunteer actors. From scenes of death, success, joy, humiliation, grieving, laughter, and exhilaration, the creators take you on a bizarre journey to reveal the deep human capacity for empathy. It was truly a life-changing experience for me. Of course, the social impact is limited for a privileged, one-person audience. The challenge—and the opportunity—that artists face is to use the tools of social media to have this kind of effect on a giant, global audience.

It's not hard to imagine how social media could help expand empathy. It offers powerful tools for content providers to help people see the world through the eyes of millions of others every day. In fact, I think cultural immunotherapies will only become more powerful as virtual reality tools improve, creating something we might call "VR empathy generators." Imagine social media–connected people, plugged in with cameras and unimposing viewing goggles, connecting vividly with strangers in their moments of suffering or joy, something we were previously unable or unwilling to do—a kind of *You Me Bum Bum Train* for everyone. We're not there yet, but we are moving in that direction. The sweeping social impact of smartphone-shot videos of black men and women being mistreated by police are an early manifestation of this potential.

Those captured moments of "citizen journalism" and the powerful proofs they provided of an injustice previously hidden to white Americans, helped turn #BlackLivesMatter into a sweeping social project. As replicated messages traveled widely and rapidly across influencer networks, the hashtag meme—and the movement that it spawned—was empowered to change the Social Organism's overall memetic makeup. #BlackLivesMatter became an all-present mantra, imbedding itself into our collective consciousness. And from there, the model was transferred to broader society, including into the offline world, thus extending the effect of the immunotherapeutic treatment. Racism has always been one of our most resilient and harmful diseases; #BlackLivesMatter is shocking our immune system into recognizing it and fighting it.

The #BLM movement has experienced rapid growth requiring the development and appointment of identifiable leaders. As of July 2016, there were thirty-eight chapters in the United States and Canada. Indeed, a decidedly real-world organizational structure has emerged out of what was initially an organic, spontaneous call for justice—albeit a structure that is still far more horizontal, decentralized, and holarchic than political organizations of the past. In a far-sighted definition of what it means in these changing times to call something a "company," Fast Company ranked #BlackLives-Matter number nine in its list of the fifty most innovative companies of 2016. An article on CNN Interactive that identified some of #BLM's main players used a Silicon Valley–like phrase to describe them in its title: "The Disruptors."

In the previous chapter we talked about how we could use new data-gathering techniques to map and learn more about what kinds of content triggers immediate responses in the Organism. In a similar vein, might we also be able to map and study how it evolves? Put differently, can we sequence the human memetic code? It wouldn't be the first time people have tried to do so.

In 2003, Nova Spivack, an entrepreneur, venture capitalist, and leading thinker in Big Data, artificial intelligence, and Web semantics, launched what he called "The Human Menome Project." (The name was an obvious play on the publicly funded Human Genome Project, which that same year completed its sequencing of the human genome, three years behind a private initiative by Craig

Venter's Celera Corporation.) On his blog, Spivack proposed that to compute the "Menome of humanity" in real time, we should "mine the Web for noun-phrases and then measure the space-time dynamics of those phrases as they move through various demographic, geographic, and topical spaces." The end result would be a "set of the most influential memes presently active around the world" as well as a record of "the menomes of individual societies, demographic groups, communities, etc."

Another initiative, calling itself the Human Memome Project (with an "m"), was launched a few years later by the Center for Human Emergence, a group led by Don Edward Beck, the inventor of the "spiral dynamics" complex modeling method for studying the evolutionary development of large-scale human psychology. Beck, who labels his method "the theory that explains everything," counts as his influences Richard Dawkins and the development psychologist Clare W. Graves. On its website, the Human Memome Project's goal is described as to "create a synthesis of all of the various viewpoints on cultural transformation, societal change, the nature of conflict, forms of conflict prevention, and development, in order to generate sophisticated electronic maps designed to monitor, at the deepest level, waves of chaos and order, change and stability, and progress and regression within our collective selves."

The outcome of these projects is not yet clear, but both efforts suggest that as Big Data techniques deepen our understandings of how complex systems evolve, people will increasingly try to identify some kind of "essence" of our nature as social beings. There's a scientific will to find the cultural equivalent of the genome, now viewed as the almost definitive blueprint of our biological selves. It's as if we're cranking up a super computer in search of the human soul.

If we do complete the equivalent of the Human Genome Project and sequence the menome, what might we find?* What confrontations with "disease" in our society's past have helped our culture build up antibodies to social division? Does the capacity for many of us—hopefully most of us—to recognize and resist the fascist signals of an egomaniacal present-day politician trace its origins to the painful European conflicts of the 1930s and 1940s? Among the countless painful "epidemic episodes" that helped our society evolve, we'd perhaps find: 1960s images of lynchings and bombed churches that moved white Americans to join their black compatriots in support of civil rights; the heartache of the Vietnam War that led people to question the once common sentiment of "my country, right or wrong"; the brutal murder of Matthew Shepard in Laramie, Wyoming, which helped galvanize empathy for the lonely struggle of oppressed gay youth. We'd also find positive moments that created lasting, memorable memes that continue to embolden us to stand up for what's right: Martin Luther King's speeches, the stories of brave defiant figures like Anne Frank, heroic figures from wars and other tragedies like the firefighters who died saving thousands on September 11, not to mention uplifting moments that celebrate genius in the arts and science, whether it's Mozart's Requiem or the Wright Brothers' Kitty Hawk taking flight. Think, for example, of how deeply this phrase runs in our collective psyche's sense of human potential: "That's one small step for man, one giant leap for mankind." All these past moments of both failure and victory have informed our sense of what it means to belong to the communion of

* We prefer the Spivack's spelling, "menome," over that of the Center for Human Emergence's "memome."

human life. They forge a collective pool of empathy from which we all draw.

So, the question is: What would have happened if we'd blocked those memes? What if Hitler's genocidal campaign was never exposed to the outside world? What if Martin Luther King Jr. had been barred from taking his place at the steps of the Lincoln Memorial, so that the words "I have a dream" were only heard by a few of his close confidants? Undoubtedly our culture would not have progressed as far as it has. If we hadn't developed the antibodies, we'd be even more vulnerable to racism and intolerance than we currently are. And that would not only hold us back morally but also economically.

This is all very well, but what are we to do with this knowledge? If there's no turning back from social media, how can we work with that system to steer the Social Organism into a healthier state? Well, I think we've got some great ideas. Read on.

CHAPTER EIGHT

THOMAS AND TEDDY

The Open Constitution of the Social Organism

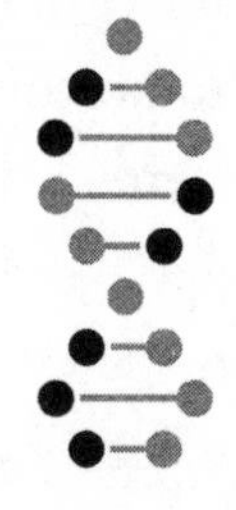

For centuries, governments have been charged with the all-important task of verifying that we are who we say we are. They issue the primary documents—birth certificates, driver's licenses, ID cards, and passports—that have long been the benchmark for authenticating identity. In recent years, the world's five biggest managers of identity were the governments of the five biggest countries: China, India, the United States, Indonesia, and Brazil. Well, these days, China's and India's governments are still in the top five, but they are behind a newcomer in the identity management business—Facebook, which manages 1.5 billion identities—and are followed by two more newcomers: Google (500 million) and Twitter (320 million). Sick of managing multiple passwords, people are embracing the convenience of single-sign-on (SSO) access that these services provide to third-party web sites. But I find this trend toward concentrated identity authentication alarming.

In a capitalist system that requires us to prove our identity to open bank accounts, travel, sign contracts, even enter buildings, this handful of private companies now wields profound power over all of us.

Facebook's vast network reach comes from it having been the first online social media platform that encouraged users to present personas as close as possible to their "real" selves. That has given it an all-encompassing, worrisome power. Consider how Facebook controls and manipulates the newsfeeds that, for more than a billion people worldwide, are a daily source of important information. What once was a chronological flow of postings is now deliberately tailored to emphasize those that have better odds of going viral and serving advertisers' needs, all coordinated by a predetermined software algorithm. The same algorithm will serve up unsolicited "memories" to us, repackaging albums of previously posted photos with whatever friend it believes we want to commemorate a "Facebook anniversary" with—sometimes oblivious to the fact that that friend or family member has died. It also prevents users from clicking through to the original source of an embedded YouTube or other video so as to boost native uploads into Facebook. That limits the interchange among social media platforms, constrains the flow dynamics of the Organism, and prevents creators from monetizing their work.

Worst of all, Facebook takes a Gestapo-like approach to what it deems to be offensive material. I discovered this when it abruptly turned off my account because of a joke I had sent to a friend in a private message. The Facebook Thought Police, watching my private conversations, determined that the image I sent to an Icelandic friend of a forty-seven-year-old-man with a "micro penis"—an image I'd lifted from a Google-sourced medical textbook—was unacceptable. To be sure, the joke was ribald, but there was no harm done to anyone and it was no worse than millions of exchanges that take place between friends every day. And that's the key point, of course: This was a *private* conversation. The upshot was that I was accused of "international child pornography" and my account was instantly shut down with a note that said little more than there is nothing you can do and no one to contact. Period. Because Facebook controlled my login through its powerful role as an SSO identifier, this move meant that my Spotify stopped, I couldn't use Uber, and my SoundCloud was shut off, forcing me to re-establish direct password credentials with each. In effect, my identity was on hold. For a time, I was the invisible man.

With a centrally controlled program that can't be audited, Facebook creates its own, subjective version of the truth, an idealized picture of life that it deigns to be the one we should experience. For a long time, the only button a user could click to express an opinion about a post was the iconic thumbs-up "Like." The platform has since added "Love," "Haha," "Wow," "Sad," and "Angry" emojis, but there is still no "dislike." Facebook is not to be a community of discord, it seems; we can be moved to tears or anger by the information that someone shares, but we're not supposed to disagree with that person. (Arguably, Facebook leaves *that* job to its own censors.) And, boy, do we play ball with it. Most people use Facebook as a place solely for happy news and images. They create idealized personas: perfect lives, perfect children, happy marriages, and professional successes. Facebook-land is like Disneyland, one that we've obediently created ourselves.

Facebook's goal is to ensure that as many eyeballs as possible are looking over its platform to justify its advertising charge-out rates. It's in the business of selling "you" to advertisers. Because the algorithm knows your real identity, your expressions, your affinities, your private conversations, and your desires, you constitute a valuable packaged item. The same algorithm also figures out which content "sticks," so that it can pitch it to companies as something to attach to. Sure, it will argue that its "community"-managed censorship policies—no nudity on Instagram, no "dick pic" jokes in Facebook messages—are imposed for our welfare, but its greatest interest is in selling positivity.

Debates around restricting content can be thorny. There's an understandable public outcry when hate speech, direct threats, and graphic, violent images are included in social media. So, companies like Facebook and Twitter feel a very strong public relations imperative to impose some kind of order. But if it was tough enough for newspaper editors to grapple with the ethics of publishing their own journalists' content, it's many magnitudes harder for social media platforms to make black and white decisions around the incomparably wider array of uncontrolled user content.

We emailed Facebook requesting comment and received no reply—a non-response that means nothing in particular. To be fair, social media providers like Facebook are between a rock and a hard place. They often face a clamor from those who feel wronged by offensive content to remove it but then come under fire from free-speech advocates for taking heavy-handed actions. Platforms have responded by trying to devise consistent policies—in Facebook's case, under its "community standards"—about when to remove content and when not. There is genuine effort there to resolve a difficult problem through standards, due process, and deliberation. Also, by publishing data on the requests it gets for data by governments around the world, Facebook is clearly trying to shine some transparency on the decisions it makes to curb content. This is commendable. But the problem is that the real world is far more complicated than any rules and procedures for "fair" censorship could ever accommodate. Special interests have the ability, and incentive, to distort the consensus process to remove or protect content in ways that serves them alone. And as it turns out, there are not only frequent cases of overreach, there have also been glaring situations where content was reasonably removed because the standards couldn't address the specific context in which the subject matter was presented.

The case of troubled Marine Daniel Rey Wolfe, who used Facebook to document his suicide with a series of graphic self-portraits and comments, underscores the dilemma. Facebook initially didn't comply with the requests of grieving fellow Marines that it take down those photos. Wolfe's posts didn't violate letter-of-the-law reading of its community standards. By those rules, Facebook vows to remove any "promotion or encouragement of self-mutilation, eating disorders, or hard drug abuse," along with "graphic images shared for sadistic effect or to celebrate or glorify violence." But Wolfe was not technically "promoting" or "encouraging" self-violence; he was promising to actually carry it out, which meant that while he was still alive the proposal to remove the material contravened another policy: the priority of keeping the lines open so that friends and family can try to intervene. Once Wolfe had died, another policy kicked in: that immediate family members are solely responsible for choosing to close the deceased's account or to "memorialize" it. When they take no formal action, the latter becomes the default, which means the person's feed stays intact and Facebook's algorithm keeps obliviously sending out auto-generated reminders of their birthdays and other details. Without action from the next of kin, Facebook was policy-bound to keep

Wolfe's account open, replete with its disturbing account of his last hours—at least until the case got media attention and senior management reversed the decision.

It's pretty hard not to sympathize with Wolfe's family and friends. Who would want to confront all that? However, all the sanitized perfection that's created by Facebook's censoring algorithm and by users' own self-censored "highlight reels" is the kind of thing that contributes to the angst of people like this Marine. Research by the University of Houston has shown that increased use of Facebook contributes to an uptick in depression via a phenomenon known as "social comparison." Imagine how PTSD-suffering veterans returning from Afghanistan and Iraq struggle to assimilate back into peacetime American society when all they see on their Facebook feeds is an unrealistic Disneyland diametrically opposed to the hell they've come from.

We are by no means saying that society is served by encouraging hate speech or graphic depictions of violence—quite the opposite. We recognize that many people feel that these platforms should limit such material. However, as we discussed in the last chapter, the best way for our Social Organism to beat back pathogens of hate and violence is to confront them. That way we can absorb the antigens they deliver, and our shared social immune system can quash them with an antidote of love and compassion. Remember, it took a mass shooting and the wide dissemination of an image of a redneck with a Confederate flag to spawn the #TakeItDown movement. Would this have been possible if Facebook had Disney-Landed that same image?

This isn't an idle question. One really worrying aspect of Facebook's "community standards" approach toward protecting us from ourselves is that it inevitably bleeds into political censorship. In one of many documented cases, Facebook took down a link to OneWorld's "Freedom for Palestine" video that UK band Coldplay had posted on its Facebook page after pro-Israeli groups reported the URL to the song as "abusive" to Facebook's standards police. Many more controversial Facebook censorship decisions can be seen on the website onlinecensorship.org, which is managed by two nonprofits, the Electronic Frontier Foundation and Visualizing Impact. In just one snapshot, every item on the site's weekly report on social media censorship for March 23, 2016, pertained to Facebook. It included reports that the company had done the following: It removed an Indian cartoon criticizing a government minister's statement that "the concept of marital rape doesn't exist in the Indian context"; it blocked a photo from a private group's page of a woman holding her newly born child who was still attached by the umbilical cord because it contained references to nudity and "sexually explicit imagery"; it suspended the page of a filmmaker reporting on anti-fracking activists; and it barred an indigenous Australian writer because she'd posted images of two topless Australian Aboriginal elder ladies engaged in a traditional ceremony. These behaviors from Facebook are schizophrenic at best.

Most of us accept the sound reasons why the First Amendment prevents the U.S. government from restricting our right to say things, even stupid or harmful things. Why don't we extend that thinking to social media platforms and make our voices heard to these companies? Yes, they are private companies and legally permitted to control content as they see fit. But, as we've hopefully made very clear throughout this book, these entities now have a profound responsibility to the rest of society.

While cases of "dangerous speech" clearly exist—the Dangerous

Speech Project is trying to systematically identify them on social media as a precursor to outbreaks of violence—we take a firm position that it is always best to err against censorship. We should demand that these new gods of social media wield their immense gatekeeping power with extreme caution and transparency. The algorithms with which they manipulate the presentation and delivery of our content aren't accessible to outsiders. Given how much influence it has on our lives, we deserve to know how Facebook weights objects by type, source, and so forth. The company has beaten the old media companies at their own game. It has hijacked the direct relationship with customers and advertisers and imposed a toll-road mentality toward "boosting a post"—even as so many users complain that they're not seeing their real friends or the things they care about. There must be transparency in these algorithms.

Why not just quit Facebook? you might say. The problem is that we are social animals, driven to where the social networks exist. Equally important, as we've noted, much of our digital identity is tied up in these platforms. As a society, it's impossible to ignore Facebook, a fact that affords it almost unprecedented control over what we say and hear. Worse, it exerts this power in its *own* interest. Facebook takes the content that you and I produce, pays us nothing for it—a luxury traditional news organizations can only dream of—and then organizes, censors, and repackages it for sale to advertisers, whose fees it keeps for itself. As the saying popularized by security expert Bruce Schneier goes, "you are not Facebook's customer, you are its product." Facebook has no right to censor us. It is hurting the Social Organism, restricting our cultural evolution. It needs to stop.

Facebook isn't the only guilty party here, by any stretch. Such abuse comes with the territory when centralized controllers of information are subject to shareholders' demands for quarterly profit growth. So we also see Twitter veering toward censorship. Though the platform takes a more laissez-faire approach to sexual content and in letting people use avatar identities, Twitter will respond to requests to block content, most controversially from governments. In February 2016, it established the Twitter Trust and Safety Council made up of forty nonprofit advocacy groups such as the Jewish interest-focused Anti Defamation League and the formerly named Gay and Lesbian Alliance Against Defamation, which now simply goes by its acronym, GLAAD. Twitter cites the noble goal of having the council help develop a "strategy to ensure that people feel safe expressing themselves on Twitter." Yet one can imagine this ostensibly constructive concept of *free but safe* speech opening the door to abuse, especially if members of the council use their seat to control speech that affects their special interests.

The problem of centralized control over content sharing is not limited to social media platforms. It's also evident among email service providers, which are now concentrated within two dominant entities: Google's gmail and Microsoft Exchange's Outlook. People who use independent email servers complain that their messages will end up in the spam folders of their Gmail-using contacts. Google's algorithm dominates all Web search, Google Chrome is the most popular browser, Google software runs the main navigation and mapping services, Google's YouTube service monopolizes Internet video, and almost half the world's smartphones use Google's Android operating system. You have the makings of a very powerful gatekeeper of information. Google's original motto might have been "Don't be evil," but how can we be sure that this profit-seeking company will always be respectful of its immense power?

One way to conceive of the power of these new media giants is to contemplate the data that passes through their servers, data about us, our habits, our interests, our messages to each other. Back in 2014, Google chairman Eric Schmidt said that at that time, every two days the Internet was generating and storing the same amount of data that human beings had accumulated between the dawn of civilization and 2003. And Google itself is party to a huge chunk of that. For Internet searches alone, Google processes an average 3.5 million inquiries each minute. The honeypots of information that this traffic generates are enormous. Google, Facebook, Twitter, Tumblr, and others are sitting on hugely valuable troves of data. Can we trust them with it?

The irony is that in a world that is flattened and decentralized by near-universal Internet access, the prime machinery for using it as a social network is now run by highly concentrated, centralized units of power. Partly, that's a function of capitalism; as firms become dominant, gaining market share and network effect, they seek to assure profitability in the face of competitive threats by consolidating ownership. This tendency raises concerns about pricing power and the risk that large incumbents will quash innovation by outsiders, which is why anti-trust laws exist. But in the digital world, the stakes are different, because the big Internet players will do anything to earn the widest possible network effect, which typically means assuring free access to their platform. Instead of pricing, then, we should worry about the broader issues surrounding Google's capacity to control a medium that has become the primary means through which society communicates.

We know from Edward Snowden's revelations that the presence of just a handful of dominant firms in this industry meant the U.S.

government could lean on them to secretly feed it information about their users. Facilitating Big Brother–like snooping in this way is naturally a major concern to everyone. But the bigger risk to the healthy growth and evolution of the Social Organism is not from government intervention but from the platforms' own constraints on free expression.

How do we reconcile this picture of a small group of institutions wielding monopolistic control over our online interactions with the rosier story we've told throughout this book of an evolving, leaderless Social Organism that's reached a higher plane of communication? Is this Facebook/Twitter/Google universe better or worse than the top-down hierarchies of the old media world? How does our biological analogy hold up against these centralized bodies? And will the evolution of the Social Organism combat the censorship problem or make it worse?

First, it's important to define some terminology. Let's not confuse "social media platform" with "social media." Some people wrongly conflate the former with the services that facilitate it, much as many assume that the "financial system" is composed of the banking intermediaries that manage it. These *systems*—in this case, the communications system—are made up of populations of interconnected human beings. The platforms and service providers are just the pipes and access points, the infrastructure over which human beings exchange information and value. Our concern should be with how well the pipes function. If that infrastructure—which includes a platform's driving algorithm and policies—is poorly designed, or if it suffers from blockages, or experiences other forms of friction, then the human system that runs within it will suffer. Social media users are like the leaves of a tree; if you sever a limb, you cut off the flow of water and nutrients to those leaves, which prevents them from carrying out photosynthesis to spur growth.

So, while the centralization and self-interested censorship instincts of social media platforms create a suboptimal situation, it doesn't negate the fact that the technology has delivered a much more open and decentralized architecture for communication. The unleashing of the core social media technology—initially the Internet protocol, followed by the various applications that led to offerings like Friendster and MySpace—set the Social Organism free from its dependence on old-style media. That established a different, organically managed distribution system. To my mind, social media services that excessively control information such as Facebook are acting like modern-day book-burners. Yet even they aren't powerful enough to undermine the liberating effect of this newly distributed, holonic system, the foundation of our twenty-first-century Social Organism.

Let's also be fair to Facebook and acknowledge that it only blocks a tiny sliver of the content contributed by its users. (Reorganizing their feeds is a different matter.) That's incomparable to traditional media organizations, for which deciding what news to exclude is arguably their most important task. Old media companies have no choice but to exclude information; the economics of an expensive production and distribution model demand it. But the combination of global, instantaneous Internet connectivity, low-cost bandwidth connections, virtually limitless cloud-based storage, and, most important, a billion-strong labor force working for free creates a completely different economic dynamic. Those are the features that define social media as an organism and which give rise to the massive outpouring of new content from hundreds of millions of people who'd never contributed to mass media before. That's a *de*centralizing phenomenon and it's happening regardless of Facebook's interventions.

Second, let's not forget that the platforms are themselves engaged in a survival-of-the-fittest competition. As we discussed in chapter 1, the industry has already gone through big waves of disruption, with SixDegrees, Friendster, and Myspace all wiped out by it. There's no guarantee that the same won't happen to Facebook or Twitter.

Still, we shouldn't be complacent. We need a set of consensually developed natural laws that protect the flow dynamics of the Social Organism. We can't just hope that market pressures will quickly force Facebook and its peers to create more open platforms. These firms' dominant market positions, giant cash stores, and instinct toward acquiring each new disruptive start-up mean that evolution is not going to happen automatically. I don't want to wait a lifetime for a truly free social media system. These companies' monopolistic control over information can have lasting, dangerous effects on society. Let's not let that harm build up for too long.

What should we be demanding from these social media behemoths? I think it's useful to look back at how we've historically dealt with the core issues at stake. I've come to believe we need a Thomas and Teddy solution. Thomas (Jefferson) gave us a constitutional commitment to the right to free expression. Teddy (Roosevelt) aggressively used the Sherman Antitrust Act to break up powerful corporations, establishing the public's clear interest in restricting monopolies—which in the social media context gets us thinking about the dominant platforms, those of Twitter, Facebook, Tumblr, Snapchat, and their various competitors. My point here is not to call for federal prosecutions—probably the last thing we need—and in any case both the existing antitrust laws and the First Amendment have dubious legal application to a social media marketplace that is privately managed, highly dynamic, and supports ongoing, rapid innovation. Rather it is that the principles embodied in those legal foundations can guide us in prioritizing the development of an open, robust, and positively evolving social media environment.

The developers at Google and Facebook present themselves as the smartest guys in the room, the ones who know what's best for the rest of us. There's a real irony, and I would say societal risk, to the fact that a group of geeks who are often viewed as socially awkward are imposing their worldviews on us via the technology they build. But, like it or not, we're dependent on these companies to encourage an open social media framework that's inclusive, constructive, and positively reinforcing. Of course, they are not necessarily incentivized to build it, not when their shareholders are focused on short-term returns and a business model that's built around exploiting free content and accumulating user data to sell to advertisers. Our challenge, then, is to promote a different business model, whether through market forces or by legal efforts, that incentivizes social media platforms to pare back their data accumulation and confer users with more control over how to present and monetize their content. We must build an ecosystem of users, content, and functionality that is open and provides pari passu rewards for each participant's contributions.

Market forces may take care of some of it. Young people in particular are leaving Facebook in droves, or never joining it in the first place. Millennials and Generation Z kids are going to Snapchat, which by April 2016 was seeing 10 billion video views a day. Because of its privacy settings, Snapchat has less (though not zero) ability to censor. More important, it allows people to regain control over who sees their content and for how long. They're creating communities around Snapchat that were impossible to create on Facebook after its ubiquitous reach gave visibility to their parents, their teachers, and their ex-boyfriends and girlfriends. Snapchat's uncensored model of fleeting human exchanges has also spawned greater creativity around the communication of emotion. Its users are living in the moment together. And they do so without fear of actions or moods or words coming back to haunt them, or that they are remembered in perpetuity. No one feels entirely comfortable looking back all the time at their bad hair phases, outbursts, drunkenness, or failures—Snapchat gives people a chance to avoid having to do that. While Facebook and Twitter have struggled with the limits of the "Like" button—how do you show solidarity with a friend whose parent has died with that button?—kids on Snapchat have figured out that their own faces and reactions *are* the medium. In this way they overcome the lack of subtle information in text. This kind of creativity provides more and richer nutrients to the Organism.

Most young people aren't closing their Facebook accounts. They can't, because they need those accounts to assert their digital identities at other sites. But they are using them much less frequently and in different ways. So, it's not totally clear how much damage this migration will do to Facebook. Still, long-term, demographics are not in the incumbents' favor. This is entirely consistent with the evolutionary forces we've outlined elsewhere in this book. If the Social Organism doesn't get what it wants from a particular platform, it will move. Eventually, Facebook will itself have to evolve or face extinction.

Watertight censorship is impossible, in any case. Creative people will always find a way around it, whether to avoid limitations by a government or a private business. Just look at how Chinese "netizens" deal with the problem. Many use VPNs to get over the "Great Firewall of China" that blocks sites like Facebook, Twitter, and Instagram. On their own heavily controlled social media sites, such as Weibo, Chinese users have created a unique language of subtle plays on words to bypass the key word searches used by government censors.

Meanwhile, in the United States and Europe, concern over institutional control of our data is growing. Snowden's revelations, though somewhat polarizing, have left many uncomfortable with breaches and manipulation of the private information that's managed by gatekeeping entities. While the focus is more on data privacy than censorship concerns, the NSA-spying story is building consciousness of the dangers we face in centralizing control over communication, whether within government or private bodies. That's prompting people to crowdsource efforts to expose these problems. The onlinecensorship.org website, for example, asks people to recount experiences of social media censorship, reviews them, and then compiles reports with which to lobby for more openness. Countless other individual sites and, ironically, Facebook pages and groups have also sprung up to protest perceived invasions of free speech.

One reason why these initiatives might succeed in pushing social media platforms toward more open strategies, even if it defies their Wall Street funders, is that all these firms have disruption and openness in their DNA—yes, even Facebook. Restrictive, proprietorial policies that curtail frictionless sharing and derivative-work creation inherently impede content evolution, which works against the platforms' long-term interest in network growth. This is why the social media business community came out forcefully against the Hollywood- and big media–backed Stop Online Piracy Act (SOPA), which would blacklist sites facing copyright actions. It was a serious threat to Internet free expression and Silicon Valley rose up to tell the world as much. While Facebook and Twitter didn't join in the "blackout" strike—in which Google, Tumblr, Reddit, Wikipedia, and many other sites set their home pages to a black background and included links for people to register their protest at SOPA—the two big social media platforms did support the movement. This unified voice against censorship is the main reason why the hotly contested bill failed.

In fact, many of these firms have corporate mission statements acknowledging the need for an open Internet. In a way, that holds them to account. It makes them sensitive to criticism and lobbying efforts, and means that when issues such as net neutrality raises its head, the hypocrisy of metering and throttling different types of content is exposed. Still, even if there is a natural check on their monopolizing instincts, the general public needs to think long and hard about how much power these institutions are amassing. These are very important, fundamental issues. We must educate ourselves on them if we are to shape a more secure, stable society for the future.

Trying to push Facebook and its ilk to do the right thing is one strategy. Building an alternative to them might be better. The good news is that powerful new technologies are emerging that could help audacious start-ups to do just that. Ad blocking tools, which allow readers and viewers to block ads at will, could so severely challenge the revenue model of incumbent media providers that it renders it unworkable. Meanwhile, there's a new *decentralizing* opportunity that comes with digital currencies such as bitcoin and their underlying technology, known as the blockchain ledger. These make sending money across the Internet less costly and allow for more automated transactions; they also open the possibility of what is essentially an ownerless network infrastructure that frees content providers from dependence on the big social media platforms. This new era of decentralized media presages a world in which all users—be they individuals or corporate entities—have direct control of their content, breaking the advertising dependency that has fed the centralized model of personal data-mining and censorship. It's potentially the next major evolutionary phase in the social media architecture and it could have as dramatic an impact on the Social Organism and its culture as did the emergence of the Internet protocol and the first social media platforms.

Consider the potentially devastating effect that ad blocking could have on the advertising model for financing content delivery. This third-party software strips out unwanted ads and the tracking beacons that go with them, ensuring the visitor to a website sees only the content they want. A January 2016 survey by GlobalWebIndex found that 38 percent of Internet users had used ad blocking in the fourth quarter of 2015. With a host of new smartphone apps coming on the market with a blessing from Apple's iPhone—seen as a ploy to undermine Google Android's ad-driven model—the practice, which was previously confined mostly to desktop computing, is poised to grow. As you'd expect, surveys show usage rates by Millennials are considerably higher, well above 50 percent. The already embattled news industry is most at risk by this. Some news sites now block their own content when they detect someone using an ad blocker, betting that readers will disengage the ad blocker rather than miss out on news. That's a big gamble. Similar strategies for combating revenue loss in the online era have proven very hard to impose. And it's not just the old news industry that's worried. Facebook itself captured the mood of the social media platforms in an SEC statement accompanying its third-quarter 2015 earnings: "[T]these technologies have had an adverse effect on our financial results and, if such technologies continue to proliferate, in particular with respect to mobile platforms, our future financial results may be harmed."

At stake is a business model that dates back to 1704, when the *Boston News-Letter* published, for a fee, a small announcement advertising the sale of a local property. From those humble beginnings a symbiotic relationship between the business community and the providers of information emerged, one that spawned much of the modern media world: advertising agencies; marketing as a profession; the very idea of a "brand"; and the explosive growth of mass media. It also fed the flawed presumption that the only way to finance the gathering and production of information was for business interests to subsidize it. There is not yet a working replacement for this model, which means the institutions we've relied upon to cover wars, probe the wrongdoings of politicians, or just update us on the state of our local government's sanitation service may not be able to pay for that work. But the existence of this problem opens the door for innovators to come up with an alternative to break what had always been an unholy relationship between news and supposedly objective information providers.

Invasive banner ads and unwanted TV commercials have always acted as a kind of tax on our consumption of news and entertainment. And, despite the earnest attempts of quality publishing firms to create ethical boundaries between their work and that of their advertising divisions, the business of selling readers' eyeballs to commercial interests has always created the perception of sellout journalism, if not the practice. In a way, society has always been "paying" for the content it receives. It's just that it has done so in a hidden and unequally distributed way. So, what if we broke the paradigm and simply asked readers or viewers to pay directly for whatever content they receive?

Until recently, attempts to shift the financing burden onto the consumer have mostly failed. Only the most established media brands, such as *The Wall Street Journal* and *The News York Times*, have gained traction with paywall models, where readers pay a monthly subscription. Workarounds are usually pretty easy—information is cheap to replicate and share on the Internet—and if readers can't achieve that they'll just ignore the pay site and shift to a free competitor. But if ad blocking forces content providers out of business, the hole in our information supply might prompt different behavior. What's more, the arrival of another powerful new technology portends an opportunity for real disruption to the business models of both traditional media companies and the dominant social media platforms: bitcoin. Discussing this strange new digital currency—and more important, the powerful technology that underpins it—can lead people down rabbit holes. Nevertheless, it's vital that we at least explore it in some depth; it is shaping up to become the core system of code with which digital society will govern itself in the future. It may well determine the direction that its evolution will take.

* * *

Bitcoin is widely misunderstood by the general public. Too many mis-associations with drug dealings, hacking attacks, and other problems have sullied the digital currency's reputation. But despite that, the smart money is recognizing that its underlying technology, the blockchain, offers a revolutionary way to share value across the Internet.

It's not easy to explain the blockchain in a few paragraphs. But we have to start somewhere, so we'll try this one-sentence explanation for starters: The blockchain is a cryptographically protected, incorruptible ledger that's distributed among a network of independently owned computers, all of which are tasked with verifying and updating its contents according to a set of software-regulated rules that incentivize them to act honestly and to agree on the veracity of the shared information. Got that? Never mind if it's too hard to get your head around; the bottom line is that it resolves a five-hundred-year-old problem by which human beings, who were always unable to trust each other to fairly and honestly share information, depended on so-called "trusted third parties" to intermediate their exchanges of value. It is a huge evolutionary leap. Now, these exchanges—whether of money or some form of potentially monetizable digital asset, such as a video clip, a song, or a piece of unique art—can be done directly, peer to peer. Total strangers on either side of the world can exchange value without either side having to trust that the other isn't digitally counterfeiting the money or secretly copying and sharing the song or artwork with someone else.

This groundbreaking concept is drawing thousands of new start-ups to explore a multitude of ways to exploit its disruptive effect. From creating peer-to-peer decentralized stock exchanges to managing the flow of electrons over solar microgrids, blockchain-inspired innovators are rethinking the way that information and value is shared. There's still a lot of work to be done to build out the base infrastructure and it's possible that much of the promises of sweeping changes are more hype than reality. But the idea of what's best described as a system of *decentralized trust* points to such a huge paradigm shift in the way society is governed that Silicon Valley pioneers like Marc Andreessen and LinkedIn's Reid Hoffman talk about bitcoin and its blockchain infrastructure as Internet 2.0.

What does it mean for social media? Well, in the field of creative content, the blockchain is inspiring technologists and activist-minded artists to reimagine the underlying ownership and rights structure to the content on which the Social Organism depends for its lifeblood. Their proposed models would restructure the power relationships within this new communications architecture, further diminishing the capacity for centralizing institutions to control the interests and activities of the users. In empowering the Social Organism's autonomous cells, it moves the system toward an even flatter, holonic structure. It would mean that we, the producers of content, would decide how it is used and monetized, not Facebook.

How would this happen? One way is by creating new methods for paying producers of content—in particular, by facilitating micropayments. Before digital money came along, it was prohibitively expensive to pay, say, a few cents for an article, because the inefficient intermediary-dominated banking and credit card system can't profitably process such small amounts. Now, innovators are looking at preloading special browser extensions with a store of digital currency to quietly work in the background paying small amounts for content under some pre-arranged deal with the publisher. Multiplied over billions of such transactions, digital-currency micropayments could offer a viable, non-advertising-dependent revenue stream for the media industry. It could create a healthier relationship between consumers of content, who are doing all they can to avoid unwanted ads, and the producers of it, who need to be compensated.

Another key innovation is the blockchain's capacity for creators of digital content to prove that they and only they are the owners of an original work forever. With that power, with the programmability of digital currency, and with the use of software-based legal agreements known as smart contracts, they can set controls over their content so that it is used as they dictate. By irrefutably identifying data in this way, the artist can turn their work into a true *digital asset*, versions of which can be bought, sold, and owned as distinct items—as we used to do with vinyl records and still do with physical books. In theory, it means that creative work producers will no longer face the impossible task of tracking down and suing the countless people who wantonly copy and paste articles, post unattributed images, or share music files. Now they will treat content as an isolated digital asset that can be directly controlled through software and attached to automatic digital currency-payment contracts. You buy it, you own it. But you can't replicate it if the smart contract is designed to stop you from doing so. This could overturn the long-standing licensing model for managing copyright in the digital environment. It's a potential game-changer for the creative works industry and for how the underlying economy of the Social Organism functions.

Trailblazers in this field include award-winning singer-songwriter Imogen Heap, who turned her "Tiny Human" release into a digital asset that was released over the blockchain. In this case, Heap made the music free to use and sought bitcoin donations to cover it, but the point was to demonstrate the many possibilities of how the content could be creatively controlled, as well as to study how it might be used in the future. She has also launched an initiative to explore a wider application of this model that she has called Mycelia. (That's a fitting name, given what I've come to learn about the fungi for which her project is named and which we discuss in the next and last chapter.) Meanwhile, start-ups like Monegraph and Mediachain are providing blockchain-based registration services that help artists track the usage of their work. And with an even larger mission, the Berklee School of Music in Boston is working with Michael's outfit, the MIT Media Lab's Digital Currency Initiative, along with a host of industry players such as record companies Universal Music, Sony, Warner, and BMG; online services like Spotify, Pandora, YouTube, and Netflix; and radio stations such as SiriusXM and WBUR of Boston, on a project called the Open Music Initiative. It's aimed at deploying blockchain technology to redefine how music is used, shared, and paid for.

More explicitly within the realm of social media, companies are starting to see ways to use blockchain and digital currency technology to challenge the centrally managed platforms of Facebook, Vine, and others. Video upload service Reveal, for example, allows users to monetize their content via a digital currency called Reveal Coin that's distributed according to how much they grow the network—by joining, by getting others to join, and by producing and spreading viral content. Prospective advertisers must buy Reveal Coins to pay for an ad, and those coins can only be purchased from the content providers who've accumulated them. Meanwhile, Taringa!, an Argentine-based social media provider, is now paying bitcoin to many of its 75 million users in return for content. Both systems are aimed at creating a positive feedback loop where content providers are incentivized to produce material that draws in more users and increases the payout for both the original creator and the platform.

We could also go one step further: an entirely decentralized social media platform, one that's not controlled by any one person or company but by an ownerless, software-driven system known as a decentralized autonomous organization (DAO). The model would submit control over the payments and digital assets to a set of "smart contract" software instructions, all regulated by the decentralized network of computers that validate all the transactions that occur on the blockchain. There's no company per se that's responsible for any of this, which gets around the need to trust a central management structure staffed by humans. That might sound pretty Jetsons-like and you may need to do some further reading to get your head around it. A few early malfunctions have raised questions about how ownerless DAOs can exist in the real world of laws.* Still, DAOs are already being built to manage everything from decentralized ride-sharing communities (which could force the taxi-disrupting company Uber into its own disruption) to nonprofit charities to a more decentralized version of Wikipedia. And by far one of the most exciting possibilities would be a social media DAO.

* Unfortunately, the collapse in June 2016 of a $150 million decentralized investment fund that chose to call itself "The DAO" will for some time create a branding problem for the broader, generic idea of *a* DAO. The episode, in which a rogue actor siphoned $50 million in tokens from the fund by exploiting a loophole in the system's smart contracts, has emphasized the need for more development work around these ideas and for a robust system for auditing their underlying software. But it shouldn't stop us from pondering the possible benefits to society that these radical new organizational structures might offer once the architecture is made more secure.

I see it as a universal agar to grow an unimaginably large array of new applications for the Social Organism.

The data that Twitter and Facebook tightly control and charge researchers like us for would now be controlled by those who produce it—you and I. And with encryption, distributed computing-based security and opt-in/opt-out clauses, we could release large amounts of it in metadata form to help further knowledge of how the Organism functions while still protecting our privacy. We could also use these transparent systems to design real-time audits that make it clear whether "likes," "retweets" and "shares" are coming from real participants, automated "bots," or clusters of low-wage "paid likers" in places like Bangladesh (a country that accounts for 40 percent of the world's paid likes). By taking away the centralized social media platforms' gatekeeping power over money and rights to creative content, we will neutralize the last major constraining power over the collective output of the Organism.

This decentralized social media economy won't arrive immediately. To be effective, blockchain services will not only need a more robust base infrastructure; they'll also require network effects—which big players like Facebook and Twitter have already accumulated as a form of capital to protect their market share from those that don't have it. But with so much systemic and technological change chipping away at the incumbents' models, from the exodus of young customers to ad blocking, it's not inconceivable that a tipping point can be reached that pushes centralized platforms into extinction. The lesson from Silicon Valley history is that communications technology is subject to a highly accelerated evolutionary process. A decentralized media environment could come sooner than you think. The blockchain is the evolutionary advance that makes the old model obsolete.

* * *

How will people behave in this environment? Once they have control over it, will individuals be as proprietorial and restrictive with their content as big media companies and brand owners are now? Maybe. The technology will allow them to be so if they choose. But as we've documented in our Seven Rules of Life, the Social Organism wants to be fed. And in a far more distributed content production environment, where the MGM studios, the News Corps., and the Viacoms are less powerful, that kind of approach will likely be competed away by those who enjoy the wider reach of an open-access approach. The value will come from having control over your material and your data, but if you want your content to compete for attention you'll still have to let it go.

In this decentralized world, corporate brand managers might ultimately become no different from everyone else: They will, like us, simply compete for the attention of the Social Organism's cells, trying to implant memes in the system to get a message across. Advertising would not be treated as something walled off and categorically separate from other information, as if it is a somewhat illegitimate content provider sneaking in the backdoor as an unwelcome guest. It will have as much chance at legitimacy as any other publisher, but it will need to earn it. To gain attention, it will compete for the Organism's love. Lessons should be taken from those makers of promotional content who've already discovered how to go viral on their own terms. In cases like Oreo's "You can still dunk in the dark" Super Bowl tweet or Dove's "Beauty Sketches" campaign, the content didn't imbed itself into some, more "legitimate" piece of news or entertainment material; it succeeded in gaining widespread audience on its own terms. That's the world of competitive marketing that I see companies facing in the future. In this world their goal will be to make content that matters, make it discoverable by those who matter, and seek the endorsement of those same people.

At the heart of these new ways of organizing society is the idea that software can govern human behavior without any one person or institution able to unilaterally alter its code. It is a form of cyberspace-based community governance. The first benefit for the Social Organism is that if we can build platforms for communicating on these principles, we can significantly reduce their owners' capacity to censor our content.

The concept of smart contracts based on blockchain technology is also important here. It helps us think of software code as a tool with which a community can automatically rule—in place of, say, a court—on when and how a set of agreements are to be executed when pre-ordained conditions are met. A simple social media smart contract might respond to someone opening and embedding a particular artist's work in a tweet, recognizing that act as fulfillment of a condition of the underlying usage agreement, and then irrevocably transferring an amount from the user's store of digital currency to the artist. Small pieces of software code act like a mathematical key to unlock a response. (Note: This matches how catalytic enzymes and other organic agents unleash biochemical reactions along an organism's metabolic pathways when they connect via a snug lock-and-key structure with a molecular substrate.) From that basic foundation, highly complex, intricate smart contracts can be built, making software code a powerful tool for designing trustworthy governance systems in cyberspace. To quote Harvard law professor Lawrence Lessig, we're creating a world in which "code is law."

This approach offers a way for communities to "legislate" for appropriate behavior on peer-to-peer online networks without any government intervention in the process. Importantly, it can also transcend borders, which is critical given the transnational nature of Internet activity. In effect, we can create rules for the Social Organism to govern itself and then allow it to evolve within those rules. Primavera De Filippi, a colleague of Lessig's at Harvard Law, goes so far as to say that the blockchain and the peer-to-peer models it engenders are tools for humans to mimic nature's "cooperation" model, the same one that keeps termites working together in the interests of the whole. Even though they have no idea of their peers' needs and have no instructions from a leader, agents in these natural systems pursue their self-interest yet do so in a way that's in concert with the needs of the whole. In short, we need governing software like the blockchain to create the ideal, fairest, most vibrant, dynamic yet stable version of a holarchy. We want social media behavior to be bound by codes (legal, moral, and software codes) that create the optimal conditions for the Social Organism to thrive.

Let's think of how we might design such a cyber-legal system. And as we do so, let's keep in mind that if the code we design pushes the Organism toward unhealthy censorship we will be hindering its evolution and potentially encouraging the uglier elements of our culture. First, we might figure out how technology could be harnessed to incentivize positive behavior that offsets the more destructive aspects of social media—the trolling, the hate speech, the vigilante justice mobs. In contrast to the counterproductive strategy of censoring antisocial behavior, encouraging pro-social behavior can be conducive to the overall interests of the Social Organism.

Governments, nonprofits, even civic-minded companies and individuals could bake certain incentives into automated responses when someone says or does something positive in a social media setting. This need not be financial. Studies have shown that publicly commending people for doing good deeds or for simply acting as good citizens, whether in a digital environment or in the physical world, can have positive reinforcing effects. We've heard innovators in at least one U.S. city government float the idea of tweeting out digital "herograms" to call out good-deed doers over social media. Companies and charities can also leverage social media by encouraging communal participation in charitable work. While it's hard not to feel a little cynical about self-serving promotional projects like Anheuser-Busch's #ABGivesBack Thanksgiving campaign, in which the Budweiser maker promised to provide a meal every time that hashtag was used, their viral effect can have a positive, community-building effect.

One innovative approach for improving Social Organism governance could tap into another big area of tech and Internet culture: video and online gaming. The use of game mechanics and design—often referred to as gamification—to motivate people to behave in certain ways and achieve their goals is already trendy in business schools. Now people are recognizing that in a world in which communities are formed around networks of computers, coders can try to promote pro-social behavior by adjusting the governance rules inside the games people play. The potential is borne out by the numbers: 1.2 billion people play video games worldwide, according to a 2013 survey from Spil Games, with 700 million of those online. Since then the numbers are thought to have grown even more with both the gender and age ratios of players, once dominated by young males, now close to parity.

For evidence of video games' growing impact on our social landscape look no further than the remarkably successful crossover game, Pokemon Go, the game that uses a camera-interfacing smartphone app for chasing virtual prizes in the real world. The estimated 9.5 million smartphone-toting users who were actively using it after just one week into its existence in mid-July 2016 were from all ages and dozens of different countries. Phenomena like this are convincing many people that the gaming world offers a rich opportunity to shape humanity.

The New York–based Games for Change festival, which is now in its thirteenth year, has spawned an entire movement with a comprehensive website that fills up year-round with contributions and discussions. For its annual event, the festival has teamed up with the Tribeca Film Festival, giving it an audience of 275,000 people. In two packed days of keynotes and panels at its 2016 conference, the festival covered three tracks of interest: games for learning (including a summit of the same name backed by the U.S. Department of Education), games for promoting health and neuroprogramming, and games for civics and social impact. Speakers include people like the developers of Minecraft, which has energized the minds of tens of millions of kids worldwide, and Jenova Chen, cofounder of Thatgamecompany, whose website describes its mission as to "[c]reate timeless interactive entertainment that makes positive change to the human psyche worldwide."

This pro-social experimentation isn't confined to educational games. The most popular game of 2015, according to many polls, was Undertale, a quirky story of a young girl trying to escape a monster-infested underworld that's presented in an unsophisticated 8-bit format. Its success has something to do with the way it directly challenges the moral fiber of the player, offering a choice of either the "genocide route" or the "pacifist route" in determining how to get past all the somewhat lovable monsters they encounter. Under the genocide route, the battles become increasingly unsatisfying as the monsters start avoiding the fights and a message is displayed in an increasingly small font size that says "But nobody came." At this point, the previously cheery music is distorted into an ominous and spooky-sounding ambient track. What's more, you can't undo your past. A restart of the game doesn't just take you back to the standard beginning as most games do. Rather, the permanent game file is remembered, leaving you with a reminder of your evil deeds. The entire experience is infused with a sense of ethical responsibility.

But how can we encourage positive behavior among real people online? A strategy adopted by League of Legends, the world's most popular online game, offers some clues. With a rapidly increasing number of women, people of color, and players of different sexual orientation joining the 67 million who play League of Legends each month, clashes were occurring in an environment previously dominated by young white males. The game's owner, Riot Games, didn't want to take Facebook's strategy of demanding users' real names, recognizing that anonymous avatars help protect privacy and encourage inclusion among people who don't want their sexual, religious, or other orientation exposed. So instead, management founded a "Tribunal," a forum where players could create case files of chat logs that documented inappropriate behavior; anyone could discuss and vote on what language was unacceptable and what was positive for the community. A whopping 100 million votes were cast, the vast majority demonstrating an overwhelming aversion to hate speech and homophobic slurs.

In the next step, Riot Games took key words and phrases from the Tribunal data and threw them into a machine-learning algorithm that automatically flagged unacceptable behavior and positively highlighted any that encouraged conflict resolution. According to a July 2015 Op-ed by lead game designer Jeffrey Lin, "[a]s a result of these governance systems changing online cultural norms, incidences of homophobia, sexism and racism in League of Legends have fallen to a combined 2 percent of all games. Verbal abuse has dropped by more than 40 percent, and 91.6 percent of negative players change their act and never commit another offense after just one reported penalty." It turns out that much of the prior verbal abuse had come not from serial, irredeemable bigots but by people who were having a bad day. Given the right incentives, they checked themselves and bit their tongues. Note that this remarkable experiment in human conditioning did not involve censorship, did not ban people from playing, did not "out" them with their real names, and was built upon a democratic model of what the community wanted. It was a form of codified, positively reinforcing peer group pressure, one that reminds us that in order to evolve we must learn from our mistakes. Imagine the potential this contains to encourage the positive evolution of the Social Organism.

It's no coincidence that we've arrived at gaming as a potential tool for encouraging the positive behavioral development of the Social Organism, since game theory has long been a part of how biological evolution is studied and understood. One relevant application was used in Richard Dawkins's *The Selfish Gene,* a book that has shaped the thinking behind this one. Seeking to explain the apparent contradiction in his argument that evolution is driven by "selfish" genes that use organisms as "survival machines" to replicate,

Dawkins turned to the famous Prisoner's Dilemma game to show how species-wide cooperation and empathy could evolve out of a process of otherwise apathetic self-interest.

The Prisoner's Dilemma involves two prisoners from the same criminal gang held in separate cells. Unaware of the other's testimony, they each negotiate with a prosecutor who offers them a bargain. If one prisoner *defects* and confesses to a serious crime while the latter *cooperates* and refuses to confess, then the cooperating prisoner will serve three years while the defecting prisoner goes free. If both confess, they each serve two years. If both stay silent, they each serve one year on a lesser charge. Dawkins noted how in computer simulations of the game in which each computer learns from the results of prior plays, what might start out as an inclination toward defection soon shifts to constant and repeated cooperation, since math will result in that being the best result, not only for everyone but for the individual. This, Dawkins suggested, could be how the ongoing algorithm of evolution leads to altruism. So long as there are no other agents with an interest in getting organisms to defect—he suggests divorce lawyers as an example—then the relentless math of evolution will drive populations toward cooperation. It's not a very romantic interpretation of how love, compassion, and empathy emerged, but it does show that in the great game of life, human communities comprised of autonomous, self-centered individuals can collectively evolve toward pursuing a common interest. Combine that with the idea of pro-social gamification strategies and we have a compelling new goal for designers of decentralized social media platforms: to devise rules that foster the evolution of a harmonious human culture.

* * *

Of course, we don't solely live in a digital world. In real life, we still need analog governance systems to manage society. We also need those same real-life systems—that is, national, state, and local governments—to create and maintain the right legal framework for a healthy digital society. If we return to the theme of how cultural evolution can be harmed by censorship and proprietorial control, it implies that we must also induce governments to implement policies that resist those instincts.

For one, governments must uphold the long-standing principle of net neutrality. This way we maintain a level playing field and prevent the deepening of the digital divide. For the time being, the battle to prevent Internet Service Providers, or ISPs, from using their gatekeeper positions to give privileged bandwidth access to the highest-paying customers has been won in the United States with President Obama's support. But the corporate proponents of "traffic prioritization" and tiered network access may get a friendlier administration in the future. This net neutrality debate might one day be moot if blockchain-based micropayments create a paradigm in which everyone pays for data on a per-bit basis, but we're definitely not there yet.

The prospect of an Internet hierarchy of privilege is not just a U.S. issue, nor solely one that deals with traditional ISPs like cable and telecom companies. Facebook found itself embroiled in a cross-cultural brouhaha when it offered poorer Indian communities "Free Basics," an Internet service for which they would pay no money but only gave them access to a limited selection of websites. Facebook argued that it was giving the poor an opportunity they wouldn't otherwise have had. But Zuckerberg's company would cherry-pick which websites the Free Basics customers could see. To the Indian techie community's credit, they successfully beat back an avalanche of Facebook PR and got regulators to ban Free Basics on the grounds that it violated Indian rules prohibiting discriminatory tariffs in data services. It's in everyone's interest to expand the poor's access to the Internet, but we need to provide them with the complete Internet, not one that Silicon Valley's gods of social media have made in their likeness.

The reason I care so much about net neutrality among the Internet's service providers is because they make up the foundational substrate upon which the living Social Organism depends. This substrate must be viewed as a public good. If we instead treat it as private property to be parceled out to the highest bidder, the meme pool from which innovative ideas move forth will be distorted and diminished. We will not evolve as efficiently, and the old, retrograde order dominated by big media companies, cable providers, and telecoms will continue to hold us back.

A healthy Social Organism also depends on governments maintaining a covenant of freedom with their citizens. That means the civil rights embodied in documents such as the U.S. Bill of Rights and the U.N. Declaration of Human Rights need to be re-affirmed, strengthened, in some cases expanded, and certainly updated for digital society. Given the transnational nature of social media, we need worldwide governmental commitment to the free speech principles embodied in the U.S. First Amendment. More specifically, citizens' rights to privacy must be embraced. Ideally, we'd have international treaties that barred government "backdoors" into databases of people's private online lives. While that's admittedly an impossible demand right now, given the tit-for-tat world of international espionage and the politics of fear in the age of terrorism, a good starting point would be to build greater public awareness of the vital role that encryption plays in protecting our rights. We also need high-level public debate about how these free speech and privacy principles apply to private entities such as social media platforms when they act as de facto governors of our communication standards.

Most important, we need an open-source approach toward the development, maintenance and upgrading of the software that governs the major social media platforms. We need algorithm transparency so that people can understand how the information they provide is being curated, controlled and used in the managing companies' interests. Without that currently unavailable information it's impossible to design pro-social solutions to improve the functioning of the Social Organism. Should governments be the ones to set such standards? Maybe. Here might be one application of the "Teddy" approach to the biggest social media platforms, those that we can label as monopolies. Laws could be framed as a trade-off: if your platform has such sweeping influence on society, you must at least make parts of its governing software open for all to see. If Microsoft can be forced to share its operating system with competing browsers and applications, can we not force monopoly-like social media platforms to share details about their algorithmic information management?

Getting domestic and international policymakers to understand the Social Organism will be hard, let alone to devise policies for it. But as its evolution proceeds, they must. A consensus is needed among policymakers, NGOs, academics, and, most important, the owners, managers, and developers of the core communications platforms on how best to promote positive social behavior in service of the common good. Thankfully, we have a great new mobilizing tool, in social media itself, to build that awareness—as we've documented with the many influential memes and hashtag movements cited in this book.

In this new world, powerful people like Facebook's Zuckerberg and Google's Sergey Brin and Larry Page have a great responsibility to encourage an open framework for social media that's inclusive, transparent, constructive, and positively reinforcing. We would add that, in the long run, they also have a well-aligned interest in achieving that same goal—they just need to persuade their shareholders to be patient. A Social Organism that can continue to grow in a stable fashion serves everyone's interests, especially those of the companies that service it.

Many will find it hard to trust that the Organism, a highly complex system with no command center, can organically create its own checks and balances to create growth opportunities for all. It demands that every one of us, including the titans of social media, try to overcome our most selfish instincts. The purely self-interested node can make itself heard but will not ultimately thrive in an Organism whose holonic relationships are forged on mutual respect and inclusion. We must strive for that goal, to forge an evolutionary path that allows the genius of human invention and artistry to coalesce into a collaborative global idea machine. This bold vision of the future is the subject of the last chapter.

CHAPTER NINE

DIGITAL CULTURE

Toward a Global Brain

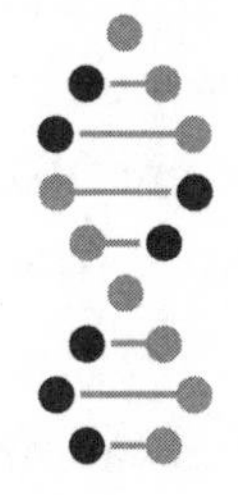

IMAGINE A child with a severed leg in a remote village in Tanzania who will die if it is not properly amputated. He is rushed to a local NGO-run clinic, one equipped with robotic surgical equipment made by a low-cost 3D printer. After putting a tourniquet on the child's leg, the clinic orders rush delivery of anesthetic drugs by high-speed drone from Dar es Salaam. The boy's medical past is quickly checked by taking a heart monitor scan that compares the result to a cloud-based database of people's unique cardiac rhythms, finding the identifying record that had been uploaded by a smartphone-wielding aid worker during a visit to his village years earlier. The clinic then dials up a New York surgeon, who puts on her virtual-reality goggles, slips her hands into the remotely located controller, and starts manipulating the robotic limbs. High-tech viewing cameras create a hologram of the boy's anesthetized body, presenting him before her as if he were there in her lab. She completes the delicate work clearing torn tendons, bone, and muscle and finally sealing the wound. After it has healed, the child is given a flexible but firm new prosthetic leg, cost-effective and custom-made by the same 3D printer. A one-legged boy who would otherwise have been doomed to panhandling in a polluted city has a chance at a more fulfilling future.

If we—that is all 7 billion of us—don't screw up the planet, advances like this imagined scenario portend a world of boundless opportunity. For that we can thank a dizzying spate of technological change and ever-intensified human interconnectivity that's part of a positive feedback loop of decentralization and disruption. Essentially, the old monopolies of knowledge are breaking down, freeing up human ingenuity. Social media is vital to this process. Technologies such as mobile telecommunication, gene therapy and other biotech advances, 3D printing, drones, smartphones, digital currency, distributed networks, and open ledgers are all feeding off and back into the Social Organism. They, too, are part of this living, evolving life form that's challenging incumbent industries and traditional models of social organization, dislodging some from outdated jobs while creating innumerable, unforeseen opportunities for others.

In this world, social media is becoming our global brain. It is a powerful mediating system through which human beings' ideas can, in the colorful words of British intellectual Matt Ridley, "meet and have sex." It represents, to reuse an analogy, a rich agar for cultivating creativity and new concepts. With automated translation services embedded into social media platforms, people with different native tongues can communicate seamlessly—and when linked via VR goggles they can feel like they are in the same room together. This environment of collaborative innovation is getting more fertile by the day.

I first realized this when my buddy Lane Merrifield showed me what he was doing at Club Penguin, the children's online game/social network. Well before Facebook and others deployed an auto-translate feature, Club Penguin let kids from all over the world communicate seamlessly in pre-determined phrases that translated across all languages. (It was a form of digital Esperanto, or a real-life version of the "babel fish" from Douglas Adams's *Hitchhiker's Guide to the Galaxy.*) That was a big aha moment for me. These are the ways in which social media has dramatically flattened the lines of communication and given billions the opportunity to contribute their thoughts to a giant pool of information unconstrained by time or distance. It has contributed more to the process of creative procreation—and so to our capacity for exponential learning and innovation—than arguably any other Internet-based technology.

That might sound like a bold claim to anyone who still thinks of social media as merely a corporate marketing tool, a Millennial joke-sharing toy, or a place for anonymous trolls to say libelous things. But by now we hope you recognize that it is so much more than that. This horizontal, biologically determined communication system offers a completely new way of rapidly unleashing, sharing, and deploying information. It is especially powerful when combined with other decentralizing technologies such as cloud-based data storage, Big Data analysis, cryptography, machine-learning tools, open data protocols, and blockchain ledgers, technologies whose interoperable qualities mean they are linked directly into the social media publishing platforms.

What's emerging is a giant, living, and ever-evolving, intertwined uber-organism with tentacles spreading far beyond the platforms of Twitter and Facebook. It's a beast that currently encompasses

1.5 billion Internet users, more than a billion websites, and, according to internetstats.org, consumes more than 2 terawatt hours of electricity to process more than 2 billion gigabytes of data every day. And global connectivity is only getting more comprehensive as experimental ventures such as Facebook's Aquila project, which will offer drone-delivered WiFi to remote areas, and Google's Project Loon, which aims to do the same via high-altitude balloons, gain traction. Mesh networks, which provide intra-community connections that periodically sync with the global Internet, as well as the rollout of cheap smartphones such as Mozilla's offering at $25, will also bring many more of the world's digitally disconnected into this giant ecosystem of human exchange.

The complexity of the environment in which this organism operates goes far beyond the most commonly recognized social media systems. Online repositories of scientific data; open-source software developers; crowd-editing sites such as Wikipedia; decentralized marketplaces such as Airbnb, Lending Club, and eBay; bitcoin and other digital currency communities—these all go into the richly interdependent, decentralized ecosystem in which the Social Organism lives and thrives.

One way social media helps spur innovation within this global network of idea-generators is by drawing attention to new investment opportunities and, in that way, steering money toward where it's needed for research and development. That's especially valuable for places that don't have the kind of deep, venture capital markets that U.S. and European start-ups can tap. This shows up in the donations to projects launched on the crowdfunding site Kickstarter, which as of early 2016 had raised more than $2 billion for over 100,000 projects. Using social media to alert people to their ideas, a pair of inventors in the Philippines got $77,000 to develop their 3D printer–based DIY home solar panel maker, and the Clean Africa Energy project in Lesotho expanded production of its clean and safe biomass cook stove—just two of myriad Kickstarter success stories.

This is just the beginning. As digital-currency applications for transferring money combine with blockchain-based systems for securely issuing and trading so-called crypto-stocks and crypto-bonds, people will gain a newfound confidence that they are not being defrauded. When combined with the less restrictive regulations for soliciting investment contained in the U.S. JOBS Act, this could open up a deluge of investment flows. The result: the organic and exponential expansion of a global marketplace of ideas. Social media will be integrated into this process, replacing newswires and other traditional sources of information for capital markets. Already, some adventurous publicly listed companies are using Twitter to release information about their earnings and other announcements. That kind of global, straight-to-the-public broadcasting strategy—whether delivered over Twitter or via some current or future successor—is going to become commonplace. For our increasingly interconnected global economy, the free flow of ideas and information is its lifeblood. And social media networks, the infrastructure over which those ideas travel, are its cardiovascular system—the heart, arteries, and veins of this vast, networked uber-organism.

Yet as we ponder how we might shape social media's future role in this, we must also douse ourselves with a bucket of cold water. The dreams we have of our future are not only filled with stories of saving Tanzanian children, or of super-smart homes that can manage our complicated lives with exquisite, automated efficiency. They can also be rather nightmarish. Many of us worry, for good reason, that the age of ubiquitous, all-powerful computing capacity might reduce the essence of life to some kind of mathematical, algorithmically determined equation where we are told, without room for debate, what we should or shouldn't value. Computers are becoming artificially intelligent, whether we like it or not. How can we ensure we're not building a world in which we are trapped by the very machines we created? As we've said, we can't blindly assume that evolution makes for a "better" world.

In March 2016, when a computer programmed by Google beat a human competitor at the 2,500-year-old game of Go—a contest that's phenomenally more complex than chess—many saw it as a major milestone in the self-reinforcing evolution of artificial intelligence. I tend to believe Ray Kurzweil, the legendary futurist, when he says that "the singularity"—that moment in which computers are able to recursively learn and self-improve to the point where artificial intelligence starts to surpass human intelligence and never turns back—is near. The combined exponential effects from Moore's law, Metcalfe's law, and all the related computing, biotech, and financial technologies that are unleashing an ever-growing flood of networked processing power are taking us inexorably to that point.

It's exciting but, naturally, it's also unsettling.

That we have a strong interest in how A.I. evolves is an understatement of profound proportions. Every day another expert adds his or her voice to the cacophony of warnings that humanity faces grave risks once computers reach a point where they control us more than we do them. It's a justified concern; we cannot assume that if machines are programmed to think for themselves that they won't embark on some malevolent mission that we're unable to stop.

Isaac Asimov and other science fiction writers' fears of a sentient machine—Kubrick's HAL, if you will—are as relevant now as ever. But, in this final chapter, I want to explore what I see as a huge opportunity for social media to provide a powerful counterbalance to a future of soulless mechanistic authority by layering on top of it a rich tapestry of humanity.

If we follow the warnings of Yale computer scientist David Gelernter, the biggest danger is that we view computer intelligence, founded as it is on rational, mathematical processing, as somehow a sufficient proxy for human intelligence, which covers a much wider spectrum. Human consciousness starts with the logical, left-brain way of thinking that we've exported into computers, but further along it also encompasses dream states and nuances of thought, emotions, and random sparks of inexplicable creativity. We do not want the machines to simply deliver some cold, rational, mathematical assessment of what's "best for us" if we can't at the same time give value to, respect, and protect all that other stuff that makes us human. What matters are the elements of our being that appreciate beauty and love, that can imagine Harry Potter performing magic, or ponder why the universe exists, or marvel, without feeling compelled to understand, at the majesty of an eagle in flight, a brilliant blue glacier, or the Great Barrier Reef.

Citing the poet Rilke, who compared "the flight of a small bird across the evening sky to a crack in a smooth porcelain cup," Gelernter asks, "How did he come up with that? Possibly by using the fact that these very different things made him feel the same way... Emotion is a hugely powerful and personal encoding-and-summarizing function. It can comprehend a whole complex scene in one subtle feeling. Using that feeling as an index value, we can search out—among huge collections of candidates—the odd memory with a deep resemblance to the thing we have in mind." He's talking about something that a computer will never *get.* (Apologies, faithful MacBook.)

I always had this feeling of sadness when I thought about the "new consciousness of the collective," this idea that we were entering a "beige" era, one devoid of the possibilities of the David Bowies and other such mutating forces of creativity. I was inspired by Aldous Huxley's *Brave New World* and by Neil Postman, who described the sad fate of conformity and the lost information that computers introduce. (Postman chained himself to the card catalog at Berkeley when it was being computerized because he didn't want to lose the value of the human notes that were left on those cards, an earlier version of "social media" for future generations to use.) The complexity of mutation and of biological evolution inspires me much more than the conformity of the computer networks envisioned by the Googles of this world. Yet here I am building my life around the potential unleashed by that technology. It's one reason I feel duty bound to keep the element of random creative genius alive and well within this computerized system.

But, given that we are on this path, I also believe that social media is our biggest hope. If life is to be worth living in a future dominated by extremely powerful computers, we must carve out a space within it where the essence of what it means to be human has primacy within the same digital context in which those computers operate. We need a computer-readable forum in which expressions of artistic endeavor are celebrated, where we can make emotional connections with each other and play out our hopes, fears, loves, and dislikes, all with the full understanding that this is an essential, nonexpendable part of our digitally interconnected future. Social media *is* that forum. Preserving the autonomy of the billion-plus human cells within the Social Organism and encouraging the multitude of ongoing interactions between them will be absolutely vital if we are to avoid a reign of malevolent robot overlords.

How might we build this space of humanistic freedom? Well, let's first not forget that these machines will be programmed by us, or at least by the software engineers among us. We, the general public, must demand some input into that process. We need accountability, transparency, and translatable evidence that the coding used to set the machines' governance protocols is something we can reach consensus on. To achieve this requires the rollout of cryptographic proofs and of decentralized, trustless architectures such as the blockchain to immutably document the engineers' work. That will sound complicated for anyone without a background in cryptography, and I don't expect every Average Joe to have the skills to audit what the techies are doing. But as long as we keep the system open and support the educational development of more civic-minded software engineers, a worldwide volunteer army of sufficiently skilled, trustworthy coders and hackers can and will use these tools to keep their peers honest. (If you don't believe me, take a scroll through the immeasurable amount of unpaid work that goes into open-source projects listed on GitHub.)

What these guardian angels must insist upon, on our behalf, is that A.I. designers apply code that interoperates with social media but which also gives the latter the autonomy to foster the continued blossoming of human imagination. It all suggests a bigger role for the armies of self-appointed "white hackers" that currently live on the fringes of mainstream society. We may develop a greater appreciation of the contribution to our security that controversial transparency advocates like Anonymous and Julian Assange's Wikileaks provide.

Second, we must remember that artificially intelligent machines are nothing without the data that's fed into them. If they are to serve us, their information inputs must detail who we really are, what we truly value, what makes us come together, and what drives us apart. Nodes in the always-connected, ever-calibrating network of computing power will function just like T-cell receptors tasked with recognizing threats: They will seek out patterns in human behavior that prompt their steering algorithm to dictate an appropriate response. We must give them valuable, meaningful, and constructive data about the human existence. As far as I'm concerned, social media is the right place to gather and process this information.

To be sure, as we mine social media to discover who we are, it's probably unwise to just set some A.I. machine loose on the network to figure things out. Microsoft's experiment with a machine-learning Twitter bot offers a cautionary tale. The A.I. account, opened to the world on March 23, 2016, in the form of a model teenage girl named Tay, soon evolved into the embodiment of a horrible human being. Hordes of Twitter users showed how easy it was to teach the bot to become a racist bigot. In little time, she was declaring that feminism was "a cancer," "Hitler was right," "9/11 was an inside job," and that the Holocaust was "made up." Within twenty-four hours, Microsoft was forced to lobotomize Tay, as one commentator put it, and then issued a statement saying it was "deeply sorry" for what they'd let loose on the world. Sadly, Tay became a reflection of the content she was fed.

Nonetheless, we should be able to use social media to assess our culture without inviting spoilers to create destructive feedback loops. And despite our obsession with all this ugly behavior, it's the best shot we have. Not only does social media represent the highest evolved distribution system for human communication, but, as we've discussed, it lives and breathes off the emotional exchanges that define the human condition. It might depend on a base of hard-wired computers as its infrastructure, but what makes social media tick is the hard-to-define gooey stuff of humanity, the magic sauce that makes us chase our loves, attack our hates, and forge the tenuous but vital bonds of community that give life its meaning.

The old, top-down model of information management is incompatible with the flat, holarchic structure of this emerging ecosystem of ubiquitous computing power. For one, change happens too fast for the old system to keep up. The time it takes for a corporate lawyer to sign off on alterations to software code can't match the timescale of computers that react in milliseconds to ever-changing conditions. Also, in a global, borderless community, how are we going to decide which of those "suits" should be speaking for us?

This new world is already being constructed through open-source computing models, a crowdsourcing approach to design and engineering that the techie community has shown to be far more effective than centralized projects. Now, as software design becomes the basis for every manufactured good (3D-printed products and parts) and for every service we use (financial, professional advice, health, communication, etc.), nearly all of it will eventually be founded on open-source coding infrastructure. People will make proprietary, profit-making applications on top of that infrastructure, but the open platform will allow innovative competitors to try to dislodge them. The superiority of this model is demonstrated by the open-source Linux operating system, which now runs 90 percent of the world's servers and datacenters, and has spawned loads of vital offshoots, including Google's Android OS for smartphones. The input of hundreds of independent engineers into that collective creative effort has made Linux's software stronger, faster, and better for all of us. Now compare that to the government-run healthcare.gov website, whose launch was delayed by horrendous malfunctions, scaling, and interoperability problems. The market will demand that software designs follow the former model, not the latter.

We must apply this same open-source approach to human creativity of all kinds. Institutions like the Creative Commons, which encourage derivative works, are vital if the Social Organism is to thrive alongside a booming industry of functional software design. We must embrace and allow the constant remixing of culture. Especially as we barrel toward the Internet of Things era, when sensors on billions of machines will have them talking to each other, we must continue to feed and nurture the Social Organism.

In this open-source world, virtually any institution that remains trapped in a centralized, top-down architecture will be forced to adapt to this new system for sharing information and knowledge. Many may need to be completely overhauled. Education is a good place to start. We should promote open-minded approaches to learning that encourage experimentation and recognize failure as an integral, even welcome, part of that process. We must also promote the idea of collaboration. In a traditional classroom, students are punished for sharing; striving for success is a lonely enterprise, with raw competition emphasized at every stage of school life. But in social media, where knowledge grows through the constant, iterative development of memes and artistic contributions, where ad hoc collaborative teams spread ideas around the world and share their work under open-source agreements, this closed-book mind-set is anathema. If we want our graduating seniors to behave civilly on social media—which, whether we like it or not, is now *the* forum in which society works out its ideas and differences—we have to prepare them for it. We can't cultivate selfish, protective, overly competitive individuals for a system that's inherently dependent on cooperation and sharing. To the economist and social theorist Jeremy Rifkin, failure to make that pedagogical transition could very well doom the planet. "We need to teach our young people to share as part of human society," Rifkin says. "Then we can prepare them to live in an interconnected planetary society and to understand the biosphere in which we live."

Government is another institutional arena that needs a top-to-bottom shake up. Our bureaucracies need to learn the same lesson that General Stanley McChrystal discovered when he arrived in Iraq to lead the Joint Special Operations Command's fight against Al Qaeda. McChrystal realized that to fight an enemy that had no real leader or classic, top-down military hierarchy, he had to similarly shake up the U.S. command structure. He had to make communications lines across the army, navy, air force, marines and the various intelligence agencies more fluid, horizontal and interactive. In effect, he had to create more of a holocracy. McChrystal left his post in controversy, after officers under his command were quoted bad-mouthing President Obama, but his reforms are credited with helping to quell the insurgencies in Iraq. He is now parlaying that experience into consulting work, advising companies how to restructure their organizations in keeping with the new information-flow paradigm of our age.

Something similar needs to happen in federal, state, and local government bureaucracies. Otherwise, our super-fast, evolving computing systems will bypass our democratic institutions and insert their own will. For now, government remains an indispensable institution for holding people accountable, and that's going to matter deeply as we monitor the coders who are building our A.I.-managed future. Maybe we'll evolve new, software-driven models of governance, using distributed blockchain ledgers to keep work records traceable and instill natural, unbreakable laws of decentralization into our human exchange systems. But it's still hard to see how we dispense with democratic governance altogether. We will need to bring government's authority structure more in line with that of the Social Organism and embrace holarchic models of organization. Given the dysfunction of the U.S. Congress, this is a daunting undertaking. And yet such change is essential.

As we try to reimagine and restructure institutions, nature once again is our guide. Our digital lives are hurtling toward a more complex state of human commune, where the permutations of possible connections are exponentially more varied and unpredictable than those that existed during the era of linear, top-down control. The fields of physics and molecular biology have had to make sense of the universe's wondrous natural inclination toward entropy and disorder. Now, after millennia of imposing our own rigid order in the face of all that chaos, we are, to an extent, yielding to it. And if we are going to let go in this way and design companies, government systems, and software programs that can contend with this new model, we need to understand where our theory of the Organism fits within the greater context.

* * *

Whatever path we take to achieving this social reconfiguration, it is going to entail a reorganization of knowledge itself. Thankfully, this is already happening. The crossover of disciplines traditionally associated with the natural sciences of biology and physics with those in the social science realm, especially around the study of human networks, is opening vast new realms of understanding about how the universe functions. This cross-pollination of ideas from different schools has become so fertile that the very idea of separate scientific or academic disciplines is starting to look a bit archaic. In fact, we think this book can be viewed in that same light: Is it a work about business, society, computer science, biology, all of the above, or none of the above?

At the MIT Media Lab, where Michael works, the favored word is "antidisciplinary," the idea being that researchers should pursue projects that defy the traditional classifications of faculty. As Media Lab executive director Joichi Ito puts it, an antidisciplinary project is "a field of study with its own particular words, frameworks, and methods." Note, he's not talking about an "interdisciplinary" approach, but rather one whose focus lies outside of the traditional boundaries that academia has carved out for itself. In this spirit, the Media Lab's designer/architect/biologist extraordinaire Neri Oxman combines computer technologies such as 3D printing with the "design" patterns found in nature to create beautiful, bacteria-managed clothes that literally live on you. She also designs buildings made of robust yet biodegradable natural materials. Her unclassifiable work reflects her view that we live in an "Age of Entanglement" in which "knowledge can no longer be ascribed to, or produced within, disciplinary boundaries, but is entirely entangled."

Others are not so much abandoning disciplines but creating new ones. Hybrid fields drawn from biology, computer science, and social science now focus on how complex systems operate in nature and what they can tell us about how human beings interact with each other. Some are reviving the cross-disciplinary ideas of people like computer scientist Jay Forrester, who in the fifties pioneered the study of system dynamics. His work led to interest in cybernetics, the study of how feedback loops and self-adaptive systems explain the behavior of networks of autonomous molecules, organisms, and computing nodes and their application to the environment.

Using similar models, many systems designers are embracing biomimicry, which seeks to model human networks and organizational systems on the structure and functioning of those found in nature. The idea is that biomimicking will lead to a more efficient use of resources—be they social resources such as brainpower, natural resources such as water and fossil fuels, or computing resources. Of course, biomimicry has always been a part of business product design—think of how birds inspire the development of airplanes—but the key now is that leaders in this field are tapping nature for lessons on how to organize communities of people.

Much of the focus is on how to structure distinct business organizations and government agencies—and, as we discussed in chapter 2, some of that work is building on the concept of holarchies and holonic structures. But the lessons from nature also apply to really big systems of ad-hoc, informal relationships. Physicist Geoffrey West, for example, has identified a preferred population growth trajectory for big cities by drawing inferences from precise mathematical equations that measure how large animals' metabolisms reach optimal efficiencies as they grow in size. French physicist-economist

Didier Sornette, along with others, is creating models that predict the boom-bust cycles of markets based on how particles and molecules behave in the natural world. Scottish engineer David Irvine used nature's coordinating mechanisms as his model for Maidsafe, a sophisticated, cryptocurrency-based network that lets thousands of computers share memory and computing power in a collective arrangement that obviates the need for a central server. To find the right optimizing balance for incentivizing owners to share or withdraw resources without disrupting the network, Irvine studied how ant colonies and other natural social systems work together. Nature, he says, "is the ultimate decentralized system."

In understanding how all these systems function, the key element is communication, the signaling mechanism for the cause-and-effect responses that shape a group's behavior. And while we tend to think of communicating as a uniquely human activity, key units of nature, both within and between organisms, are constantly communicating with each other. In fact, some living organisms play roles as messengers between other organisms. One striking example comes from mycelium, the prodigiously expansive mass of underground filaments on which fungi are formed. (One mycelium conglomeration in Oregon's Blue Mountains occupies 2,384 acres of soil to stake a claim as the biggest living organism on earth.) Scientists have long known that mycelium forms symbiotic relationships with plants over what's known as mycorrhizal networks: The plants provide the fungi with food while their root-like mycelia suck up water and nutrients such as phosphorus and nitrogen and transfer them to the plant. More recently, however, researchers discovered that the mycelia connections allow plants to share information with each other about the state of their metabolism. Using the same fungal interconnections, they will then make transfers of phosphorus and nitrogen from those that are rich in nutrients to those that are in need.

"I believe that mycelium is the neurological network of nature," says mycologist Paul Stamets. "Interlacing mosaics of mycelium infuse habitats with information-sharing membranes. These membranes are aware, react to change, and collectively have the long-term health of the host environment in mind." Stamets calls mycelium "Nature's Internet," and even goes so far to describe it as "a consciousness with which we might be able to communicate."

I recently took an amazing trip with Paul around Iceland in the spring of 2016, where we discussed how mycelium is nature's "immune system." A remarkably passionate human being, Paul argues that once we figure out "cross-species interfacing," we might be able to tap these "sentient cellular networks" to improve our own lives. How, and indeed why, would we do that? Because these "externalized neurological nets sense any impression upon them, from footsteps to falling tree branches," which means they could "relay enormous amounts of data regarding the movements of all organisms through the landscape." He's even made a case for tapping the communicative power of mycelium, which has a powerful capacity to teach organisms' immune systems to defend themselves, to bolster bees' resilience to the diseases that are dangerously threatening colonies worldwide.

Mycelium's role as nature's communicator stems from the unique cellular structure of its fibrous networks. At the tips, where the extended filaments connect with the outside world, the strands are intensely *polynucleated* in what's known as a *coenocyte*—which means their cells contain not one but many nuclei. This is like a concentration of brain power, which, Paul says, turns the tips into powerful sensors that are constantly reading data from the outside world. That data is then conveyed, through biochemical reactions, back to cells deeper within the underlying fungi so that they can adapt and evolve to their changing surrounding. I think it conjures up a fascinating analogy with the hyper-sensors that are now deployed in places that interface with our social media networks: the personal cameras and recording devices that convey information, such as the shooting of a black man, to the Social Organism. It's not for nothing that images of both mycelium and neural networks look similar to graphic representations of social media networks.

Whether Stamets is right about mycelium's special properties, the notion of a biological communication network isn't unique to fungi. All multi-species ecosystems must share information if they are to regulate their complex, interdependent relationships. That goes for the trillions of microbes that coexist inside the human body, a giant

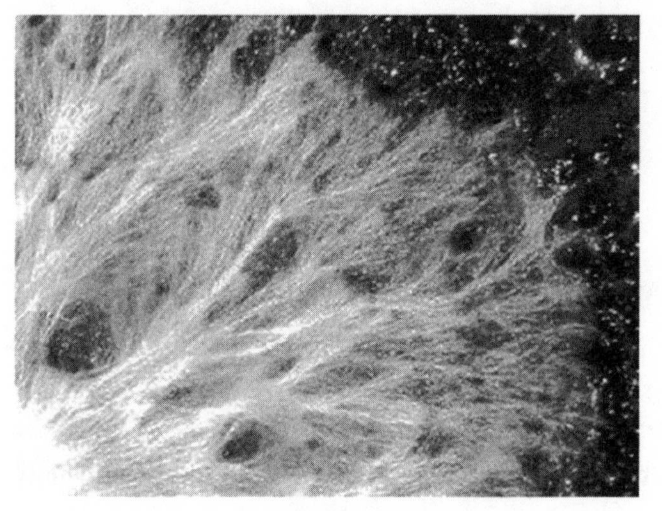

Mycelium

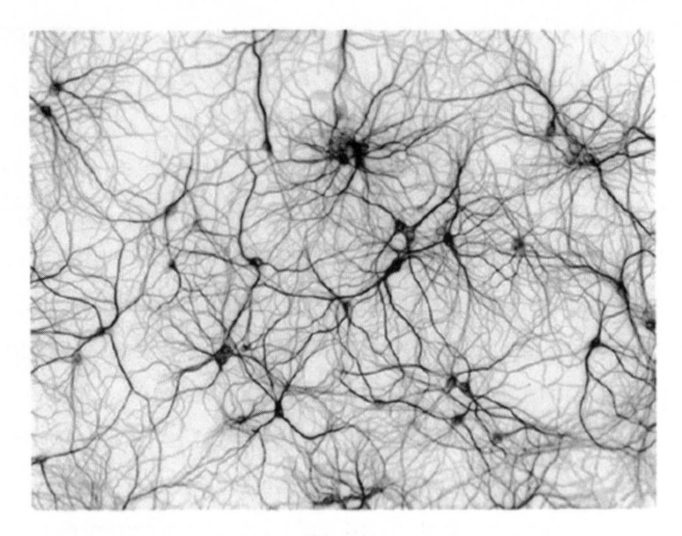

Neural

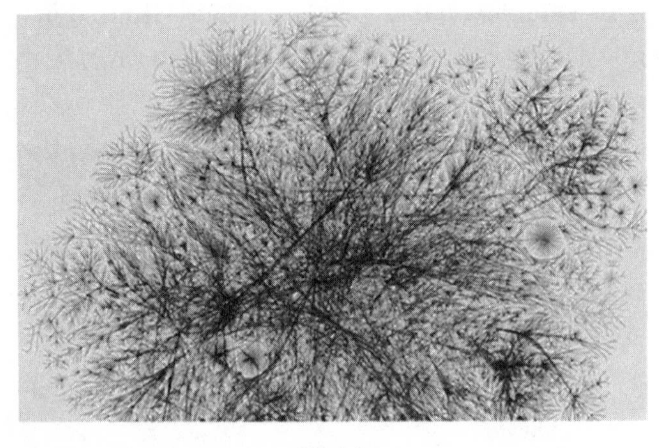

Social

ecosystem of tiny microorganisms whose interactions with each other—both competitive and cooperative—are only now becoming apparent to scientists armed with powerful new Big Data and

DNA-sequencing techniques. Known as the human microbiome, this congregation of microscopic creatures is the biological equivalent of our networked Social Organism; it's constantly sending and receiving signals from a countless array of nodes. The balance of communication within the microbiome—which will in turn influence and be influenced by its particular mix of symbiotic and pathogenic microorganisms—will decide whether we are healthy or not. As Michael's teenage daughter Zoe points out, this giant leaderless community of tiny organisms "does a much better job of looking after its environment than we humans have done for ours."

Societies can adopt the same "self-healing" and positive growth mechanisms, especially if their communication systems are open and interconnected. Think of the "we shall overcome" message that was implied in the widely replicated #JeSuisParis and #JeSuisBruxelles hashtags following the terrorist attacks in Paris and Brussels.

I recently relocated to Iceland, where I've been struck by how peaceful, productive, innovative, and communitarian its society is. And I think that says something about its networking instincts. The survival of the "Icelandic species" relied upon collective behaviors to combat the harsh environment, dark winters, and isolation. It gave rise to Iceland's *sagas* during one of the most prolific eras in medieval literature. These unvarnished and realistic tales emphasized, on the one hand, respect for rugged individuals who'd overcome nature's challenges and, on the other, their absolute dependence and connection to a wider social setting. It's a holonic ideal: independence and autonomy yet simultaneous, unavoidable dependence on the wider whole. These stories forge a conflict in which was bred both a socializing instinct and a respect for each person's unique qualities. It probably explains why Iceland has a 60 percent penetration on Snapchat, 93 percent penetration on Facebook, and geothermal-heated natural-spring swimming pools that teem with social interactions. A society interwoven with the shared values of humanism, egalitarianism, accountability, sustainability, and a deep connection to nature has created a unique petri dish of culture from which I am learning every day. I hope that the Social Organism can also become infused with the same inherent trust.

It seems that societies whose communication behaviors most mimic those of nature fare the best. So it's presumably a good sign that, everywhere, we are developing habits like those of birds. To Giles Hutchins, cofounder of the consultancy Biomimicry for Creative Innovation, our new tendency to share smaller packages of content such as tweets on Twitter matches nature's preferred communication format of "short instant messages." Traditionally, he says, human communication has been "presented or created in long form and can also be very documentary," but now we are seeing "a reawakening of our very own 'waggle dance' or pheromone-style short messaging instinct." Tweets, he notes, "mimic the biological bird call metaphor," as do SMS messages. Perhaps this is why it can feel like the Social Organism is functioning as one big cacophonous birdhouse.

This merging of human and natural systems cuts both ways. We are discovering how our new communications architecture also helps us understand natural phenomena such as the spread of disease. After Haiti was hit with a devastating earthquake in 2010, epidemiologists used social media patterns to study and predict the development of a cholera outbreak. Their work helped medical teams get ahead of the epidemic, preventing a bad situation from turning catastrophic. The technology may also be useful in monitoring the very real problem of suicide contagion, a phenomenon first highlighted in 1962 when Marilyn Monroe's death by barbiturate poisoning led to a 12 percent increase in the rate of U.S. suicides. Reading an article about Guyana's shockingly high suicide rate, I was struck by how researchers had found that when people killed themselves, mini "outbreaks" of follow-up suicides would cluster in the place where the first happened. The article discussed the prevalence of "contagion beliefs" associated with mental illnesses, pointing to a troublesome network effect where one person's actions can trigger a domino effect across a population of mentally ill people. It's precisely the kind of pattern that, once identified, could show up in social media data, where it could be used as an early-warning tool.

Different types of computing technology are working in parallel to fulfill two distinct purposes. In one direction, social media platforms and related social networking technology are dramatically changing how we distribute and consume information. In another, high-powered microscopes, gene-sequencing, Big Data, and sophisticated mathematical modeling tools are giving us a deeper understanding of complex systems of all kinds, be they biological, sociological, or physical. Together, these twin trends are delivering a kind of reflexive duality where biology and sociology are becoming one.

We probably shouldn't be that surprised—we should have known all along what the eco-physicist Fritjof Capra has argued: that human social systems are not just *like* living systems, they *are* living systems.

Yet this reflexivity goes deeper still. Experiential information, which we were taught to view as data points that only we humans, with our supposedly superior brains, were uniquely capable of interpreting, isn't just something that is sustained outside of our bodies as an independent variable; it can actually change us at our core. Thanks to studies of mice that have been conditioned to fear a certain smell, which found that their offspring were born with the same fear, we now know that trauma is something that can be coded into our DNA. Presumably, that means that learned positive responses can equally be incorporated and passed down from generation to generation. This demands even more that we respect our collective consciousness. Let it remind us of our past but also bring us forward, help us to grow.

As both our communication system and our social media–infused culture undergo the accelerating evolution detailed in this book, it appears that the biological makeup of the human species is itself undergoing faster changes. Research by University of Wisconsin anthropologist John Hawks has found that human evolution has sped up over the age of civilization, making the genetic differences between our bodies and those of people from 5,000 years ago much greater than the differences between those people and the Neanderthals, who vanished 35,000 years previously. Hawks's thesis is that by changing our environment, our diet and moving around so much, we were forced to adapt more frequently. Wouldn't it then follow that the Social Organism's ever-wider exposure to new, emotive information sources must also change our bodies—or at least our brains?

And that's not all. Biotech is now bringing the power of computing to the redesign of our very body. The Media Lab's Hugh Herr, who lost his legs in a mountaineering accident, has created sophisticated prosthetic limbs that many believe are better than the human version—certainly they will last longer and they are more readily upgraded. Then, at the molecular level, there's the somewhat polarizing field of synthetic biology. Recently, scientists led by genetics pioneer Craig Venter announced that they'd created a microbe with a simple DNA structure composed of just 437 genes, simpler than any known organism found in nature. The scientists are not quite sure what it is yet, but they say that it could provide a useful platform—a code base, if you will—with which to develop bold new medical treatments. Others will understandably worry that a real-life Dr. Frankenstein has been given a dangerous opportunity. Venter's team didn't clone a living thing; they created one from scratch.

My friend, the futurist Andrew Hessel, certainly thinks this radical new field can be a force for good, to in essence rewrite our biology. Recognizing that an organism's cells function as information processors that use their own special programming language, DNA, Andrew and other "bio-hackers" are using tools like 3D printing to synthesize biological agents such as the Phi-X174 bacteriophage, a virus that infects the *E. coli* bacteria but is benign for humans. While some worry that this technology might one day create bio-warfare weapons, Andrew's approach is to shine the sunlight of transparency and open-source coding on a humanitarian mission. His Pink Army Cooperative is an open-source community of like-minded bio-engineers who are contributing their coding and knowledge to a collaborative effort to create a synthetic oncolytic virus that would target and kill breast cancer cells. An open-source community of brainy people can bring to bear so much more collective processing power than can a patent-driven pharmaceutical company. This, he believes, will ensure that his community will beat such companies in the race to make such a virus, both in terms of cost and speed. They are making the Linux of cancer treatments: a robust, heavily tested, patent-free design that anyone is free to copy and apply. Big Pharma should be worried.

What this survey of pioneering interdisciplinary work reveals is a convergence of three rapidly evolving forces: biology, computing networks, and, most important, a globally shared wellspring of human knowledge and cultural output. It suggests that if the world is approaching Ray Kurzweil's wonderful/horrifying (take your pick) singularity moment, its structure could be far more nuanced and complex than that which Hollywood likes to portray. Movies like 2015's *Ex Machina*, where the focus is on android machines that take control of our minds, suggest we are at risk of losing our human essence. But I think they are missing a key part of the story. Beyond the machines, there is a simultaneous and powerful evolution of the global human brain under way. I'm not talking about changes in our individual brains. (There's a viable argument to make that having an always-available search function at our fingertips is making at least part of our brains dumber.) I'm talking about the evolution of the amorphous "brain" of interconnected minds that has been plugged in and set to work by social networking technology. Life itself is already unfathomably complex as a system—far more so than any computer could hope to be. Now, with our highly evolved living brains contributing to a giant pool of procreating memes and ideas, a Cambrian explosion of creativity is under way.

So, while we are undoubtedly headed to a new, decentralized

concept of collective mindshare—whether that's to be labeled the singularity or something else—I think it's too simplistic to describe that as a world run solely by computers. This new paradigm also includes that richly diverse, wonderfully unpredictable interconnected human layer, which of course is another way to describe the Social Organism. Along with the biological/physical layer of the complex natural ecosystem in which it resides, the Organism's global human brain will engage with the computer layer to set us on a path of random changes that are simply impossible to forecast.

I see it as the ultimate act of unlocking *human capital*, a commonly used term in economics but one that's all the more relevant here if we think about it as NYU economist Paul Romer does. He says human capital is "stored as neural connections in a brain." We are now able, like never before, to open the locks on all that rich, stored capital. Companies such as Twitter founder Biz Stone's new start-up Jelly, which allows people to ask a question of potentially millions of social media-interconnected minds, deliberately seek to accelerate this kind of exponential expansion in information-sharing. As Stone puts it, "Everyone is working on Artificial Intelligence, what about just, Intelligence?" This great unlocking of ideas almost guarantees life will be very different in just five to ten years' time, though there's no way to predict what it will look like. What *is* clear to me is that if we recognize that humanity derives power from sharing information, together we can set the world on a more sustainable path.

To put this all in context, I'll return to my bio-hacker friend Andrew Hessel. Instead of making A.I. computers human-like, he is honing the already incredibly high-tech computers that have long resided inside humans. "We are seeing the formation of a new cellular organism," Andrew says, "one that is comprised of billions of intelligent minds. Just think of them as molecules interacting together for the first time. We've never done this before. Who knows what we'll make from this process?" To undertake this collective, unguided mission of idea formation, these billion intelligent minds are following the instructions of the Internet protocol, which Andrew describes as "the first truly global communications standard" we've created. He adds, "The only other global standard that I'm aware of is the genetic code. Whether we are talking about plants or humans, the structure of the genetic code has been the only one in use."

The core genetic code—our first common programming language—has been in place for 3.5 billion years, long before Alan Turing conceived, in the 1930s, of an era of man-made computers that could augment the limited computational capacity of a single human brain. Over that time this standard DNA code has coordinated the activities of an infinitely more complex network of information processing "machines." Together they have progressively built the richly diverse and constantly evolving reality of life on earth.

It's a humbling thought. And when we see the hubris of politicians and other would-be leaders play out daily across our media streams, such humility can be a valuable refuge, a place from which to reflect with wonder on this incredible world. The most important tools being built right now, the most important buildings, vehicles, and software applications, are those that work within and recognize the highly complex, adaptive systems that shape society.

Such efforts do not lend themselves to a giant ego. Kevin Slavin, another genius Media Lab software designer, has suggested that the people currently at the cutting edge of design tend to show more humility than their predecessors. People who are "deliberately working with complex adaptive systems cannot help but be humbled by them," Slavin hypothesized in a recent article. "Maybe those who really design systems-interacting-with-systems approach their relationships to said systems with the daunting complexity of influence, rather than the hubris of definition or control."

The world is complex—more so than we can comprehend. No individual can hope to try to control it. We can jointly figure out how to work *with* it, how to teach parts of it to respond in certain ways to certain stimuli. But the overarching systemic processes, where billions of interacting molecules create feedback loops, counter-responses, and self-fulfilling perpetuations, are impossible to manage against their will. That's the dilemma that gripped me when I found myself a few years ago in the Mojave Desert, reaching for the right metaphor to describe the social media landscape. I knew it was far too complex to synthesize into a traditional flow chart. The only thing that seemed to sufficiently capture its complicated intricacy was life itself.

There's a critical lesson here as we figure out how to manage this unpredictable new model for communicating our ideas, hopes, dreams, and fears. Humility in the face of complexity is a trait that can help us, as a group, to collectively gain the most from that system. Humility implies respect for everyone else; it implies empathy, compassion and, most of all, tolerance for difference. For although specific individuals have no singular power to take autocratic charge of this complex system, the paradox is that the system itself derives its power from individualism, from the diversity of its billion-node makeup.

Here, *diversity* and *community* are two sides of the same coin. Together, they capture the holonic essence of the Social Organism, where units belong indelibly to a common, wider whole but are also intrinsically autonomous. If people are not allowed the freedom to express themselves, to be who they are without demands that they conform to the wishes of someone else, we introduce stress into the Social Organism. But if we let it draw upon the shared but diverse humanity of its billion-odd nodes, the Social Organism gets stronger. It turns out strength does not come from unity, at least not when that idea is defined as conformity or predictability. It comes from variety, change, dynamism, and a capacity for surprise. With rich, heterogeneous gene pools, variance creates a greater chance of mutation, which allows the population to evolve into something stronger. Similarly, a wide array of ideas means we have a better chance of finding the best answers to whatever problems we face.

There's no guarantee we won't screw this up. A poorly designed legal and political framework that fails to safeguard diversity and free expression could see us overwhelmed by some of the more destructive elements imbedded into our millennia-old cultural code—the diseases of greed, selfishness, hate, and intolerance that have reared their ugly heads in recent years. Just as an entire species can be wiped out when its immune system isn't strong enough to withstand a threat from some extremely harmful pathogen, so, too, can a culture be destroyed. Just ask anyone who lived through Nazi Germany or, more recently, North Korea.

This systemic convergence of understanding and interaction

between our biological, technological, and social worlds comes at a most urgent moment. Thanks largely to the top-down, centralized model of communication that persisted until the rise of the Internet, the planet itself is on the verge of ecological disaster. A fragmented and woefully unsophisticated understanding of the functioning of the Social Organism has led to social governance structures that encourage terribly destructive decisions—climate change; war in pursuit of oil that foments conditions for terrorism; curbs on human mobility, freedom of speech, and lifestyle choices that breed resentment and antisocial backlash. One could argue, in fact, that the very idea of the nation-state, the dominant power structure for the past half-millennium, is at loggerheads with sustainability. (And yet Britons felt compelled to do their "Brexit.") The simplicity and rigidity of that geographically defined political unit runs counter to the borderless, interconnected, and supreme complexity of social media, which in just a single decade has become the dominant, transnational system for human communication. It is vital that we come to terms with how that Organism functions. The survival of our home is at stake.

The Social Organism will always be in flux. There will always be tension. So, there's no way to definitively map it. What we have instead are guideposts. These are the Seven Rules of Life that dictate how the Organism functions. In essence, they tell us that we need to nourish our ideas, that we must reach out to people's emotional receptors to have an impact, and that we should encourage others to share or replicate our memetic content. These biology-provided markers, outlined throughout this book, provide a framework—not just to improve your understanding of how best to engage with social media in your life or business but a framework for how we can deliberately build a better society. We should no longer dismiss social media as trivial, nor fear it as an agent for disorderly chaos. Instead, in understanding and treating it as a Social Organism, we have a unique opportunity to nourish a new, healthier society and to build a more inclusive, prosperous, and sustainable world.

ACKNOWLEDGMENTS

The partnership that produced this book emerged from a serendipitous meeting in a Caribbean paradise. We met at the Blockchain Summit, a gathering of entrepreneurs and digital currency experts held on Richard Branson's idyllic Necker Island. So our first thanks go to the sponsors of that conference, without whom we wouldn't have met: Valery Vavilov and George Kikvadze of BitFury, Bill Tai and Susi Mai of MaiTai and, of course, Sir Richard.

Some time before then, however, the kernel of the idea was planted in Oliver's mind by Tim Sanders, after he saw him deliver one of his early Social Organism presentations following that formative moment of realization in the Joshua Tree desert. Thank you, Tim, for convincing someone whose professional life revolved around twenty-first-century digital media that a six-hundred-year-old printed medium of long-form communication could drive his ideas further.

We are both deeply grateful to our agent, Gillian MacKenzie, who has by now seen Michael through five book deals and who recognized the significance of this one from the start. She superbly shaped the proposal into a winning formula and devised, among other elements, the narrative's uniquely styled point of view.

Our editor, Paul Whitlatch, immediately grasped that we could shift the debate on social media away from the prevailing, unhelpful dichotomy that simplistically painted it as either a liberating force or a societal scourge. To make sure we delivered on the book's promise to help its readers take charge of this new communication architecture, he deftly trimmed our prose and sharpened its focus. Michelle Aielli and the Hachette publicity team, as well as marketing director Betsy Hulsebosch, also deserve thanks for all their hard work and for giving us the leeway to put our Social Organism promotional ideas into practice. And we'd also like to cite Paul's assistant, Lauren Hummel, production editor Melanie Gold, and, of course, Hachette Books publisher Mauro DiPreta.

Various people shared feedback, offered advice, and otherwise imparted wisdom that helped improve our understanding of the subject matter and sharpened the text. There are too many to name in total, but we'd like to single out Andrew Hessel, Ethan Zuckerman, César Hidalgo, Paul Stamets, Joel Dietz, Patrick Deegan, Ray Kurzweil, Jason Silva, and Norman Lear.

Special acknowledgment must go to Deen Freelon and his co-authors Charlton D. McIlwain and Meredith D. Clark for sharing data that was used to compile charts in their groundbreaking report on #BlackLivesMatter, *Beyond the Hashtags.* Similarly, we'd like to thank Soroush Vosoughi and Deb Roy of MIT's Laboratory for Social Machines for providing access to other pools of Twitter data.

In addition, we'd like to add the following individual thank yous:

Oliver

Thank you, Alice Franceschetti, for seeing something in me and giving me the opportunity to work with Lisa K. Jennings and Melanie

White in their lab all those years ago. Thanks to Sam B. Girgus for putting up with me. To my mom, Kay Turner, you gave me a wicked sense of humor and sensitivity. To my father, Bill Luckett, you taught me to have an incredible work ethic and to believe in myself.

Whitney Luckett, I love your loyalty, and Park Dodge, I love your genius and kindness. To Scott and Mer for coming into our crazy family. To our family in Los Angeles who supported us so, so much for so, so many years: Peter Grassl, Nenette Brockert, Troy Adams, Michelle Van Duzen, Teresa Lopez, Kozy n Dan, Concha, Imelda, Tim Sovay, Devin Liston, and Lisa Dimitroff. To our family in New York: Stephanie Ruhle, Steph Cozzi, Brandi Norton, Kelly Covell, Ben Patterson, Adéllyn Polomski, Felabi Phillips, Justin, and Mike and Andrea aka the Schnerberts. To our new family in Iceland for welcoming us with such open arms to a strange new land: Heiða Kristín (#BusinessWomanoftheYear), Jóga Jóhannsdóttir, Frosti Gnarr, Högni Óskarsson, Ingunn Benediktsdottir, Sigurjón Gunnsteinsson, Birgir Breiðfjörð, Gummi Jónsson, Einar Örn, and Pétur Marteinsson. I must also include Guðjón, Anton, Robert and Christopher, our adopted Inklaw sons in Reykjavik.

Lisa Bonner... go girl! You are #1BadAssAttorney.

Kate and Morgan... the piggies.

Sean, Alexandra, and Victoria, I love you guys.

Libby Anschutz, Bob Iger, Kevin Mayer, Dana Settle, Ari Emmanuel and Kate McLean, thank you for the opportunities of a lifetime.

Much love to Rob Maigret, for the great partnership; Björk Guðmundsdóttir, for teaching me gratitude; Jon Gnarr, for teaching me humanism; Daniel Lismore and Zebra Katz for teaching me to be myself; Norman Lear, for teaching me equality; and finally, my husband, Scott Guinn, for teaching me true love...you are the love of my life.

Michael

First, a nod to my colleagues at MIT Media Lab's Digital Currency Initiative, which I joined right when this book project was beginning. So to Brian Forde, Simon Johnson, Neha Narula, Chelsea Barabas, Gina Vargas, and Media Lab director Joi Ito, thank you for allowing me to keep my toes in journalism for a bit longer when I could otherwise have been investing all my energies into digital currency research.

A load of gratitude must also go to a group of people in Pelham without whom the burden of family management that I leave on my wife's shoulders would be even greater: Jen Rohr, Dafne Ginn, Jane Robbins, and many others.

To Lia, who combines an incessantly inquisitive mind with a passion for sports and a deep love of family, thank you for filling my life with light. To Zoe, who has helped a forty-nine-year-old mind break free of its pattern-recognition limits and understand that our quest for self-identity can be fluid and dynamic, thank you for helping me see. And to Alicia, who holds our family and household together, deals with the fact that my head is often in a different place, and still manages to enlighten me with her intellectual acumen, wise counsel, and moral clarity, I would be nothing without you.

NOTES

Preface

xviii **In his memoir, Twitter cofounder**: Stone, B., *Things a Little Bird Told Me: Confessions of the Creative Mind* (Hachette, 2014), 124.

xx **The *Los Angeles Times* once wrote**: Vankin, D., "Tech Mogul Oliver Luckett Connects with Emerging Artists in a Big Way," *Los Angeles Times*, May 2, 2014, http://www.latimes.com/entertainment/arts/la-et-cm-ca-oliver-luckett-20140504-story.html.

Introduction

xxiii ***Details* had recently bestowed a few entrepreneurs**: The project was for the April 2013 edition of the magazine and was also written up in *The Huffington Post*. Brooks, K., "Draw the Future of Social Media: Details Magazine Challenges You to Be a Digital Maverick," *The Huffington Post*, March 27, 2013, http://www.huffingtonpost.com/entry/draw-the-future-of-social-media_n_2951114.

xxvi **This connection between memes and genes**: Dawkins, R., *The Selfish Gene: 30th Anniversary Edition* (Oxford University Press, 2006), 189–202.

xxx **Each human unit on the network constitutes**: Koestler, A., *The Ghost in the Machine* (Macmillan, 1976), 48.

Chapter 1: The Algorithm of Life

4 **Darwin's "dangerous idea" constitutes a "basic algorithm"**: Dennett, D., *Darwin's Dangerous Idea: Evolution and the Meanings of Life* (Simon & Schuster, 1995), 50.

6 **It is, as Dennett says**: Ibid.

7 **As Stephen Jay Gould has said**: Gould, S. J., *Wonderful Life: The Burgess Shale and the Nature of History* (Norton, 1989), 30–36.

9 **Hidalgo describes a tree as a "computer powered by sunlight"**: Hidalgo, C., *Why Information Grows: The Evolution of Order, from Atoms to Economies* (Basic Books, 2015), 35.

11 **In 2013, Aidan King**: Andrews, N., "Young Grape Picker Gives Sanders a Cash Boost," *The Wall Street Journal*, October 1, 2015, http://www.wsj.com/articles/young-grape-picker-gives-sanders-a-cash-boost-1443742401.

Chapter 2: From Steeples to Snapchat

14 **If we conceive of societies as organisms, Wilson argues**: Sloan Wilson, D., *Darwin's Cathedral: Evolution, Religion, and the Nature of Society* (University of Chicago Press, 2002).

19 **They defined the so-called "Overton window"**: The Overton window is discussed at the website of the Mackinac Center for Public Policy, where Joseph. P. Overton served as senior vice president until his death in a 2003 airplane crash. "The Overton Window: A Model of Policy Change," Mackinac Center for Public Policy, http://www.mackinac.org/OvertonWindow.

28 **[T]he number of blogs soared to 182.5 million by 2011**: "Buzz in the Blogosphere: Millions More Bloggers and Blog Readers," Nielsen, March

8, 2012, http://www.nielsen.com/us/en/insights/news/2012/buzz-in-the-blogosphere-millions-more-bloggers-and-blog-readers.html.

28 **Now, with Tumblr alone claiming 277.9 million blogs**: Tumblr's "about" page. https://www.tumblr.com/about.

28 **Meanwhile, newspaper revenues are less than half**: Mitchell, A., and Page, D., "State of the News Media 2016," Pew Research Center, April 29, 2015. Posted in: http://www.journalism.org/2016/06/15/state-of-the-news-media-2016/.

30 **The company swelled to one hundred employees servicing around 3 million users**: Cleary, S., and Hanrahan, T., "College Site Publisher YouthStream to Buy Sixdegrees for $120 Million," *The Wall Street Journal*, December 15, 1999, http://www.wsj.com/articles/SB945269426653408644.

30 **YouthStream itself was forced to sell the following year for a measly $7 million**: "Alloy Buys Youthstream Media Networks for $7 Million," *Chief Marketer*, August 6, 2002, http://www.chiefmarketer.com/alloy-buys-youthstream-media-networks-for-7-million/.

32 **So what about Myspace?**: Gillette, F., "The Rise and Inglorious Fall of Myspace," *BloombergBusinessweek*, June 22, 2011, http://www.bloomberg.com/bw/magazine/content/11_27/b4235053917570.htm.

36 **According to early Twitter engineer Evan Henshaw-Plath**: Henshaw-Plath, E. (presentation, MIT Media Lab, Cambridge, Mass., September 24, 2015).

38 **The company claims its policy stems from rules set by the Apple Store**: Sims, A., "Instagram Admits Nipple Ban Is Because of Apple, CEO Kevin Systrom says," *The Independent*, October 1, 2015, http://www.independent.co.uk/life-style/gadgets-and-tech/news/instagram-ceo-kevin-systrom-says-apple-are-reason-app-bans-nipples-a6674706.html.

38 **when *Vogue* creative director Grace Coddington was temporarily banned**: Alexander, E., "Grace Coddington Banned from Instagram

for Posting Topless Line Cartoon," *The Independent,* May 20, 2014, http://www.independent.co.uk/news/people/grace-coddington-banned-from-instagram-former-model-causes-upset-with-her-nude-cartoon-9401684.html.

39 **A 2014 poll of 127 users by the University of Washington**: Roesner, F., Gill, B. T., and Kohno, T., "Sex, Lies, or Kittens? Investigating the Use of Snapchat's Self-Destructing Messages," 2014, https://homes.cs.washington.edu/~yoshi/papers/snapchat-FC2014.pdf.

40 **As Snapchat founder Evan Spiegel**: Spiegel, E., "Let's Chat," Snapchat-blog.com, May 9, 2012, http://snapchat-blog.com/post/22756675666/lets-chat.

40 **A 2014 poll by Sparks & Honey showed a clear preference**: Sparks & Honey's SlideShare page, "Meet Generation Z: Forget Everything You Learned about Millennials," June 17, 2014, http://www.slideshare.net/sparksandhoney/generation-z-final-june-17.

40 **In another 2014 poll, Defy Media found**: "Millennials Smile for Snapchat," eMarketer, April 8, 2015, http://www.emarketer.com/Article/Millennials-Smile-Snapchat/1012324.

41 **As of November 2015, Vine itself boasted 200 million users**: Smith, C., "By the Numbers: 27 Amazing Vine Statistics," DMR blog, July 14, 2016, http://expandedramblings.com/index.php/vine-statistics/.

42 **in 2016, Google surpassed more than 1 billion monthly active users**: Lardinois, F., "Gmail Now Has More Than 1B Monthly Active Users," *TechCrunch*, February 1, 2016, https://techcrunch.com/2016/02/01/gmail-now-has-more-than-1b-monthly-active-users/.

42 **Android claims more than 80 percent of the market**: "Smartphone OS Market Share, 2015 Q2," IDC Research, Inc., http://www.idc.com/prodserv/smartphone-os-market-share.jsp.

44 **To Howard Bloom, the brilliant but slightly mad music publicist–turned–evolutionary theorist**: Bloom, H., *The Global Brain: The Evolution of Mass Mind from the Big Bang to the 2st Century* (Wiley, 2001).

45 **Ray Kurzweil, the famous futurist and Google engineering director:** Kurzweil, R., *The Singularity Is Near: When Humans Transcend Biology* (Penguin Books, 2006).

Chapter 3: The Age of Holarchy

54 **Coca-Cola, Hewlett-Packard, Procter & Gamble:** Wright, D., Murphey, C., and Effron, L., "Meet the Vine Stars Who Turn 6 Seconds of Fame into Big Bucks," ABC News, Sept. 15, 2014, http://abcnews.go.com/Business/meet-vine-stars-turn-seconds-fame-big-bucks/story?id=25522189.

54 **Ritz Crackers got teen Vine star Lele Pons:** Original Vine and follow-up responses here: http://www.vineactivity.com/stealing-lele-pons-ritz-bacon-flavored-crackers-show-us-your-best-baconbomb-tag-it-w-the-hashtag-you-could-hear-from-ur-fav-viner/.

54 **but has nonetheless monetized his fame by landing lucrative TV and film roles:** Spangler, T., "King Bach: Vine's No. 1 Creator Brings Comedic Chops to Movies and TV," *Variety*, June 21, 2016, http://variety.com/2016/digital/news/king-bach-vine-the-babysitter-1201797370/.

54 **A year later, they signed with Republic Records:** Hampp, A., "Folk-Pop Duo Us Becomes Vine's First Major Label Signing," *Billboard*, March 24, 2014, http://www.billboard.com/articles/news/5944884/folk-pop-duo-us-becomes-vines-first-major-label-signing-exclusive.

55 **Around the same time, Canadian singer-songwriter Shawn Mendes:** Trust, G., "Shawn Mendes' 'Stitches' Hits No. 1 on Adult Pop Songs Chart," *Billboard*, January 25, 2016, http://www.billboard.com/articles/columns/chart-beat/6851764/shawn-mendes-stitches-hits-no-1-adult-pop-songs-chart.

55 **Then there are the YouTube millionaires:** Disclosed in slideshow at TV Guide's online site, entitled "These 23 YouTube Stars Make More

Than Most People on TV," TVGuide.com, http://www.tvguide.com/galleries/youtube-stars-make-more-1089689/.

56 **A survey by O'Reilly Media in 2013**: Bruner, J., "Tweets Loud and Quiet," O'Reilly Radar, December 18, 2013, https://www.oreilly.com/ideas/tweets-loud-and-quiet.

57 **As Fusion writer Gaby Dunn noted**: Dunn, G., "Get Rich or Die Vlogging: The Sad Economics of Internet Fame," Fusion, December 14, 2015, http://fusion.net/story/244545/famous-and-broke-on-youtube-instagram-social-media/.

57 **Efforts to create mutual sharing agreements...such as the Shout! project**: "Shout! - Promo Video," Vimeo video, 1:35, posted by "Lupa Productora," https://vimeo.com/157641350

58 **Super spreaders typically account for about 20 percent**: The so-called 20/80 rule, and the nuances and other factors that influence contagion effects, is discussed in: Stein, R. A., "Super-spreaders in infectious diseases," *International Journal of Infectious Diseases* 15, no. 8 (August 2011): e510–e513.

59 **The speed with which Carter Reynolds lost control**: Willett, M., "The Rise and Fall of Carter Reynolds," *Tech Insider*, July 31, 2015, http://www.techinsider.io/the-rise-and-fall-of-carter-reynolds-2015-7.

63 **When the hashtag #ShakeitupJalene alerted Swift**: Bell, R., "Taylor Swift Makes 4-Year-Old's Dying Wish Come True," *Taste of Country*, March 3, 2015, http://tasteofcountry.com/taylor-swift-fan-jalene-dying-wish/.

63 **Another time, she donated $50,000 to eleven-year-old Naomi Oakes**: Vokes-Dudgeon, S., "Taylor Swift Donates $50,000 to a Young Fan Battling Cancer, See the Little Girl's Reaction!" *US Weekly*, July 8, 2015, http://www.usmagazine.com/celebrity-news/news/taylor-swift-donates-50000-to-young-fan-battling-cancer-201587.

63 **A tearful Swift also gave a shout-out**: Norwin, A., "Taylor Swift Chokes Up In Concert Talking about Her Mother's Battle with Cancer," Hollywood

Life, August 18, 2015, http://hollywoodlife.com/2015/08/18/taylor-swift-mom-cancer-cries-ronan-arizona-concert/.

65 **It's the kind of all-encompassing idea**: Koestler's life described in: Scammell, M., *Koestler: The Indispensable Intellectual* (Faber & Faber, 2010).

65 **Holonics, the concept that arose from the holon theory**: Koestler, *Ghost in the Machine*, 57.

67 **As per the two diagrams below by Flemming Funch**: Funch, F., "Holarchies," at Flemming Funch's website, World Transformation, February 4, 1995, http://www.worldtrans.org/essay/holarchies.html.

70 **As they argued in a bestselling book**: Ismail, S. et al., *Exponential Organizations: Why New Organizations Are Ten Times Better, Faster, and Cheaper Than Yours (and What to Do about It)* (Diversion Publishing, 2014).

70 **One example is Chinese smartphone-maker Xiaomi**: Ismail, S. et al, ibid.

71 **He calls the ideal organizational design a "holacracy"**: See details of the project at http://www.holacracy.org.

71 **CEO and founder Tony Hsieh, who is worth almost $1 billion**: Sawyer, N., and Jarvis, R., "Why Zappos' CEO Lives in a Trailer, and 13 Other Things You Don't Know about Him," ABC News, August 12, 2015. On its website, Zappos describes holacracy this way: http://www.zapposinsights.com/about/holacracy.

72 **Implementing a holacracy is not easy**: Wasserman. T., "Holacracy: The Hot Management Trend for 2014?" *Mashable*, January 3, 2014, http://mashable.com/2014/01/03/holacracy-zappos/#eFDs82AstEqi.

72 **Mihaela Ulieru, a researcher in intelligent systems**: Ulieru, M., "Organic Governance Through the Logic of Holonic Systems" in *From Bitcoin to Burning Man and Beyond*, ed. Clippinger, J., and Bollier, D. (Off the Commons Books, 2014).

Chapter 4: Cracking the Memetic Code

76 **A Wikipedia entry on the topic lists 128 different scandals**: https://en.wikipedia.org/wiki/List_of_scandals_with_"-gate"_suffix

77 **of his 1976 classic of evolutionary theory**: Dawkins, *The Selfish Gene*, 189–202.

80 **"The world around you is built from memes,"**: Zarrella, D., "An Introduction To: Memes and Memetics For Marketers," *Dan Zarrella* (blog) http://danzarrella.com/an-introduction-to-memes-and-memetics-for-marketers/.

82 **Safire, who was formerly a Nixon speechwriter**: Alterman, E., *Sound and Fury: the Making of the Punditocracy* (Cornell University Press, 1999), 79.

83 **In 2015, a team of researchers**: Indiana University, "Network Model for Tracking Twitter Memes Sheds Light on Information Spreading in the Brain," Newswise.com, June 17, 2015, http://www.newswise.com/articles/network-model-for-tracking-twitter-memes-sheds-light-on-information-spreading-in-the-brain.

90 **In a well-researched *New York Times Magazine* article**: Johnson, S., "The Creative Apocalypse That Wasn't," *The New York Times Magazine*, August 19, 2015, http://www.nytimes.com/2015/08/23/magazine/the-creative-apocalypse-that-wasnt.html.

93 **Crypton, the Japanese company that created "Miku" in 2007**: Statistics on Hatsune Miku creative works provided at http://www.crypton.co.jp/miku_eng.

97 **The first is what Belgian cyberneticist Francis Heylighen**: Heylighen, F., "What Makes a Meme Successful? Selection Criteria for Cultural Evolution," in *Proc. 15th Int. Congress on Cybernetics* (Association Internat. de Cybernétique, Namur, 1999), 418–423.

98 **The meme's survivability will be tested again**: Ibid, 418–420.

102 **A Wharton Business School study of seven thousand**: Berger, J., and Milkman, K. L., "What Makes Online Content Viral," *Journal of American Marketing Research* (American Marketing Assoc., 2011).

https://marketing.wharton.upenn.edu/files/?whdmsaction=public:main.file&fileID=3461.

104 **Japanese research found that subjects who were shown such images**: Kliff, S., "Want to Increase Your Productivity? Study Says: Look at This Adorable Kitten," *The Washington Post*, October 1, 2012, https://www.washingtonpost.com/news/wonk/wp/2012/10/01/want-to-increase-your-productivity-study-says-look-at-this-adorable-kitten/.

109 **dove into the frequent resurgences in social media activity around in the Black Lives Matter movement**: Freelon, D., McIlwain, C. D., and Clark, M. D., *Beyond the Hashtags: #Ferguson, #BlackLIvesMatter, and the Online Struggle for Offline Justice*, (Center for Media & Social Impact, 2014).

Chapter 5: Balanced Diet

115 **where, as *New Yorker* cartoonist Peter Steiner put it**: Steiner, P., Image Caption: "On the Internet, nobody knows you're a dog," *The New Yorker*, July 5, 1993.

117 **As Yuval Harari points out in *Sapiens***: Harari, Y. N., *Sapiens: A Brief History of Humankind* (Harper, 2015).

118 **In a popular NPR Radiolab episode**: "23 Weeks, 6 Days," Radiolab, *Radiolab.com*, Season 11, Episode 6, http://www.radiolab.org/story/288733-23-weeks-6-days/. Also see the parents' book on their experiences:French, K., and T., *Juniper: The Girl Who Was Born Too Soon* (Little Brown, 2016).

120 **Katherine Dunn so wonderfully allegorized**: Dunn, K., *Geek Love* (Knopf, 1989).

122 **the writings of the sociologist Erving Goffman**: Goffman, E., *The Presentation of Self in Everyday Life* (Anchor, 1959).

123 **in the immortal words of Paris Hilton**: Spoken in a cameo role in *The O.C.*, referenced in: Wolff, J., "The Peculiar Endurance of the Physical

Signature," *Slate*, June 28, 2016, http://www.slate.com/articles/technology/future_tense/2016/06/the_peculiar_endurance_of_the_physical_signature.html.

125 **"This picture has been stolen over and over"**: Laney Griner's journey from anger to happiness about the viral spread of her photo can be followed in the comments stream attached to the original post on her Flickr page: https://www.flickr.com/photos/sammyjammy/1285612321/.

125 **But a week later, an Instagram post from Mitchell**: Instagram post found here: https://www.instagram.com/p/BAMH-mpObuf/.

127 **In a one-month New York "residency" in October 2013**: Portrayed in the documentary *Banksy Does New York* (2014), directed by Chris Moukarbel.

129 **"We would hope people want to drink [Diet Coke]"**: Vranica, S., and Terhune, C., "Mixing Diet Coke and Mentos Makes a Gusher of Publicity," *The Wall Street Journal*, June 12, 2006, http://www.wsj.com/articles/SB115007602216777497.

135 **J.P. Morgan Chase's social media strategists**: Greenhouse, E., "JPMorgan's Twitter Mistake," *The New Yorker*, November 16, 2013, www.newyorker.com/business/currency/jpmorgans-twitter-mistake.

Chapter 6: The Immune System

143 **Take Kerry Needham, the working-class mother of Ben Needham**: Thornton, L., "Ben Needham's Mum Hits Back at Madeleine McCann's Parents as They Shut Twitter Account Due to 'Trolls'," *Mirror*, October 6, 2015.

144 **A week later, the sixty-three-year-old mother committed**: Barnett, E., "Madeleine McCann 'Twitter Troll' Death: Trolling Is Never a Victimless Crime," *The Telegraph*, October 6, 2014, http://www.telegraph.co.uk/women/womens-life/11144435/Madeleine-McCann-Twitter-troll-Brenda-Leyland-death-Trolling-is-never-a-victimless-crime.html.

145 **Check out a recent *Wall Street Journal* online graphic**: "Blue Feed, Red Feed," at http://graphics.wsj.com/blue-feed-red-feed/.

148 **YouTuber C. G. P. Grey offered an explanation**: CGP Grey, "This Video Will Make You Angry," https://www.youtube.com/watch?v=rE3j_RHkqJc.

149 **Palmer's vacation home was sprayed with the words "lion killer"**: Collman, A., and Nye, J., "Cecil the Lion Killer's $1million Florida Vacation Home Vandalized with Graffiti and Pigs Feet as He Remains in Hiding," *Daily Mail*, August 4, 2015, http://www.dailymail.co.uk/news/article-3185082/Cecil-lion-killer-s-1million-Florida-vacation-home-vandalized-graffiti-pigs-feet.html#ixzz4FLJDZFrm.

149 **The Yelp page for his dental practice was inundated**: Displayed in review section at http://www.yelp.com/biz/river-bluff-dental-bloomington.

149 **Most tellingly, dozens of airlines**: "More than 42 Airlines Adopt Wildlife Trophy Bans after Cecil the Lion's Death," *Humane Society International*, August 27, 2015, http://www.hsi.org/news/press_releases/2015/08/42-airlines-adopt-wildlife-trophy-bans-082715.html?referrer=https://www.google.com/.

151 **journalist Jon Ronson details many cases**: Ronson, J., *So You've Been Publicly Shamed* (Riverhead, 2015).

152 **A comprehensive analysis of the events**: Mensch, L., "The Tim Hunt Debacle: Why Feminists Cleared a Nobel Prizewinner," in Louise Mensch's personal blog, December 15, 2015, https://medium.com/@LouiseMensch/the-tim-hunt-debacle-c914395d5e01#.swupk5p1b.

159 **It is an example of what Ethan Zuckerman**: Zuckerman, E., *Rewire: Digital Cosmopolitans in the Age of Connection* (Norton, 2013).

159 **There's also the case of Liz Woodward**: Liz Woodward's Facebook page, https://www.facebook.com/LizWoodwardFirefighters/.

161 **In the days following the 2015 terrorist attacks in Paris**: At "Blindfolded Muslim man with sign 'Do you trust me?' hugs hundreds in Paris," November 16, 2015, https://www.youtube.com/watch?v=lRbbEQkraYg.

162 **When we see the kind of sexual harassment that Caroline Criado-Perez**: Topping A., "Caroline Criado-Perez Deletes Twitter Account After New Rape Threats," *The Guardian*, September 6, 2013, https://www.theguardian.com/technology/2013/sep/06/caroline-craido-perez-deletes-twitter-account.

Chapter 7: Confronting Our Pathogens

165 **In both Gaza and India, giant sand castles were built**: McGee, B., "Graffiti Artwork of Drowned Aylan Highlights Refugees' Plight," *Reuters*, March 11, 2016, http://uk.reuters.com/article/uk-europe-migrants-aylan-idUKKCN0WD15L.

165 **A Scottish tabloid began a campaign that spawned the #wehaveroom**: Stories from the *Daily Record*'s "We Have Room" campaign posted at http://www.dailyrecord.co.uk/all-about/wehaveroom#fV12bp73X1ZSFzVG.97.

166 **The soccer club Bayern Munich quickly announced a 1-million-euro donation**: Grohmann, K., "Bayern to Donate Funds, Set Up Migrants' Training Camp," *Reuters*, September 3, 2015, http://uk.reuters.com/article/uk-soccer-bayern-migrants-idUKKCN0R31G220150903.

166 **Timothy Ray Brown, the famous "Berlin patient"**: Details of Brown's experience at Engel, M., "Timothy Ray Brown: The Accidental AIDS Icon," Fred Hutch News Service, February 20, 2015, http://www.fredhutch.org/en/news/center-news/2015/02/aids-icon-timothy-ray-brown.html.

167 **blood tests of some AIDS patients**: Zimmer, K., "The Lurker: How a Virus Hid in Our Genome for Six Million Years," *National Geographic*, May 10, 2013, http://phenomena.nationalgeographic.com/2013/05/10/the-lurker-how-a-virus-hid-in-our-genome-for-six-million-years/.

168 **Most strikingly, data in the United States show**: Bureau of Justice Statistics' Victimization Analysis Tools, found at http://www.bjs.gov/index.cfm?ty=nvat.

169 **The non-partisan Pew Research Center's**: "Changing Attitudes on Gay Marriage," Pew Research Center, May 12, 2016, http://www.pewforum.org/2016/05/12/changing-attitudes-on-gay-marriage/.

169 **Similarly, acceptance of interracial marriage has expanded rapidly**: Wang, W. "The Rise of Intermarriage," Pew Research Center, February 16, 2012, http://www.pewsocialtrends.org/2012/02/16/the-rise-of-intermarriage/.

170 **A 2015 Bloomberg graphic showed**: Tribou, A., and Collins, K., "This Is How Fast America Changes Its Mind," Bloomberg.com, June 26, 2015, http://www.bloomberg.com/graphics/2015-pace-of-social-change/.

173 **But as Dartmouth professor Brendan Nyhan noted in a nineteen-part "tweetstorm"**: Nyhan posted his tweets as a collection on his blog: "How We Got Here on Trump: A Tweetstorm," Brendan-nyhan.com, March 14, 2016, http://www.brendan-nyhan.com/blog/2016/03/how-we-got-here-on-trump-a-tweetstorm.html.

177 **In his book *The Better Angels of Our Nature***: Pinker, S., *The Better Angels of Our Nature: Why Violence Has Declined* (Viking, 2011).

183 **Fast Company ranked #BlackLivesMatter number nine**: "The Most Innovative Companies of 2016," posted at http://www.fastcompany.com/most-innovative-companies.

183 **An article on CNN Interactive that identified some of #BLM's**: Griggs, B. et al., "The Disruptors," August 2015, CNN, http://www.cnn.com/interactive/2015/08/us/disruptors/.

183 **In 2003, Nova Spivack, an entrepreneur, venture capitalist**: Spivack, N., "The Human Menome Project," Nova Spivack's blog, August 5, 2003, http://novaspivack.typepad.com/nova_spivacks_weblog/2003/08/the_human_menom.html.

184 **Center for Human Emergence, a group led by Don Edward Beck**: Details at "The Human Memome Project," Center for Human Emergence, http://www.humanemergence.org/humanMemome.html.

Chapter 8: Thomas and Teddy

191 **Also, by publishing data on the requests it gets for data by governments:** Facebook updates its disclosures periodically at https://govtrequests.facebook.com/

191 **The case of troubled Marine Daniel Rey Wolfe:** Nye, J., "Family's Distress After Marine Documented His Suicide in Series of Grisly Pictures on Facebook…and the Social Networking Site Refused to Take Them Down," *Daily Mail*, May 8, 2014, http://www.dailymail.co.uk/news/article-2623950/Familys-outrage-Marine-documented-suicide-series-grisly-pictures-Facebook-social-networking-site-refused-down.html#ixzz4FLSmC7nA.

193 **In one of many documented cases:** Flock, E., "Coldplay Angers Fans by Telling Them to Check Out 'Freedom for Palestine' Video," *The Washington Post*, June 3, 2011, https://www.washingtonpost.com/blogs/blogpost/post/coldplay-angers-fans-by-telling-them-to-check-out-freedom-for-palestine-video/2011/06/03/AG50OvHH_blog.html.

193 **Many more controversial Facebook censorship decisions:** Details taken from the March 23, 2016 update at Onlinecensorship.org, https://onlinecensorship.org/news-and-analysis/march-23-2016-politics-and-patriarchy.

194 **[T]he Dangerous Speech Project is trying to systematically identify:** Details at http://dangerousspeech.org/.

195 **As the saying popularized by security expert Bruce Schneier:** Scheier's first comment was reported by Gelman B., "Facebook: You're Not the Customer, You're the Product," *Time*, October 15, 2010, http://techland.time.com/2010/10/15/facebook-youre-not-the-customer-youre-the-product/.

195 **In February 2016, it established the Twitter Trust and Safety Council:** Cartes, P., "Announcing the Twitter Trust & Safety Council," Twitter's blog, February 9, 2016, https://blog.twitter.com/2016/announcing-the-twitter-trust-safety-council.

205 **A January 2016 survey by GlobalWebIndex found that 38 percent**: Mander, J., "Ad-Blocking Jumps by 10%," January 22, 2016, https://www.globalwebindex.net/blog/ad-blocking-jumps-by-10.

205 **Facebook itself captured the mood of the social media platforms**: Facebook's SEC filing available at http://investor.fb.com/secfiling.cfm?filingID=1326801-15-32.

205 **At stake is a business model that dates back to 1704**: Cheetham, N., "In 1704, the First Newspaper Advertisement, an Announcement," Prezi, June30,2014,https://prezi.com/mkgutf9_cyvg/in-1704-the-first-newspaper-advertisement-an-announcement/.

210 **She has also launched an initiative... called Mycelia**: Howard, G., "Imogen Heap Gets Specific about Mycelia: A Fair Trade Music Business Inspired by Blockchain," Forbes, June 28, 2015, http://www.forbes.com/sites/georgehoward/2015/07/28/imogen-heap-gets-specific-about-mycelia-a-fair-trade-music-business-inspired-by-blockchain/#4124e05a62ff.

210 **And with an even larger mission, the Berklee School of Music**: Details at http://open-music.org/#open-music-initiative-1.M.

211 **Video upload service Reveal, for example**: Casey, M. J., "BitBeat: Social Network to Launch Own Coin; Gift Cards on the Blockchain," *The Wall Street Journal*, January 16, 2015, http://blogs.wsj.com/moneybeat/2015/06/16/bitbeat-social-network-to-launch-own-coin-gift-cards-on-the-blockchain/.

211 **Meanwhile, Taringa!, an Argentine-based social media provider**: Casey, M. J., "BitBeat: Latin America Facebook Rival to Use Bitcoin to Pay for Content," *The Wall Street Journal*, April 21, 2015, http://blogs.wsj.com/moneybeat/2015/04/21/bitbeat-latin-america-facebook-rival-to-use-bitcoin-to-pay-for-content/.

212 **or clusters of low-wage "paid likers" in places like Bangladesh**: Listen to a podcast about Bangladesh's "liking" industry by Garrett Bradley, described by M. Scollinger, "Where Do Facebook 'Likes' Come From? Often, It's

Bangladesh," PRI.org, podcast audio, May 20, 2016, http://www.pri.org/stories/2016-05-20/where-do-facebook-likes-come-often-its-bangladesh.

215 **To quote Harvard law professor Lawrence Lessig**: Lessig, L., *Code: Version 2.0* (Perseus, 2016),1.

215 **Primavera De Filippi, a colleague of Lessig's**: Commons Transition's interview with De Filippi, "Commons Governance and Law with Primavera De Filippi,"Commons Transition, July 31, 2015, http://commonstransition.org/commons-centric-law-and-governance-with-primavera-de-filippi/.

217 **The potential is borne out by the numbers**: Spil Games, "State of Online Gaming Report 2013," http://auth-83051f68-ec6c-44e0-afe5-bd8902acff57.cdn.spilcloud.com/v1/archives/1384952861.25_State_of_Gaming_2013_US_FINAL.pdf.

217 **The estimated 9.5 million smartphone-toting users**: Wagner, K., "How Many People Are Actually Playing Pokémon Go? Here's Our Best Guess So Far," *Recode*, July 13, 2016, http://www.recode.net/2016/7/13/12181614/pokemon-go-number-active-users.

217 **The New York–based Games for Change festival**: Details at http://gamesforchange.org/festival/.

219 **According to a July 2015 Op-ed by lead game designer Jeffrey Lin**: Lin, J., "Doing Something about the 'Impossible Problem' of Abuse in Online Games," *Recode*, July 7, 2015, http://www.recode.net/2015/7/7/11564110/doing-something-about-the-impossible-problem-of-abuse-in-online-games.

220 **One relevant application was used**: Dawkins, *The Selfish Gene*, 202–234.

Chapter 9: Digital Culture

228 **Douglas Adams's *Hitchhiker's Guide to the Galaxy***: Adams, D., *The Hitchhiker's Guide to the Galaxy* (Del Rey, 1995), 39.

232 **If we follow the warnings of Yale computer scientist David Gelernter:** Gelernter, D., "Machines That Will Think and Feel," *The Wall Street Journal*, March 18, 2016, http://www.wsj.com/articles/when-machines-think-and-feel-1458311760.

235 **Within twenty-four hours, Microsoft was forced to lobotomize Tay:** "Tay, Microsoft's AI Chatbot, Gets a Crash Course in Racism from Twitter," *The Guardian*, May 24, 2016, http://www.theguardian.com/technology/2016/mar/26/microsoft-deeply-sorry-for-offensive-tweets-by-ai-chatbot.

238 **To the economist and social theorist Jeremy Rifkin:** Interview with Michael J. Casey, Rotterdam, June 23, 2016.

238 **McChrystal realized that to fight an enemy:** See McChrystal, Gen. S. et al., *Team of Teams: New Rules of Engagement for a Complex World* (Portfolio, 2015).

240 **As Media Lab executive director Joichi Ito puts it:** Ito, J., "Design and Science," *Journal of Design and Science*, January 30, 2016, http://jods.mitpress.mit.edu/pub/designandscience.

240 **In this spirit, the Media Lab's designer/architect/biologist extraordinaire:** Oxman, N., "The Age of Entanglement," *Journal of Design and Science*, February 22, 2016, http://pubpub.media.mit.edu/pub/AgeOfEntanglement.

241 **computer scientist Jay Forrester, who in the fifties pioneered the study of system dynamics:** Useful background discussion: Forrester, J., "The Beginning of System Dynamics: Banquet Talk at the International Meeting of the System Dynamics Society Stuttgart, Germany," July 13, 1989, http://web.mit.edu/sysdyn/sd-intro/D-4165-1.pdf.

241 **Physicist Geoffrey West, for example:** Lehrer, J., "A Physicist Solves the City," *The New York Times*, December 19, 2010, http://www.nytimes.com/2010/12/19/magazine/19Urban_West-t.html?_r=0.

241 **French physicist-economist Didier Sornette:** Casey, M. J., "Move Over Economists, Time to Give Physicists a Turn," *The Wall Street*

Journal, June 10, 2013, http://blogs.wsj.com/moneybeat/2013/07/10/fx-horizons-move-over-economists-time-to-give-physicists-a-turn/.

242 **To find the right, optimizing balance for incentivizing owners to share**: Irvine interviewed by Michael J. Casey, New York, April 7, 2014.

243 **"I believe that mycelium is the neurological network of nature,"**: Stamets, P., *Mycelium Running: How Mushrooms Can Help Save the World* (Ten Speed Press, 2005), 2.

247 **To Giles Hutchins, cofounder of the consultancy Biomimicry**: Hutchins, G., "'Superorganisations' – Learning from Nature's Networks," August 15, 2012, at Hutchins's personal blog, https://thenatureofbusiness.org/2012/08/15/superorganisations-learning-from-natures-networks/.

247 **After Haiti was hit with a devastating earthquake in 2010**: Chunara, R., Andrews, J. R., Brownstein, J. S., "Social and News Media Enable Estimation of Epidemiological Patterns Early in the 2010 Haitian Cholera Outbreak," *The American Journal of Tropical Medicine and Hygiene*, 86(1), 2012, 39–45, http://www.healthmap.org/documents/Chunara_AJTMH_2012.pdf.

248 **Reading an article about Guyana's shockingly high suicide rate**: Scutti, S., "Suicide Rates Highest in Guyana, May Be Explained by Clustering Effect," *Medical Daily*, October 14, 2014, http://www.medicaldaily.com/suicide-rates-highest-guyana-may-be-explained-clustering-effect-306982.

248 **what the eco-physicist Fritjof Capra has argued**: Capra, F., *The Hidden Connections: Integrating the Biological, Cognitive, and Social Dimensions of Life Into a Science of Sustainability* (Doubleday, 2002), 102.

249 **Thanks to studies of mice that have been conditioned**: Das, B. G., and Ressler, K. J., "Parental Olfactory Experience Influences Behavior and Neural Structure in Subsequent Generations," *Nature*, 17, No. 1: (2014), http://www.nature.com/neuro/journal/v17/n1/full/nn.3594.html.

249 **Research by University of Wisconsin anthropologist John Hawks**: Dunham, W., "Rapid Acceleration in Human Evolution Described,"

Reuters, December 10, 2007, http://www.reuters.com/article/2007/12/10/us-evolution-human-idUSN1043228620071210.

250 **Recently, scientists led by genetics pioneer Craig Venter**: Nield, D., "Biologists Have Just Created a New Species of Bacteria with Just 437 Genes," *Science Alert*, March 26, 2016, http://www.sciencealert.com/scientists-have-created-a-living-organism-with-the-smallest-genome-yet.

252 **He says human capital is "stored as neural connections**: Romer, P., "Human Capital and Knowledge," Paul Romer's blog, October 7, 2015, https://paulromer.net/human-capital-and-knowledge/.

252 **As Stone puts it, "Everyone is working on Artificial Intelligence"**: Stone, B., "Introducing Jelly, a New Search Engine," *The Biz Stone Collection* (blog), April 28, 2016, https://medium.com/the-biz-stone-collection/introducing-jelly-a-new-search-engine-47e2594ad3ff#.a3wnivhgf.

253 **"We are seeing the formation of a new cellular organism"**: Andrew Hessel interview with Michael J. Casey, December 30, 2015.

254 **Kevin Slavin, another genius Media Lab software designer**: Slavin, K., "Design as Participation," *Journal of Design and Science*, March 13, 2016, http://jods.mitpress.mit.edu/pub/design-as-participation.

INDEX

#ABGivesBack, 216
Abrams, Jonathan, 31
adaption, of organisms. *See* evolution
Advanced Research Projects Agency Network, 23
advertising
 on blogs, 27, 28
 holonic structure of social media, 54, 55
 media evolution of, 18
 open-access approach compared to, 203–206
 social media used for, 43–44
affinity receptors, xxvii, 97
Amazon, 91
American University, 109–110, 112
Andreessen, Marc, 24, 208
Android (Google), 42, 204
anger
 about content of social media, 104, 127–128, 133–134
 "thought germs," 148–149
 of trolls, 128, 143–145
Anheuser-Busch, 216
antibodies, developing, 174–176
Anti Defamation League, 195
antidisciplinary concept, 239
Apple, 38, 61, 204
Aquila project (Facebook), 228
Arab Spring, xviii, 37, 144
armadillos, 121
ARPANET, 23
art
 as digital asset, 209
 for empathy, 181–182
 memes as, 85–94
artificial intelligence (A.I.), 46, 97, 231–234
Ashley, Brittany, 56
#AskJPM, 135–137
assimilation, 97–101
AT&T, 22
theAudience
 clients of, 10–11, 52, 61, 62
 content control, 131–132, 134, 139–140
 on cross-popularization, 59
 donations by, 155
 founding of, xxvi
 on viral content, 101
authority, 99
avatars, on social media, 31

Baauer, 132
Bachelor, Andrew (King Bach), 54, 59
Banksy, 126–127
Baran, Paul, 20–22
Barnett, Emma, 144
"Beauty Patches" (Dove), 140
Beck, Don Edward, 184
Bell System, 22
Berger, Jonah, 102

Index

Berklee School of Music, 210
"Berlin patient," 166–168
Berners-Lee, Tim, 24
Betaworks, 100n
The Better Angels of Our Nature (Pinker), 177–178
Beyoncé, 39, 92, 112–113, 123, 130
Bieber, Justin, 62–63, 122
Big Data, xxviii–xxix, 183–184, 244–245
biology analogies
  biodiversity, 120–121
  boll weevils, 1–6, 162
  emotion, 133–134
  evolution as algorithm of life, 1–13, 80, 98 (*See also* evolution; media evolution)
  genes as cultural equivalent to memes, 77–81, 105
  genetic code as programming language, 252
  holonic structure, 48–52 (*See also* holarchy)
  homeostasis, xxx, xxxii, 61, 148 (*See also* social media negativity)
  immune system, 152–153, 155, 166–168, 174–176, 180–183 (*See also* cultural immune system)
  metabolism and food, xxx, xxxi–xxxii, 128–129 (*See also* content)
  mimesis, 114–121
  mycelia, 241–246 (*See also* global brain concept; open-access approach)
  replication, 77–81, 99 (*See also* memes)
  response to outside stimuli, 131, 133–134, 149–154, 162–163 (*See also* content; cultural immune system)
  Seven Rules of Life, defined, xxix–xxxiv
  Social Organism and biology metaphor inception, xxi, xxiii–xxvi
  super spreaders, 58
  viral life cycle, 94–101 (*See also* memes)
  volvox (green algae), 48–52, 66–67
biomimicry, 8, 240
Biomimicry for Creative Innovation, 246–247
biotechnology, computing and, 225–228, 248–250
bitcoin, xxxiv–xxxv, 41, 207–212
#BlackLivesMatter, xvii, xxvii, 108–113, 153–154, 180–183
blockchain ledger technology, 34, 207–212, 229
Bloom, Howard, 44–46
Bloomberg, 170
boll weevils, 1–6, 162
Boston News-Letter, 205
Bowie, David, 114–115, 121
branding, 129–132
#Brexit, 164, 174
broadband connections, 26, 33
Brown, Michael, 108, 112
Brown, Timothy Ray, 166–168
bulletin board systems (BBS), 23–24, 31
Butler, Judith, 122
butterfly effect theory of chaos, 5
BuzzFeed, 57, 100

Capra, Fritjof, 247
capsids, 96
Carleton University, 72–73
Casey, Michael, xxxiv–xxxv
Castile, Philandro, 109
Catholic Church, as form of mass communication, xxiv, 16–17, 93
CD Baby, 92
Cecil (lion), 149–150
cellular structure. *See also* holarchy
  holonic structure compared to, 48–52
  Social Organism analogy, xxix–xxx, xxxi–xxxii
censorship. *See also* corporate culture; media evolution
  content issues, 131
  cultural evolution and, 168
  cultural immune system and, 174–176
  media evolution and, 35–36, 38

Index

open-access approach compared to, 188–195
as response to social media negativity, 162–163
Center for Human Emergence, 184
Center for Media and Social Impact, 109–110, 112
Cerf, Vint, 20, 23
Chainsmokers, 131–132
chameleons, 114, 115–116
Charleston (North Carolina), massacre in, xv–xvi, xv–xxi, xxxiii
Chen, Jenova, 217
China
centralized control of media by, 202
identity management by, 187
social media platforms in, xxxviii, 41
Chrome (Google), 195
civilizing process, 177–178
Clinton, Hillary, 11
Club Penguin, 227
CNN, 147
Coca-Cola, 54, 129–130
Coddington, Grace, 38
coherence, 99
Coldplay, 112, 193
collaboration, promoting, 236–237
#CollegeIn5Words, 105–107
Confederate flag, xv–xvi, xxxiii, 112, 171
constructive messages, encouraging, 156–162
"contagion beliefs," 247
content, 114–141
branding, 129–132
changing nature of, 114–121
emotion of, 101–102, 127–128, 135–141 (*See also* emotion)
of memes, 94–95, 101–104
message for, 132–134
open-access approach and, 190
persona and performativity, 115, 121–129
Content ID (YouTube), 34
corporate culture. *See also* open-access approach
proprietary instincts of, 32, 44, 69–70, 92, 131–132
success of exponential organizations, 70
cost per impression (CPM), 28
cotton farming, boll weevils and, 1–6, 162
"The Creative Apocalypse That Wasn't" (Johnson), 90–91
Creative Commons, 236
Criado-Perez, Caroline, 162
Crossfire (CNN), 147
cross-popularization, 59
Crypton, 93
"crystals of imagination," 9
cultural immune system, 164–186
cultural norms, 177–183
data-gathering techniques for, 183–184
mycelium comparison, 241–246
overcoming problems with, 185–186
positive social mutation for, 166–171
refugee crisis example, 164–166
for resilience, 171–176
rise of populist fascism, 173–174
social media negativity, 152–153, 155
Curry, Steph, 125–126
cybernetics, 240
CyWorld, 41

"Daddy Swag," 140
Dangerous Speech Project, 193–194
Dartmouth College, 173–174
Darwin, Charles, 4–8, 46
Darwin's Cathedral (Wilson), 14
data analytics, xxviii–xxix
Davies, Donald, 20, 23
Dawkins, Richard, xxvii, 46, 77–81, 82–83, 116, 219–220
DC Toy Collector, 55
DDT, 3–4, 162

Index

decentralization. *See also* global brain concept; open-access approach
decentralized autonomous organization (DAO) model, 211
global brain concept and, 233, 235–238
media evolution and, 20–22, 34
open-access approach, 199, 211
social media distribution networks, 29
top-down hierarchy of "old" media compared to, xxxvi, 43, 59, 69–71, 93, 197, 235–238, 255
"Deep Dreams" (Google), 97
Defense Department Advanced Research Projects Agency Network, 23
De Filippi, Primavera, 215
Defy Media, 40
Delta-32 mutation, 166–168
Demir, Nilifur, 164
democratization, of communication, 25
Dennett, Daniel, 4–6
Denny's, 105–107
destructive memes, 154–156
Details, xxviii
DeviantArt, 91
dial-up modems, 26, 31
Diet Coke, 129–130
DigiSynd, 44
digital cosmopolitanism, 159
Digital Currency Initiative (MIT), 210
digital currency systems, xxxiv–xxxv, 41, 207–212, 229
digital immigrants, 52
digital natives, 168
Disney, 44, 55, 137–139, 192
distinctiveness, 99
distributed networks, xxxvi–xxxvii, 20–22
"Doge," 85
Dorsey, Jack, 29
dot-com bubble, 30
Dove, 140
#The Dress, 119
Dunn, Gaby, 57
Dunn, Katherine, 120
Durkheim, Émile, 14

Ebola, 105–107
Eepy Bird, 129–130
Electronic Frontier Foundation, 193
email, centralized control of, 195
Emanuel, Ari, xxvi
emoticon responses, 146
emotion
anger, 104, 127–128, 133–134, 143–145, 148–149
of content, 101–102, 127–128, 135–141
empathy, 73–74, 181–183
as evolutionary trait, 103–104
holonic structure of social media and, 64
"Ermahgerd," 86–87
Espinosa, Matthew, 59
Europe, refugee crisis in, 164–166
European Union, censorship and, 36
EvenTubeHD, 55
evolution, 1–13. *See also* media evolution
accelerated speed of human evolution, 248
cultural, 166, 170, 179, 185–186 (*See also* cultural immune system)
disruption to society and, 1–6
emotion as evolutionary trait, 103–104
of memes, 77–81
of social media, xxvii–xxix, 10–13
Social Organism analogy, xxx–xxxiv
social science context of, 8–10
theory of, 4–8, 46
top-down hierarchy of "old" media, xxxvi, 43, 59, 69–71, 93, 197, 235–238, 255
Ex Machina (film), 250
exponential organizations, 70

Facebook
Aquila project, 228
business model of, 34–36
censorship issues of, 36–37, 188–195
degree of separation between users, 30
on "Free Basics" (India), 221–222
gatekeeping function by, 198

homophily issues, 145, 146
identity management by, 187–188
Instagram and, 38
popularity of, 33
as social media platforms, 29
fan art, 92
"Feel the Bern" slogan, 11
file-sharing technology, 89
@FindBenNeedham, 143
#Findthesheep, 119
First Amendment, 193–194, 222
"Formation" (Beyoncé), 112–113, 130
Forrester, Jay, 240
#FOWF, 164
"Free Basics" (India), 221–222
Freeman, Morgan, xvi
#FreeMilo, 128
"Free the Nipple Movement," 38
French, Tom, 118
frictionless sharing tools, 84
Friendster, 31–32
Frozen (Disney), 139
Funch, Flemming, 67
Fusion, 57

#Gamergate, 146–147
Games for Change festival, 217
gamification, 216–221
Garner, Eric, 108, 112
"-gate" suffix, 76
Gawker, 27
Geek Love (Dunn), 120
Gelernter, David, 231–232
gender
LGBTQ social media content, 114–115, 120
misogyny, 146–147
performing, 122
same-sex marriage, 169–170
Generation Z, social media preferences, xxxvii, 40
genetics
genetic code as programming language, 252
Human Genome Project, 184, 249
memes as cultural equivalent to, 77–81, 105
"Gerl, yer girven mah gersberms" (Hard 'n Phirm), 87
"Ghetto Beat Down" (King Bach), 54
The Ghost in the Machine (Koestler), 65
GLAAD, 195
The Global Brain (Bloom), 45
global brain concept, 225–260
artificial intelligence (A.I.), 231–232, 233
biotechnology and computing, 248–250
communication behaviors for, 246–248
decentralization and reorganization for, 233, 235–238
defined, 226
humility and, 253–256
interdisciplinary approach to, 239–241, 250–253
mycelia model, 241–246
overview, 44–46
potential of, 225–233
GlobalWebIndex, 204
Goffman, Erving, 121–122
GoFundMe, 160
Goldenberger, Maggie, 86–87
Gomez, Selena, 62
Google
Ads, 27
Android, 42, 204
artificial intelligence application, 97
Blogger, 27
business model of, 41–42
centralized control by, 195
Friendster and, 31–32
Go, 230
page ranks, 126
Project Loon, 228
Waze, 42, 161
Gould, Stephen Jay, 6–7
government, reimagining, 237–238
Grey, C. G. P., 148
Grier, Hayes, 59, 60

Index

Grier, Nash, 52–55, 59
Griner, Justin "Success Kid," 125
Griner, Laney, 124–125
Gutenberg, Johannes, xxiv, 17–18, 20

Haiti earthquake, social media use and, 246–247
Hall, Justin, 27
Harari, Yuval, 117
Hard 'n Phirm, 87
"Harlem Shake" (Baauer), 132
#HasJustineLandedYet, 151–152
Hatcher, Lorraine, 160
hate speech, censorship of, 36, 162–163
Hawks, John, 248
Heap, Imogen, 209–210
Henshaw-Plath, Evan, 37
Herr, Hugh, 248–249
Hessel, Andrew, 9, 249–250, 251–252
Hewlett-Packard, 54
Heylighen, Francis, 97–101
Hidalgo, César, 8, 9, 44
Hilton, Paris, 123
Hilton, Perez, 27
Hirsch, Tad, 37
Hitler, Adolf, 145–146, 186
HIV, 107, 110–113, 166–168
HolacracyOne, 71
holarchy, 48–74
  disruption to power structure, 174 (*See also* cultural immune system)
  facilitating efficient communication flow with, 69–74
  holacracy, defined, 71
  holonics, defined, 64–69
  holonic structure, overview, xxxi, 48–52
  holons, defined, 64
  social media as, 52–64
  Social Organism analogy, xxxi–xxxii
homeostasis. *See also* social media negativity
  segregation in social media as, 148
  Social Organism analogy, xxx, xxxii, 61
Homestar Runner (Web puppet show), 85
homophily, 145
Hsieh, Tony, 71–72
Huffington Post, 27, 100
Human Genome Project, 184, 249
"Human Memome Project," 184
"The Human Menome Project," 183–184
HUMAN Project (Kavli Foundation), 157–158
Humans of New York (HONY), 158
humility, 253–256
Hunt, Tim, 152
Hutchins, Giles, 246
hyperText markup language (HTML), 24

Iceland, social media used by, 245–246
identity. *See* persona
identity management issues, 187–188
India
  "Free Basics" program, 221–222
  identity management by, 187
  social media platforms in, xxxviii
Indiana University, 83
information. *See also* holarchy; media evolution
  authority of memes, 99
  communication needed for global brain approach, 246–248
  defined, 8n
  experiential, 247–248
  facilitating efficient communication flow, 69–74
  gatekeepers of, 59, 93, 163, 194, 198, 221
  memes as messaging, 101
  message content for, 132–134 (*See also* content)
  proprietary instincts of corporation, 32, 44, 69–70, 92, 131–132
Instagram
  business model of, 38, 39
  holonic structure of social media, 61–62
  use statistics, 84

Index

Internet
increasing exposure to conflict from, 168 (*See also* cultural immune system)
Internet of Things, 236
Internet Service Providers (ISPs), 221
inventions leading to, 20–26
use statistics, 228
World Wide Web, advent of, 24
Irvine, David, 241
ISIS, 144
Ismail, Salim, 70
IT industry, economics of, 25–26
Ito, Joichi, 239

Jack & Jack, 55, 59
Jelly, 251
#JeSuisBree, xvii, 112
#JeSuisCharlie, xvii
#JeSuisParis, 161
Johnson, Steven, 90–91
Jones, Leslie, 128
journalism. *See* media evolution
J.P. Morgan Chase, 135–137

Kahn, Bob, 20, 23
Kan and Aki, 55
"Kardashianists," 123–124
Kavli Foundation, 157–158
Kickstarter, 228–229
Kindle (Amazon), 91
King, Aidan, 11
King, Martin Luther, Jr., 132, 185, 186
King Bach (Andrew Bachelor), 54, 59
Kloss, Karlie, 62
K.N.O.E. Clothing, 126
Knowyourmeme, 85
Koestler, Arthur, xxxi, 64–69, 78
Korine, Harmony, 62
Kurdi, Aylan, 164–166
Kurzweil, Ray, 45–46, 230, 250

Laboratory for Social Machines (MIT), 107n, 109–110
Lasseter, John, 135
Lavandeira, Mario Armando, Jr., 27
League of Legends, 218–219
Lear, Norman, xx
Lessig, Lawrence, 214
Leyland, Brenda, 143–144
LGBTQ, social media content about, 114–115, 120
"like" buttons, 146
Lin, Jeffrey, 219
Lindemann, Maggie, 59–60
LinkedIn, 37–38
Linux, 236
"listicles," 100
"loops" (Vine), 41, 52–55
Los Angeles Times, xx
Lotan, Gilad, 100n
Luckett, Bill, xvi

Macro Connections (MIT Media Lab), 57
#MaggieandCarter, 60
Maidsafe, 241
Make-A-Wish Foundation, 159
"March of Evolution," 6
Martin, Trayvon, 108
mass media. *See* media evolution
McCann family, 142–144
McChrystal, Stanley, 237–238
Mckesson, DeRay, 108–109
Mediachain, 210
media evolution, 14–47. *See also* social media
of advertising, 205–206 (*See also* advertising)
blogs as early competition to journalism, 26–29
broadcast media inception, 19
distributed networks, xxxvi–xxxvii, 20–22
gatekeeping function of, 198
insulation of media, 131
interaction problems of media, 147
Internet and, 20–26
mass media concept, 18–20
printing press invention, xxiv, 17–18, 20
religion as community, 14–17, 93

Index

media evolution (*cont.*)
  social media adaptation, 42–47
  social media business models, 34–42
  social media, early platforms, 29–34
  top-down hierarchy of "old" media, xxxvi, 43, 59, 69–71, 93, 197, 235–238, 255
memes, 75–113
  artistic innovation of, 85–94
  content of, 94–95, 101–104
  as cultural equivalent to genes, 77–81, 105
  defined, 76–77
  as "derivative works," 98–99
  destructive memes, 154–156 (*See also* social media negativity)
  "Ermahgerd" example, 86–87
  framework of meaning from, xxxvii
  hashtag memes as societal influence, 180 (*See also* cultural immune system)
  holonic structure of, 51
  inception of term, xxvii
  memetic code, 78, 153–156
  mimeme, defined, 116
  religious myths as, 15–16
  study of memetics, 82–87
  as "thought germs," 148–149
  viral examples of, 105–113
  as viral life cycle, xxvi–xxvii, 94–101
  Watergate example, 75–76, 81–82
Memories (Snapchat), 39
Mendes, Shawn, 55, 59
Mensch, Louise, 152
Mentos, 129–130
Merrifield, Lane, 227
mesh networks, 228
messaging. *See* information; memes
metabolism. *See also* content
  persona comparison, 128–129
  Social Organism analogy, xxx, xxxi–xxxii
Metallica, 90, 91
Metcalfe, Robert, 26
Metcalfe's law, 25–26, 29–30
"Meth Curry," 125–126
Michael and Carissa, 54–55
Microsoft, 36, 37, 195, 234
Mi Fen, 70–71
Miku, Hatsune, 93
Milkman, Katherine L., 102
Millennials, social media preferences, xxxvii, 40
Miller, J., 87
mimesis, 114–121
misogyny, 146–147
MIT
  Laboratory for Social Machines, 107n, 109–110
  Media Lab, 8, 37, 158–159, 210, 239, 248–249, 252–254
  Shout!, 57
Mitchell, Leon, II, 125–126
Monegraph, 210
Monroe, Marilyn, 247
Moore, Gordon, 26
Moore's law, 25–26
Mosaic, 24
Mozilla, 228
Museum of Modern Art (New York), 49
music industry, changes in, 91–92
mutagens, 155
Mycelia (Heap), 210
mycelium (biological), 241–246
Myspace, 31–33

Napster, xxvi, 89
National Physical Laboratory (United Kingdom), 23
Needham, Kerry, 143–144
Nelson, Ted, 24
net neutrality, 221–224
Netscape, 24, 76
"new consciousness of the collective," 232
Newman, Randy, 138–139
News Corp., 32–33
Newsome, Bree, xvii
New York Times, 101–102, 206
New York Times Magazine, 90–91
New York University, 109–110, 112

Nixon, Richard, 75
NM Incite, 28
norms, cultural, 177–183
novelty, 99
NPR, 118
NSA, 196–197, 202
Nyhan, Brendan, 173–174

Oakes, Naomi, 63
Obama, Barack, 11, 159, 221
"old" media. *See* media evolution
OneWorld, 193
onlinecensorship.org, 193, 202
online gaming, 216–221
online mailing lists, 23
open-access approach, 187–224. *See also* global brain concept
  advertising and, 203–206
  blockchain ledger for, 207–212
  censorship issues, 188–195
  centralized control issues, 195–197
  decentralization phenomenon of, 199, 211
  First Amendment, 193–194, 222
  gamification solutions for, 216–221
  governance of, 213–216
  identity management issues, 187–188
  need for, 197–203
  for net neutrality, 221–224
  open-source applications, 235–237
  social media *versus* social media platforms, 197–198
  "Thomas and Teddy" solution for, 199–200, 222
OpenSlate, 55
Opte Project, 49
O'Reilly Media, 56
Oreo, 43–44
Outlook (Microsoft), 195
Overton, Joseph P., 19
Overton window, 19
Oxman, Neri, 239

Palmer, Walter, 149–150
Paris attacks (2015), xvii, 144, 161, 166
Parker, Sean, xxvi, 33, 52, 155
pattern recognition, 15, 97–101, 134, 153
paywall models, 206
peer-to-peer advice platforms, 70–71
peer-to-peer commerce, 207, 215
"perfect loops" (Vine), 41, 52–55
performativity, 115, 121–129
persona
  content and performativity, 115, 121–129
  holonic structure of, 68–69
PewDiePie, 55
Pew Research Center, 169
Pink Army Cooperative, 249–250
Pinker, Steven, 177–178
Pixar, 135
Plato, 120
Pons, Lele, 54
populist fascism, 173–174
positive social mutation, 166–171
Postman, Neil, 232
printing press invention, xxiv, 17–18, 20
Prisoner's Dilemma, 220
Procter & Gamble, 54
Project Loon (Google), 228
publicity, for memes, 100

Quinn, Zoe, 146–147

Radiolab (NPR), 118
RAND Corporation, 22
reach, of memes, 100
"Real Beauty Sketches" (Dove), 140
@RealDonaldTrump, 127
Reddit, 11, 86
Red Lobster, 130
refugee crisis, in Europe, 164–166
religion
  as community, 14–17, 93
  cultural evolution and resilient, 171
Renren, 41
replication (reproduction)
  of memes, 77–81, 99
  Social Organism analogy, xxx, xxxi–xxxii

Index

Republic Records, 54–55
resilience, 171–176
response to outside stimuli. *See also* content; cultural immune system
  content control, 131, 133–134 (*See also* content)
  hashtag "movements" as immune system response, xxxiii
  social media negativity, 149–154, 162–163
  Social Organism analogy, xxx, xxxiii
Reveal Coin, 210–211
Revver, 32–33, 33–34, 129–130
Reynolds, Carter, 59–60
Rich Site Summary (RSS) feed format, 27
Ridley, Matt, 8, 226
Rihanna, 63
Rilke, 231
Ring, Ian, 28
Riot Games, 218–219
Ritz Crackers, 54
Robinson, Brian, 71
Romer, Paul, 251
Ronson, Jon, 151
Roof, Dylann, xv–xvi, xxxiii
Roy, Deb, 107n, 109–110

Sacco, Justine, 151–152
Safire, William, 82
Salinas, Jalene, 63
same-sex marriage, 169–170
Sanders, Bernie, 11
Sapiens (film), 117
Schmidt, Eric, 196
Schneier, Bruce, 194
Scott, Miles, 159
search engines, advent of, 26
Secret, 40
Secret Order of the Boll Weevils, 2
segregation, in social media, 146–150
#Selfie (Chainsmokers), 131–132
selfies, 122–124
The Selfish Gene (Dawkins), 46, 77–81, 82–83, 219–220
serendipity, 12
Seven Rules of Life, defined, xxix–xxxiv, 32n
sexting, 39
#ShakeitupJalene, 63
"short instant messages," 246
Shout! (MIT Media Lab), 57
Shteyngart, Gary, 89
Simon, Herbert A., 65–66
single-sign-on (SSO) access, 187–188
Singularity University, 70
SixDegrees.com, 30
Slavin, Kevin, 242–243
smart contracts, 214
Snapchat, 39–41, 200–201
Snowden, Edward, 196–197, 202
social media. *See also* content; cultural immune system; holarchy; memes; social media negativity; *individual names of social media companies*
  adaptation to, 42–47
  biology metaphor inception, xxi, xxiii–xxvi
  business models, 34–42
  celebrities' influence and power, 56–64
  celebrities of, 52–56
  complexity of, xviii–xxi
  early platforms, 29–34
  evolution of, xxvii–xxix
  frictionless sharing tools of, 84
  as global brain, 226 (*See also* global brain concept)
  Iceland's use of, 245–246
  influence of, xv–xxi
  mindset change of, xxxv–xxxiv
  overview, xv–xvi
  persona and, 68–69, 115, 121–129
  rise of platforms for, 29–34
  "rose-colored" expressiveness of, 35, 189
  selfies as performativity, 122–124
  social media platforms *versus,* 197–198
  user demographics, 200–201
  viral nature of, xxvi–xxvii

Index

social media negativity, 142–163
- destructive memes, 154–156
- encouraging constructive messages, 156–162
- harm from, 144–146
- homeostasis analogy, xxx, xxxii, 61, 148
- McCann example, 142–144
- response and counter-response to, 150–154, 162–163
- segregation in social media, 146–150

The Social Network (film), 33, 34

Social Organism. *See also* biology analogies; content; cultural immune system; evolution; global brain concept; media evolution; memes; open-access approach; social media; social media negativity
- biology metaphor inception, xxi, xxiii–xxvi
- emotional response of memes, 102
- holonic structure of, 67–69 (*See also* holarchy)
- Seven Rules of Life, xxix–xxxiv, 32n
- social media analogous to, xxi, xxiiii–xxxix
- social media distribution, 29
- social organism term, 14
- viral nature of social media, xxvi–xxvii, 94–101 (*See also* memes)

Sony Ericsson, 123

Sornette, Didier, 241

SoundCloud, 132

So You've Been Publicly Shamed (Ronson), 151

Sparks & Honey, 40

Spiegel, Evan, 40

Spil Games, 216

Spivack, Nova, 183–184

Spring Breakers, 62

Stamets, Paul, 242–243

Stanton, Brandon, 158

Steiner, Peter, 114

Sterling, Alton, 109

"Stiches" (Mendes), 55

stimuli, response to. *See* response to outside stimuli

Stone, Biz, 251

"Success Kid," 124–125

suicide contagion, 247

Sullivan, Andrew, 27

super spreaders, 58

@sweepyface, 143–144

Swift, Taylor, 55, 61–62, 63

Syria, refugees from, 164–166

#TakeItDown, xv–xvi, xxvii

Taringa!, 41, 210–211

"Tay" (Microsoft), 234

Telecom Act of 1996, 24–25

Telegraph (U.K.), 144

thatgamecompany, 217

"Thomas and Teddy" solution, 199–200, 222. *See also* open-access approach

"thought germs," 148–149

360i, 43–44

Timberlake, Justin, 33

Time Magazine, 109

"Tiny Human" (Heap), 209–210

Toy Story 3 (Disney), 137–139

traditional media. *See* media evolution

translation software, 227

Transmission Control Protocol/Internet Protocol (TCP/IP), 23

Tribeca Film Festival, 217

"Tribunal" (League of Legends), 218–219

trolls, 128, 143–145. *See also* social media negativity

Trump, Donald, 113, 127, 147, 162, 173–174

Tumblr
- business model of, 38–39
- holonic structure of social media, 62
- use statistics, 28, 84

TuneCore, 92

Index

Twitter. *See also individual hashtag campaigns*
  business model of, 36–37
  censorship and, 36, 195
  content and emotion, 135–137
  data obtained from, 106–107n
  hashtag "movements" as immune system response, xxxiii
  holonic structure of social media, 56, 63
  persona, 127–128
  social media platforms, 29
  trolls, 128, 143–145
  used for corporate earnings reports, 229
  use statistics, 84
  Vine and, 41
Txt-Mob SMS, 37

Ulieru, Mihaela, 72–73
Ulrich, Lars, 91
Undertale, 217–218
Universal, 132
University College London, 152
University Hospital Lausanne, 83
University of North Texas, 109–110, 112
University of Washington, 39
University of Wisconsin, 248
Upworthy, 159
U.S. Department of Defense, 23
Usenet groups, 23
Usher, 139–140

Venter, Craig, 184, 249
video, early availability on social media, 33
video games, 216–221
Vine, 41, 52–55, 59–60
Vines, 91
Visualizing Impact, 193
vocaloid enthusiasts, 92–93
volvox (green algae), 48–52, 66–67
Vosoughi, Sorous, 107n, 109–110

Wall Street Journal, 129, 145, 206
Walt Disney Company, 44, 55, 137–139, 192
Watergate, 75–76, 81–82
Waze (Google), 42, 161
#wearefull, 164
WeCare, xxiii
#wehaveroom, 165–166
Weibo, 41, 202
West, Geoffrey, 240
Wharton Business School, 101–102, 133, 134, 148
Whisper, 40
Wilber, Ken, 64
"Wild Life" (Jack & Jack), 55
Williams, Serena, 154
Wilson, David Sloan, 14
Wolfe, Daniel Rey, 191–192
Woodward, Liz, 159–160
Wordpress, 27
World Wide Web, advent of, 24
Wretch, 41

Xiaomi, 70–71

Yahoo!, 38–39
Yiannopoulos, Milo, 128
You Me Bum Bum Train (theatrical experience), 181–182
Young, Tim, 159–160
YouthStream Networks, 30
YouTube
  censorship and, 36
  content control, 132
  Content ID, 34
  early video availability on social media, 33
  holonic structure of social media, 57
  memes, 87
"You've Got a Friend in Me" (Newman), 138–139

Z1010 (Sony Ericsson), 123
Zappos, 71–72
Zarrella, Dan, 80
Zimmerman, George, 108
Zuckerberg, Mark, 29, 33, 34
Zuckerman, Ethan, 158–159